HAND BOOK OF PRINTING PROCESSES TECHNOLOGIES & INDUSTRIES

The unique book on Printing & Printing Processes, Technologies & Industries containing various manufacturing technologies & processes of different printings alongwith the addresses of plant, machinery and raw material suppliers with the valuable addresses of All India Trade & Industry Organisation and Financial Institutions in India for the aggrassive entrepreneurs & industrialists.

By:
EIRI Technocrats
&
Sudhir Gupta

Recipient of Udyog Rattan Award
and
15 years experienced Industrial consultant.

PUBLICATION DIVISION

ENGINEERS INDIA RESEARCH INSTITUTE

4449, Nai Sarak, Main Road, New Delhi - 110 006 (INDIA)
Phones : 291 8117, 291 6431, 292 0361 ◆ Fax : 91-11-291 6431

Printed & Published by

ENGINEERS INDIA RESEARCH INSTITUTE

Regd. Office : 4449, Nai Sarak, Main Road, New Delhi - 110 006 (INDIA)
Phones : 291 8117, 291 6431, 292 0361 • Fax : 91-11-291 6431

Distributed by

SMALL INDUSTRY RESEARCH INSTITUTE

New Delhi (INDIA)

ISBN : 81-86732-07-1
Printed in New Delhi (India)

Rs. 375

Printed & Published by **Sudhir Gupta** for **'Engineers India Research Institute'**, and Laser Type Set by **Dharmender** at Engineers India Research Institute, and Printed at 'Kumar Offset Press', 251/8, Padam Nagar, New Delhi - 110 007

PREFACE

The Printing Industry now-a-days in India are increasingly day by day. New technologies, methods & processes are being developed gradually. The Printing sector plays a vital role towards recording, disseminating, preserving and updating data, information, knowledge, news, views, opinions & expertise from domestic and foreign sources.

The contribution of printing industry is all pervading and touches various aspects of the economy, education, administration and day to day life of people. The Printing industry has got tremendous demand in India as well as in abroad.

The Indian printing industry comprises 1,32,000 small, medium and large printing presses spread all over the country, involves a capital investment of about Rs. 6,500 crore, and provides direct and indirect livelihood to over 5,25,000 and 2,50,000 people, respectively. It plays a vital role in meeting the needs of adult education, universal primary education, secondary and territory education, distance learning, the press media, and the trade and industry in India. It also actively promotes the purposes of India's Mass Literacy Mission of achieving a literacy rate of well over 50 per cent as well as the official recognition accorded to 16 Indian languages for their intensive standardisation and extensive adoption and usage. Thus the multi-faceted role of the printing industry directly aids the endeavours of putting Indian masses and Indian languages in the mainstream of India's socio-economic development as well as of breaking the vicious circle of poverty. Further, it has a direct bearing on the process of globalising Indian trade and industry.

The book deals in three parts. The first part of the book deals with the technologies of printing & printing processes, the second part of the book covers the various project profiles on printing which are most indispensable now-a-days for every entrepreneur and industrialist who are venturing for new unit. Part third the last but the most important, covers the various sources/suppliers for plant & machinery, materials and the technologies.

Director

ENGINEERS INDIA RESEARCH INSTITUTE

Nai Sarak, New Delhi.

Contents

Part - 1

TECHNOLOGIES OF PRINTING & PRINTING PROCESSES

1

AUTOMATIC BLANK DIE CUT STICKERS WITH FLAT DIES

Impracticability from many aspects was being experienced so far by the printers for the production of blank stickers, which was mainly owing to steep rise in prices. An Australian company viz. RAPID PACKAGING SERVICES PVT. LTD., due to their deep research as well as engineering competence, has been able to develop a new, fast, easy to operate, "Blank Die Cut Stickers" machine through Automation and Flat Dies. This system enables printers to make their own blank Labels/Stickers of short runs and at a speed of 15,00 impressions per hour. With this introduction, no need to keep the stock in pile has been felt, since it is always available for day to day requirements. Cost of the production has been reduced to the extent and to the barest minimum. Mostly, this has proved conducive to the Screen Printers. Due to low cost, this system has turned to be a most accomplished in house configuration. This facility is also extended to the Computers at an additional cost - to hole-punch on both sides of the paper - comprehensively. Before the start of the machine can produce Labels/Stickers from upto 1,000 meters long rolls and to a maximum size of 130 x 180 mm. It has a 'waste-rewind' system also. The main attraction of this machine is that one has not to pay attention constantly, while the machine is in operation, but undoubtedly you are to take care that the paper does not fear-off from the roll.

2
DIGITAL PRINTING

There is no exact definition of 'digital printing', which in itself makes the term open to debate. There are two basic approaches: one, the computer industry and two, the print industry.

To the computer industry, any data output on paper is a printout, whether it is in black and white or colour. So they use the term 'printers' - a term used in the print industry to describe press operatives.

To the print industry, digital printing is where the computer is on-line to the press and data is transferred directly from the computer to the press. Other options are plateless information transfer, non impact printing and plate manufacture on-press (masters). Some experts disagree as to whether masters are a true digital print procedure, but this is irrelevant if we are talking of 'computer to paper' rather than 'computer to press'. To the printer, there is yet another meaning, that of digital platemaking off-press, combined with rapid plate change over on-press; but this is not called digital printing.

3
GRAVURE PRINTING

PRINTING FORMS: OFFSET Vs GRAVURE

At Klambt, gravure cylinders are electro-mechanically engraved using a bromide derivative. Direct engraving is projected to be perfected for production applications in one to two years. Checking is done via digital proofs and economical form proofs. A comparison of the costs involved reveals that the preparation of an impression cylinder of 32 pages is approximately five times more expensive than an eight-page offset plate. A cylinder takes approximately 2.5 hours to prepare as compared with 1.5 hours for an offset printing form.

The reproducibility of the print quality of reprints is extremely high when preparing new cylinders. Despite high power scanners and stored in profiles as employed in offset printing nowadays, the values common for gravure printing do no even begin to be reach. The resolving power in the bow-5 per cent range in offset is considerably poorer as compared with gravure printing even when using heat-fused plates. The facility also includes a flexo imprinting unit for the single-colour printing of prices and addresses. This imprinting unit enables non-step alternate imprinting for runs 10,000 in size.

Gravure printing is characterized by constant high quality throughout the entire run, especially when it comes to flesh tones, colour trueness, flatness of the product (no offset buckling, paper does not turn brittle), soft tone transitions, high colour intensity, as well as maintenance of high quality also when simple stocks are involved.

Ink fading, streaking, off-setting, slurring, ghosting, picking, blistering and dot gain are unknown. The only thing which occasionally happens is that the blade ruptures. Gravure printing is characterized by high availability, high capacity utilization of the facility and stable production extending over hours and even days.

LARGER VARIETY OF PAPER TYPES ENABLED BY OFFSET

On average, paper costs account for approximately 50 percent of a job. Owing to the format variability offered by gravure printing, the paper can be used to full advantage (can be printed all over). Consequently, paper waste is minimal. At Klambt, the gravure cylinder is sometimes modified to a certain diameter by milling off the copperplate base. Gravure printing is also advantageous in that coated papers can be purchased at more favorable terms than for offset. Offset, on the other hand, offers the advantages that a considerably larger variety of papers can be printed.

When productivity and straight investment costs are considered, gravure printing and rotary offset are almost on par with one another. Prices for both gravure and offset products are on the decline, however, this has affected offset more dramatically than gravure printing. Thus, for example, good prices are still being paid for high-quality fashion catalogues.

4
HOLOGRAMS

A hologram is a three-dimensional image created by sophisticated techniques involving lasers and precise optical instruments. Although hologram technology is 25 years old, it was not until American Bank Note Company began to mass-produce quality holograms at a reasonable cost that commercial applications were feasible.

In the early 1980s, the issuers of Master-Card and Vias credit conferred with American Bank Note about using holograms as security devices a process for which American Bank Note holds the patents Credit card industry security analysis determined that holograms are perhaps the most effective means of halting the proliferation of counterfeit cards that cost the industry millions annually. A hologram on each card verifies its authenticity and prevents counterfeiting.

In addition to security applications, holograms have many uses as marketing tools. The world-renowned November 1985 National Geographic, contained 54 pages of advertising, the most in a quarter century. National Geographic convinced advertisers that the Taung skull hologram was such a unique cover that the readership would surely increase.

Zebra Books uses a hologram as the log for its line of historical differentiates its books from competitors on the shelves of drugstores, supermarkets, and card shops. Zebra is so pleased with consumer response to this holographic logo, they plant to use a second American Bank Note hologram for another line of books.

Tonka Toys includes a hologram sticker as a means to distinguish its Gobots from similar competitive toys. The robotic-like toy segment of the toy market has been one of the faster-growing and most profitable over the last three years. Tonka's expectation is that the free hologram will help its share of the market to grow even faster.

American Bank Note Company holograms also have appeared on school notebooks and binders, magazine cards, product labels, point-of-sales displays, company logos and the covers of Fortune 1000 company annual reports.

The hologram is a pre-eminent example of the union of creativity and technology, according to Salvatore F. D'Amoto, Vice Chairman of American Bank Note Company. If you're ambition is to attract consumers with eye-catching packaging or thwart counter-feiters and holster security. American Bank Note Company holograms are a high technology answer available today.

5

NEWSPAPER TECHNOLOGY

The newspaper offset preprintstage, including repro and ad processing, has become fully digitized, making much use of the fourth roller technique ('mainstream'), which enabled it to absorb all software updates and advances in hardware. Using generally accessible programmes such as Quark-XPress, full page makeup became affordable even for small newspaper publishers.

In addition to digitization of in-house processes, there has been digitization of supplied products: agency copy, agency photos and some advertisements already. Press photographers are now making increasing use of digital cameras, and there are mobile satellite transmission units available to send the photos to the editorial offices. Digitation has also made newspapers independent of any particular edition or issue, os that the newspaper content, the actual product of newspaper publishers, can be forwarded to all corners of the world via telecommunication lines.

THE COMPACT FOUR-HIGH TOWERS

As regards the present state of play in newspaper rotary presses, this year's trade fairs - NEXPO and IFRA - have shown that the favorite design is the four-high tower option in the form of stacked letter press units. The criticism of this design by advocates of the satellite system is that they are not so good at holding the register marks. Although this is true in principle, it has been shown in practice that these marks can be kept below the visibility limit by inexpensive means.

Besides the compact desing of the four-high towers, this year's NEXPO also brought a break through for the non-zonal inking technique in newspaper offset machines. There are two versions here: the European version with anilox roller and the American-Japanese version without anilox rollers. The European-style offset inking units employ an anilox roller which, together with the doctor blade, performs two functions: first removal of the residual ink relief coming back from the inking rollers, namely by dipping in fresh ink; secondly, continuous metering of the ink film to be applied to the inking roller via screen cells with a defined volume. To ensure that this residual ink relief does not appear as a pattern on the printed product, an inking roller of a size 1:1 relative to the plate cylinder has been introduced. The non-zonal offset inking units in the American and Japanese style use a very different approach. These are inking units with definable or adjustable inking. They get along without any metering roller, that is, they have no anilox roller, os they are very much like conventional inking units. However, a blade roller with a doctor blade is connected to the distributor, so that it is possible to do without the division into zones in the ink feed.

ISSINGLE-FLUIDINKONITSWAY

According to Rockwell, the American-Japanese desing will come into its own once the single-fluid inks developed by this firm come to the market. Then, it should be possible to dispense with the damping unit, since this printing ink moves the damping fluid to the plate at the same time. Rockwell stresses that only the non-zonal inking unit without an anilox roller is in a position to process the single-fluid ink or to perform the separating process at the correct point. The single-fluid ink developed by Rockwell splits into free surface water and residual emulsified ink precisely where the greatest shearing force acts on the single-fluid ink.

Fluid-free offset printing using the silicone separating layer in the printing plate (Today) still comes up against tool life problems in the printing form for newspapers, and the developments now announced have still to prove that they can cope with print runs of up to 1,50,000 copies.

6

OVER-PRINTING BY FLEXOGRAPHY

Normally, acquiring of hi-technology and sophisticated machinery is beyond the reach of a common man, who although possesses fondness, his aspirations remain dormant for want of funds and the capital investment. He tries to exert himself to reach the pinnacle of his carrier; but non-availability of tremendous funds fails him.

A British company, by the name of FOCUM LABEL MACHINERY LTD, with a long and in-depth experience to their credit, in manufacturing label printing machines, by Flexo process, has now manufactured an high speed, but small from single to multi-colour over-printing machine by Flexo to print to pre-die cut stickers with pin-registration. By setting up this small machine having excellent features, extra expenditure is curtailed. This machine requires only one operator. By installing this machine, printers can derive much benefit out of this unit and can outwit in price-line as compared to their brethren. This machine, popularly called OV-175 has been manufactured by the FOCUS LABEL MACHINERY LTD UK, possesses variable speed of upto 9,500 impressions per hour with accurate registration across web. Having Digital Counter of five digits and automatic unwind and rewind system, this machine can print stickers of 175 x 130 mm, in a single phase supply. If can print on plain self-adhesive labels, tapes, foils and most of the material in reel form. Through multiple passes, multi-colours can be printed. Right from the big houses, stores, manufacturing companies, to small offices, stores, godowns, this machine has proved marvellous with low investment, especially in view of the fact that over-printing such as prices, expiry dates, any other additional information on already printed labels, is required to be exhibited, with perfection. With the introduction of the above mentioned machine - OV-175, (a concise and compact unit), FOCUS LABEL MACHINERY LTD UK, has filled up the void for the future generation. Utilizing minimum space, low capital investment, without involving labour, high quality and quantity output, fast speed to meet the time schedules, are the main features of this machine.

7

SILK SCREEN PROCESS (THE PRINTING UNIT)

In constructing the frame shown in Fig., well-seasoned wood such as hemlock, knot free fir or white pine could be used. It need not be made of any particular kind of wood but the three mentioned above are inexpensive and any be bought at any lumber yard. It is important that the wood be well cured and straight grained. The frame must be set absolutely flat on the printing base when completed.

Keep Silk tight while forcing rope in Groove

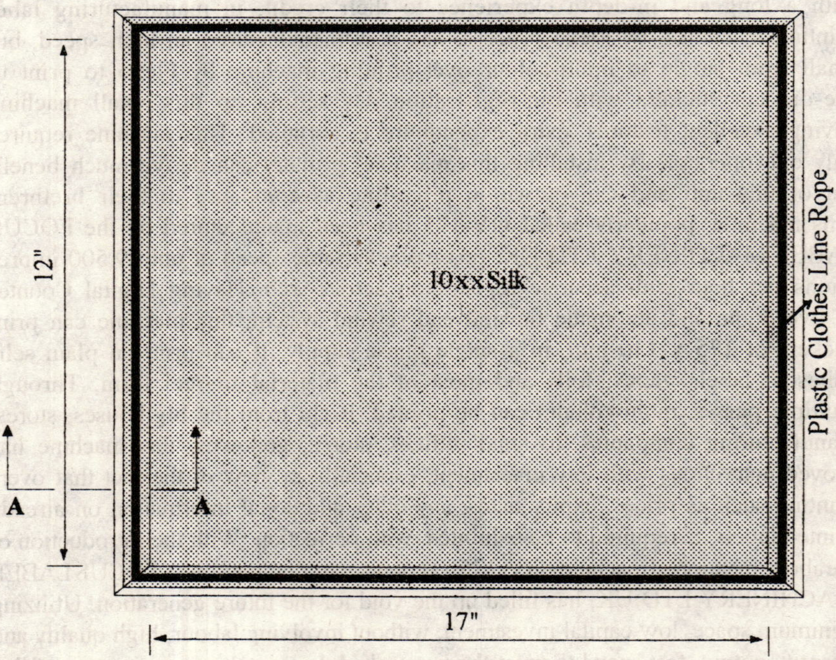

The finished frame should be sanded to remove any splinters or rough places; then shellacked, allowed to dry, then resented and shellacked again. This preparation of the frame usually prevents warping and makes cleaning easier.

There are a number of fabrics that can be used for screen printing; such as silk bolting cloth, copper or bronze mesh, stainless steel mesh, a number of synthetic fabrics, and organdy. Since some of the synthetic fabrics can be dissolved with some of the chemicals used in screen printing and some of the metal meshes need special treating before using, for simplicity, only bolting silk is used.

In order to stretch the silk, first place the frame on a flat smooth table. Center the silk ever the frame. Begin at the center of one side and gentle hammer the rope into the groove of the frame, pinching the fabric under it. Next do the same on the opposite side but pull the cloth tightly as the rope is forced into the groove. Next do the same on both ends, then cut off the excess fabric. The silk is then ready for washing. Although the cloth appears clean when bought it usually has some starch and factory greases and oil in it. These must be removed or the first stencil will not adhere properly to the fabric. This is done by washing with warm water and a good grade of soap. When the silk is dry, clean it with lacquer thinner. Cover the rope all the way around the frame with white paper tape, then turn the frame basin

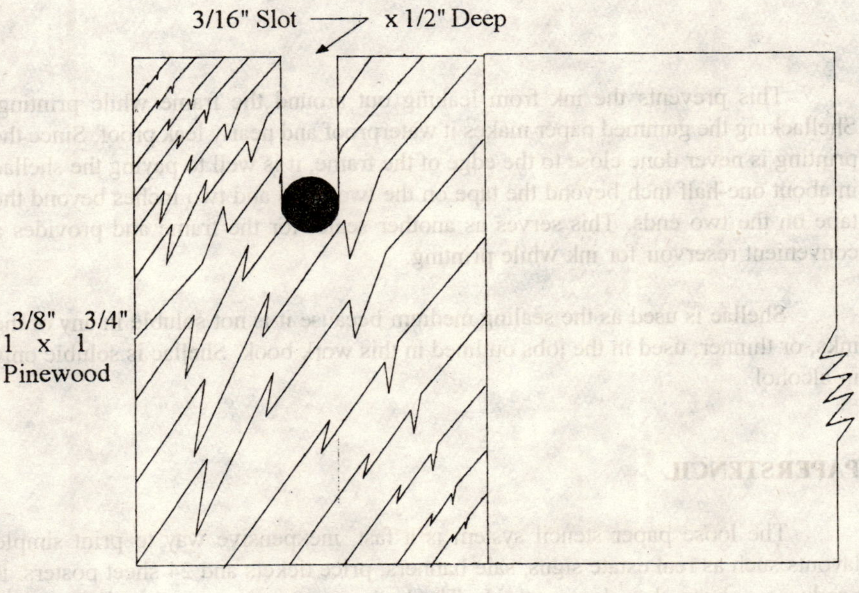

Section A - A

side up and, folding the gummed paper in half lengthwise with the unglued sides together, paste it all the way around the inside of the frame so that half sticks to the frame and half to the silk.

Hand Operated Squeegee about 20 Lbs. Pressure Required

This prevents the ink from leaking out around the frame while printing. Shellacking the gummed paper makes it waterproof and nearly leak proof. Since the printing is never done close to the edge of the frame, it is well to paying the shellac in about one-half inch beyond the tape on the two sides and two inches beyond the tape on the two ends. This serves as another sealer for the frame and provides a convenient reservoir for ink while printing..

Shellac is used as the sealing medium because it is not soluble in any of the inks, or thinner, used in the jobs outlined in this work book. Shellac is soluble only in alcohol.

PAPERSTENCIL

The loose paper stencil system is a fast, inexpensive way to print simple layouts such as real estate signs, sale banners, price tickets and 24 sheet posters. It produces a sharp clean line methods. The low cost of paper stencils and the small amount of preparation necessary makes this the ideal system to use when there is no small detail in the design and less than five hundred copies ordered.

HOW TO DO IT

Step 1. - Using ordinary wrapping paper, cut a sheet one inch smaller in each direction than the frame to be used. By using paper this size, it will need no additional taping or blocking out.

Step 2. - Shellac one side of the stencil in order to make ti transparent. This makes it easier to see through the paper well enough to cut the stencil. Allow the paper to dry.

Step 3. - Tape the original illustration to the drawing board. Center the shellacked paper over the drawing and tape all four corners. Cut out and remove all the parts that appear as black on the original.

Step 4. - Remove the cut stencil from the drawing. Remove original from drawing board and center it under ringed silk screen frame.

Step 5. - Place cut stencil in register on top of original art and lower the hinged silk screen frame into contact with the stencil.

Step 6. - Pour a small out of poster ink into the silk in areas that will not be part of the print. This ink will hold the stencil to the silk.

Step 7. - Lift the screen just enough to remove the original art and replace with a blank sheet.

Step 8. - Pour in a little more poster ink and squeezee it over all the area to be printed.

Step 9. - Remove the printed copy and place on rack to dry. Repeat the printing until there are the needed number of good copies.

Step 10. - Wash the silk with the appropriate thinner and wipe clean. Here you will find that the loose paper stencil washes off with the ink leaving no additional cleanup problem, another big reason why this stencil system should be used when ever possible.

8

FLEXOGRAPHIC PRINTING

Rotary letterpress printing from rubber stereos originated about 1800 and took the name "aniline printing" from the aniline dyes dissolved in water or alcohol which constituted the ink. The machines were crude and the inks used left much to be desire. So long as these conditions held the process had little appeal for printers of quality and development was slow.

The possibilities of the process led to increasing advances both in machines and in inks since about 1935, and the scene is now completely transformed, as is also the name of the process, now generally known as flexographic printing. Far from being confined to the printing of grocers bags and the like, flexographic printing is now being used to produce a wide variety of printed material, including waxed wrappers, decorative wrappers, toffee twist, regenerated cellulose film packs, corrugated papers, cartons aluminium foil, plastic films and newsprint. Modern flexographic machines using pigmented inks can produce work which compares favorably with that of older established printing methods.

FLEXOGRAPHICPRINTINGMACHINE

While their has been no change in principle in recent years there have been great changes in detail. These changes have greatly increased the prospects of the flexographic process as a competitor, not only of photogravure, but also of conventional letterpress and litho printing. Much greater attention has been paid to refinements lead it to close control at all stages of printing, so that it is now possible to obtain results which compare favorably with the other methods of printing.

Modern flexographic printing presses are constructed on much more robust lines than formerly and this has made fine control possible. As in any other high-speed process the moving parts must be stout enough to prevent whip and vibration.

All cylinders are precision-made and precision-mounted on generous soundless and bearings. Apart from sharpness of printing the need for this stability is more obvious when it is remembered that ink control is done by pressure on the end bearings of the inking rollers. This pressure introduces a leverage on the shafts at each and tending to force the roller apart at the centre . Even heavy rollers suffer from distortion when pressure is increased and at high speeds the ink itself exerts a distinct pressure in the same outward direction.

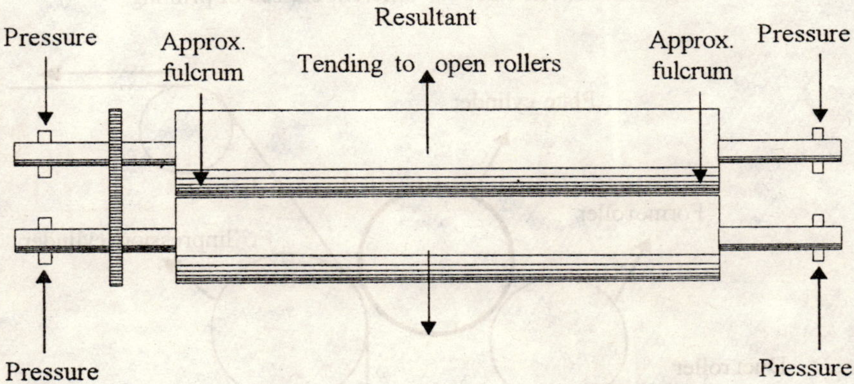

Forces operating on Inking Rollers

Many devices have been introduced to give continuous fine control of pressure and correct alignment of rollers. This control is quite as important in flexographic printing as in other processes; indeed, it is probable that it is more important. In Letterpress printing, pressure may vary quite appreciably without impairing the result, but in flexography no tolerance is permissible; the pressure must remain constant at practically zero, usually described as a "kiss" touch. All modern machines give this control and older machines lacking it cannot compete in finished results.

PRINTING UNIT

Various designations can be applied to the rollers in the printing unit, but for convenience those have been used in this chapter.

On most machines the duct roller is rubber covered, while the forme roller may be of rubber but is more generally of steel. It is seldom that both rollers rotate in the ink. Normally, the forme roller is clear of the ink surface. When the letter is a steel roller it is engraved or grained in order to carry a heavier but more controllable ink feed.

The two inking rollers usually operate at the same surface speed, but in a few designs there is a small differential, giving a shear to the ink.

In the "Anilox" inking system there is a single chromium plated steel engraved inking cylinder which rotates in the ink duct. This cylinder is engraved by a special mechanical process to produce many thousands of small, identical square cells. The surplus ink is wiped off with a doctor blade or hard rubber doctor roll and the cells convey the appropriate volume of ink to the stereo, there being different cell sizes for different classes of printing.

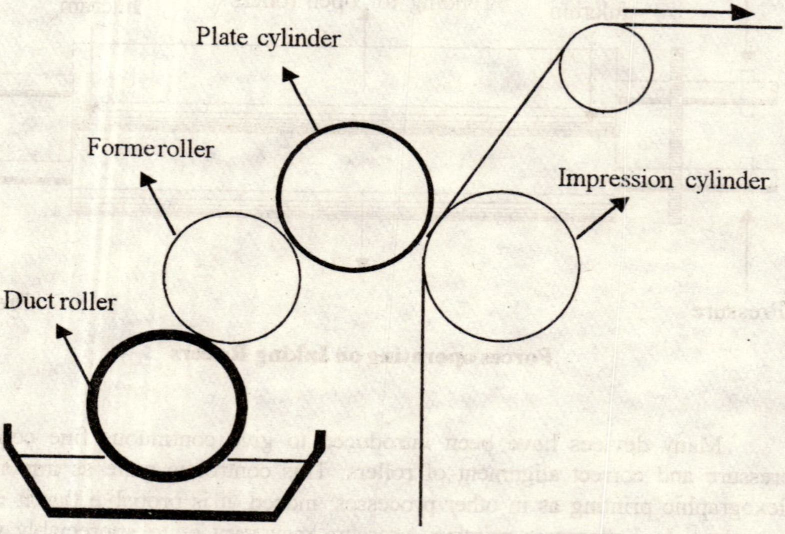

Members of Aniline Printing Unit

The engraving or graining of the forme roller has made it possible to deliver a greater volume of ink to the stereo than can be done with plain rollers without developing the usual ill effects of over-inking or variation in volume with press speed.

On many machines provision is made for maintaining the inking rollers at a slow speed of rotation by an auxiliary motor. Whenever the machine as a whole stops, the inking rollers are thrown clear of the stereo or plat e cylinder and take up the auxiliary drive. By means of a free-wheel they pick up the speed of the press when it restarts. This arrangement prevents the ink from drying on the rollers and keeps the ink well agitated in the duct.

Pigmented inks are kept in suspension either by agitators within the duct or by a circulating system from a reservoir fitted with a pump.

STEREOS

The stereo is the most troublesome item in the printing unit and its preparation requires great securacy. Imperfection in the gauge of the stereo cannot be corrected by the adjustment of the machine. Where the stereo is mounted on a backing sheet for clipping to the plate, cylinder make-ready can be carried out. When the job is a continuous design of accuracy. This is the most critical point in flexographic printing and is the most frequent cause of poor quality. Unfortunately, the effect this has on the job is not always traced to its correct cause.

The only exception to the rule of uniformity of gauge occurs when the desing has large solids with isolated small type-matter or design. It may be an advantage to have the small type-matter a fraction lower than the main solids to allow for a slight pressure on the solids. It is difficult to adjust the press to the correct minimum pressure on a very large solid, and although the solid can absorb slight pressure without showing much sign, small type-matter immediately shows "squash".

DRYINGSYSTEMS

The drying of flexographic inks takes place by evaporation, and two main factors influence the rate of drying apart from drying by absorption into the paper. These factors are (1) the amount of heat available to provide the latent heat of evaporation of the solvents, and (2) the efficiency of ventilation to remove the solvent vapours.

In printing dye-type flexographic inks on absorbent sulphite papers little trouble is experience except at high speeds. Atmospheric heat and the drought caused by the moving web are sufficient to drive off the solvents. When inks containing pigments are employed dying requires special provisions; the pigment interferes with the release of the solvent and the greater thickness of the ink film, as compared with dye-type flexographic inks, adds to the time required for drying.

There are many different designs of heaters in use, of which the following systems are most common:-

Steam or electrically heated drums,
Infra-red lamps or tubes above the paper,
Heated panels over which the web travels,
Hot air blast within a tunnel.

Steam heated and electrically heated drums are both employed. The latter can be set thermostatically to operate at the required temperature. Hated drums are very useful for general work both, as speeds increase, their capacity to provide sufficient heat for the fast moving web becomes stretched to the limit. Larger drum diameters and higher temperatures become necessary and these introduce new problems.

Infra-red lamps or tubes above the paper have the advantage of quick shut down at stoppages, especially if a cold air drought is also available for automatic use when the machine stops. The heat is applied to the printed side and not through the paper or film, so that the insulating effect of the web is avoided. As with drums, the quantity of heat available is limited.

Heated panel systems are similar in effect to drying by rotating drums. They have the advantage that scorching of the web can be prevented by dropping the panels away from the paper when the machine stops.

A novel arrangement of such panels (Timson Standard Four colour Press), where the heat is supplied by a number of panels within the chamber. The web can be made to pass into the hot are before printing an also between each colour. The panels reinforce one another and maximum use is made of the heat available. The heating systems is insulated from the printing units to prevent evaporation of the solvents in the ducts.

More important even than the provision of heat is the efficient and rapid removal of solvent vapour-laden air from the surface of the printed web. This is best achieved by a high-speed turbulent air flow directed on to the surface. Such an air flow sweeps away the thin, nearly stagnant, solvent-saturated air close to the wet print. Solvents cannot evaporate into air already saturated with their own vapours, and even a thin layer of such air near the surface can check the rate of drying.

The evaporation of the solvents absorbs heat from the paper and ink, chilling them. This heat is replaced much rapidly by high velocity air than by slow currents and the rat of evaporation is maintained.

When the air is preheated the rate of evaporation is greatly increased. A greater amount of heat is then available to supply the latent heat of evaporation and in addition, the vapour pressure of the solvents is increased.

This principle has been applied in the machine a Halley four-colour flexographic press. Hot air is supplied between colours and hot or cold air in the chamber above the machine to complete drying.

Drying between colours on a multi-colour machine is most important for good trapping. Owing to their liquid nature flexographic inks are more difficult in this respect than letterpress inks. Wet printing is very difficult to achieve successfully unless there is some provision to harden each print before it arrives at the next unit. The air space between printing units on a multi-colour machine is usually bounded by the web of paper and by the projecting masses of the units themselves. Unless forced ventilation is applied the air in this box-like space can become sufficiently solvent-laden to retard drying.

After heat application it is frequently necessary to chill the surface of the print before re-reeling to prevent set-off or blocking. The ink may be dry enough but the resin is soft and tacky due to the heat.

MACHINESPEEDS

As speeds increase the amount of heat and energy necessary to dry flexographic inks becomes a very serious problem. Already the power consumption of electrical drier on flexographic presses is assuming large proportions, and each increase in speed involves a greater than proportionate increase in heat supply. As a result, economic speeds will be determined as much by the efficiency of the application of heat as by improvements in machines or in ink formulation.

Many different factors govern actual working speeds. A machine may be designed to operate at a high speed, but in practice it will be found that there is an optimum speed for each class of work. Some of the factors involved are:-

1. Efficiency of the drying system,
2. Length of travel,
3. Enclosure of duct,
4. Nature of printed material,
5. Choice of solvents,
6. Rate of solvent release of resins,
7. Rate of loss of tack of pigment/resin system,
8. Rate of viscosity increase with loss of solvent,
9. Type of ink,
10. Weight of ink carried,
11. Adjustment of printing units.

Certain of these factors are not the concern of the ink-maker. In those factors in which ink formulation has a direct bearing the choice of materials is not always a straightforward matter of selecting those contributing to the fastest possible drying. For highest speeds it is necessary to seek such materials, but when printing on surfaces which must be used at lower speeds, other considerations arise. The rat of drying of the solvents must be reduced by the use of higher boiling solvents in order to give good working properties at the printing unit. If the ink dries too rapidly for the speed of printing, the stereo will begin to fill in with partially-dried syrupy ink.

In addition, the rates of solvent release and of losses of tack of pigment/resin systems vary with different resin. However, resins are not judged solely on this property, and other advantages such as adhesion and efficiency in pigment dispersion may out weight drying performance.

Fastest drying is associated with dye-type flexographic inks, semi-pigmented inks are intermediate and pigmented inks slowest under like conditions.

While dealing with this question of machine speeds it is important to recognize that a fault in the adjustment of the printing until can make a satisfactory ink appear to be slow drying. If the stereo is slightly irregular and requires pressure to bring up the whole design, or if there is accidental pressure somewhere in the system, the ink may be squashed to the edges of the design. A fine outline of the design in heavy inking in transferred and these areas cannot dry in the travel allowed and marking-off on turner rollers or set-off in the reel occurs. This is no fault of the ink and must be watched for before adjusting the solvents.

Machine speeds vary from less than 100 ft. per min. to over 1,000 ft. per min. according to the nature of the work. Cellulose and other films are worked in the lower ranges up to 300 ft. per min., while sulphite papers enable speeds up to 1,000 ft. in bag-making and re-re-recyling. Much paper converting is done in the 400-800 ft. range.

9
PHOTO POLYMER PLATE

The Photo Polymer Plate, a water soluble plate, used for letter press printing consists of a light sensitive layer protected by transparent foil firmly mounted to a backing of either a film or metal or aluminium base. The plates can be used for printing by flexo or rotary processes. In respect of the former, the plates are processed in solvents. The thickness of the light sensitive layer is variable, being relatable to the extent of relief required. Thus these plates are available in different thicknesses and hardnesses but for mounting on rotary cylinders soft and flexible plates are available for use.

APPLICATIONS

Primarily, the plates can be employed for printing of labels, packaging, embossing, business forms, newspapers, imprinting, dry offset, metal and pantography both on sheet-fed and rotary presses.

The plates can also be used for printing labels on fabrics by specially developed rotary letter presses.

For achieving perfect finish of labels, the plates can be used for printing of sticker labels by flexo on very fast machines.

With the use of magnetic base, photo polymer plates can be used on platen press and flat-bed cylinder presses.

For foil printing pantograph dies can be fabricated by employing photo polymer plates. The plates can also be used for embossing as counter dies.

The small rubber stamp industry is also now exposed to the positive influence of photo polymer plate, in that a very sharp impression with a far more lasting product would be ensured with the use of this revolutionizing plate.

PROCESSING UNITS

Photo polymer plate was first perfected in Holland for a unique compact for fast and safe production on steel, aluminium or foil backing. This industry has now a capacity to produce over 1500 units per annum which are being exported to about 85 countries including India.

The units comprise of a exposure segment, a wash-out segment and a drier until by hot air.

Two kinds of wash out units are available-one, an absolutely pollution free water base unit for letterpress printing and two, a solvent base unit for printing by flexo. Both the units are either free standing compact units or in table models.

The units are easy to operate and a plate can be ready in about 11 minutes with the use of a negative, preferably a matted one.

The attachable wash-out unit is made os stainless steel and is operated with a flat brush and a rotating plate on top. Plates can be secured to this plate with adhesive or magnetic foil.

The wash-out unit is fitted with temperature gauge and an outlet. The dryer is fitted with an efficient hot air circulation and has two shelves and a fume outlet.

Production of both water and solvent base printing plates can be realized by adding a second wash out unit for a continuous operation.

The normal sizes in which the units are available are 8"x12", 12"x23", 23"x33", 25"x32", 31"x40" and 43"x63". In accordance with the individual customer requirement the specially constructed cabinets of bigger sizes are also available.

10

SHEET-FED PRINTING

The printing industry, in particular, are undergoing structural change of a fundamental nature which are proving more fat-reaching than the transition from letter press to offset printing. Critically Mr. Wachter added: "If pre-press and printing processes play only a secondary role in this scenario, what virtually insignificant part is being played by sheet-fed printing in its present form within printing's secondary role?"

The somewhat extreme view is put into perspective, however, when institutions such as the German National Printing Association depict print products as a permanent, modern medium with a future and forecast annual growth rates of 2 to 2.5 per cent. However the market for printed information is stagnating to a certain extent, meaning the proportion of print products in the exchange of information is on the decline. In view of figures like these, playing a secondary role is not exactly the end of the world.

Print products currently produced on sheet-fed presses include:

* Printed information, for example, product catalogues, retailer information and similar items in small to medium-size runs.
* Advertising in the form of brochures, direct-distribution advertising, leaflets, inserts, etc. in small to medium-sized runs.
* Documentation, image brochures, books, calendars in small to medium-sized runs.
* Packaging and packaging accessories such as folding boxes and labels in all run sizes.

As a consequence, the sheet fed offset printing segment is currently defined by virtue of run size and format as compared with small offset and by virtue of run size for the most part as compared with rotary offset printing. However, every new rotary offset printing press generation shifts this segment downwards with regard to run size (currently between 15,000 and 20,000).

This development is being counteracted in sheet-fed offset printing by new technologies for enhancing run sizes and automation with the objective of minimizing make ready and down times.

WEB OFFSET PRINTING

As the Web Offset printing process matures, it continues to improve. Over the past year, web offset has maintained its position as the dominant printing process because of this. Although gravure and flexography also improve and grow, neither has matched the growth of web offset. In 1986, web offset is projected to achieve a 38.5 percent share of the commercial printing market, a position that reflects a real growth rate of 8.5 percent annually.

New developments in high-speed press equipment, long life plates, paper, ink and chemicals have contributed to improvements in offset printing. To keep pace with high-speed presses and the dynamic requirements of customers, web press control systems have burst upon the scene. They have improved print quality, reduced manning requirements and upped productivity. fundamental elements such as pin register systems, quality improvements and training programs also have contributed significantly.

With all the resources being applied to web offset, the process will continue to make major strides. It is dynamic, and must be classified as a "process on the move" What is moving web offset and influencing its evolution?

Several key factors that determine printing process selection are identified in a recent study conducted by the Graphic Arts Marketing Information Service (GAMIS/PIA). Ranked one, tow, three in importance are: quality, price and service. All three can be derived from web offset and have a major impact on its success. Without question, they are the primary elements assessed by the web offset printer who must meet product/market requirements in order to survive in the competitive print arena.

The term "quality" means different things to different people. In web offset, color register, separation, grade of paper and ink coverage all contribute to quality printing. The web offset manager must control these variables on each job. Control of the press system is essential. If not, hickies, linting, color variation, dot gain, non-uniform ink laydown, misregister, ghosting and marking can appear as unwanted by products. Consistency of quality over long runs is a primary concern.

Press automation has improved color registration. Closed loop color-to-color systems simplify registration on press, improve color quality and consistency, and reduce waste. The electronic explosion within the graphic arts has sent shock waves throughout the color separation area. Electronic color scanning, digitizing and separation systems have vastly improved the prepress department's ability to produce high quality separations.

At the same time, the transition of electronics and technology into the prepress area continues to spawn new products for web offset application. The interation of electronic prepress may eventually unmask itself and produce an effective color proofing system.

Integration of the prepress area and web offset press has occurred through plate and film scanning systems that are linked with automatically preset, ink fountain keys. These systems have simplified the task of achieving color on press, while reducing make ready.

The ability to produce quality printing is largely dependent on the substrate and materials. In most print market segments, the cost of paper far outweighs the cost of printing and binding. The challenge is to maintain a high degree of print quality on lower-cost paper grades.

The web offset insert/flyer printer is requesting a brighter or whiter, light weight offset sheet, which has a better finish, greater opacity and more bulk than super-calendered and machine-coated stocks. Some paper mills have responded by offering a new "O" is being accepted by printers and their customers.

Paper and usage trends are driven by several factors. Paper upgrading drives many print market segments served by web offset. It is often reflected in the use of heavier basis weights and brighter sheet within a particular grade category. A shift upward in paper grade often represents a critical decision for the customer and printer. But once customer acceptance is established, it may be impossible to reverse the decision.

Growing acceptability of color printing has spawned demand for coated paper and facilitated continued growth of heat set web offset. As demand for heat set and increased color grows, the drive for coated papers will continue.

A by product of interest in coated papers and print quality is the emergence of the supercalendered paper classification. In 1984, paper mills produced nearly one million tons of this grade. However, the classification for supercalendered sheets remains unsettled. This is largely due to different nomenclatures used by paper mills.

Supercalendered paper represents an important range of grades for achieving quality and appearance similar to coated groundwood grades-at considerably less expense. When printing heavy coverages, it often is difficult to determine the difference between a lightweight coated and a supercalendered sheet.

Ink is also a critical element in achieving good print quality. In fact, the amount of printed coverage is often the basis for determining quality. Ink manufacturers have responded well to the dynamics of web offset and kept pace with changing conditions. Environmental Protection Agency (EPA) guidelines and regulations governing air pollution have influenced development of higher solid inks, chemically reactive inks, radiation curable inks and water-based inks, Development of higher solid inks for heat set printing is considered an interim solution to the overall air pollution problem.

With a shift toward lower, basis-weight coated and supercalendered sheets, the ink manufacturer has assumed responsibility to maintain and enhance print film properties, especially on lower grade papers. To further complicate ink-related issues, press speeds continue to increase. Speeds exceeding 2,000 fpm. require adjustments in ink tack, rheology solids contents and other properties for effective printing. Ink manufacturers must resolve the picking and linting problems that occur at high speeds.

EPA pressure also has prompted development of substitutes for isopropyl alcohol in web offset. Some of these new substances have had detrimental effects on ink performance and paper coatings.

To satisfy demand for improvements in ink gloss and physical properties of ink, manufacturers must continue research and development. Greater understanding of paper and ink reactions, press dynamics, thermal characteristics and press speeds is critical to efforts aimed at improving the physical properties of ink.

To promote quality improvement within the non-heat set segment of the web offset industry, Printing Industries of American (PIA) development Specifications for Non-Heat set Advertising Printing (SNAP). SNAP was originally designed as a communications tool to specify color standards, proofing, film densities and tone reproduction aim points, screen ruling, four-color reverses, color bars and proofing stock recommendations. A test plate incorporating SNAP specifications is available from PIA along with targets to monitor dot gain, ink trap and hue error.

Despite the development of SNAP and Specifications for Web Offset Publication (SWOP), there is still room for printing and proofing to attain results anticipated by the customer, printer and separation house. Color analysis and densitometry will continue to develop as demand for more color in web offset increases.

Considerable emphasis is being placed on dot gain in an effort to control color variability-a primary contributor to waste in ink, paper and downtime. The Graphic Communications Asso. (GCA) Print Properties Committee has analyzed the effect of dot gain on ad reproductions, along with variables affecting it and, ultimately, color variability.

Finally, the quality arena continues to feature a battle between heat set and non-heat set printing. Heat set offset is expected to continue making market share gains in various end-use printing markets. The gains are largely attributed to print customer's desire to enhance their quality image by upgrading to better paper and improving reproduction.

Part - 2

PROJECT PROFILES ON PRINTING

11

COMPUTER CONTINUOUS STATIONERY (FORMS)

INTRODUCTION

Information means paper on which to print it, and computer-processed information usually means high speed line printers and continuous forms business forms are usually printed on web off set presses of the unit in line design with a steel impression cylinder in each units, as the printing is done only one side of the paper.

Presses are equipped with a number of auxiliary functions such as punching numbering, slitting sheeting gluing or rewinding. Many business forms are printed for computer and punching of the hole is critical as these are used to position the sheet in the print out devices. Also many business. Forms are used in optical character reading (OCR) equipment. The paper used for this type of printing must meet stringent requirements especially in cleanliness.

The multiplication of computers has caused an unexpected proliferation of business-forms. The use of forms in computers has increased demands of the paper used for business forms.

Different raw materials are used for the manufacture of different grades of paper required for the use in computer stationary. The main criteria is low cost paper conforming side by side to the requisite properties with the advents of computers and its use in almost all walks of life it is expected that computers will use maximum production of paper.

USES AND APPLICATION

As the name suggest these papers are used in computer for data input as well as data output. Computer prints the data with the help of printer on it, to be output, on these papers which are very clean smooth and its mechanical strength is sufficient high to not tear during operation. It has high durability and reliability capacity to handle and undergoes high productivity.

Since computer operates at high speed it consumes much more stationary/ spurs than hundreds of clerks. We are listing the papers required by different computer units below:

Unit

1. Computer papers of various sheets size but of some hole diameter and Hard copy hole pitch perforated terminal
2. Computer papers of various sheet sizes but of same hole diameter Printer and hole pitch perforated.
3. Computer papers of same sizes 15" as for sheets also having same holes pitch and hole pitch and hole Printer diameter. These are also perforated.

MARKET SURVEY

To use computer for any task require first of all to communicate the data of the concerned problem to the computer and similarly to provide answers, computer requires to communicate results to the user. This to and fro communication is done through various media - one of which is stationery. Computer stationery is normally defined as the papers pre-printed or otherwise used to communicate data to computer or to user. Such communication normally is being done continuously by computer and so requires stationery in huge amount. Computer stationery many a times is known as Continuous Stationery.

Continuous Stationery is normally divided in two groups:

1. Single Ply Stationery.
2. Multi-Part Stationery.

Single Ply Stationery is used normally for simple tasks like preparing pay rolls or for training in computer programming, where computer at one point of time - performs only one duty.

As against this Multi-Part Stationery is used in computers having more than one terminals. When various jobs are handled by computer at a time and job is very complex, multi-part stationery is used. It facilitates to get different output at a time on different terminals and even to have more than one copies at a time from the same result. All large frame and medium computers use multi-part stationery.

PRESENT MANUFACTURERS OF COMPUTER STATIONERY

Continental Forms (P) Ltd.
B-9, G.T. Karnal Road Indl. Area,
Delhi - 110 033
Phones : 712 6464, 712 3347, 724 9503
Fax : 011-724 9502

Glaxy Forms
G-13, Udyog Nagar,
Rohtak Road,
Delhi - 110 041
Phone : 547 3285

Nipoon Computer Aids (Pvt.) Ltd.
A-17, Shalimar Apartments,
Masjid Moth, N.D.S.E.-II,
New Delhi - 110 019
Phones : 621 2660, 623 1208

Glaxy Forms Ltd.
1340 A, M.I.E.,
Bahadurgarh - 124 507
(Haryana)
Phones : 314019, 314029

Indus Forms Private Limited
31-B, Sector 31,
Faridabad - 121 003
(Haryana)
Phones : 8-212050

Arun Graphic Computer Forms (P) Ltd.
E-13, Sector-7,
Noida - 201 301
(U.P.)
Phone : 522584

MANUFACTURINGPROCESS

The sort of paper for printers you need depends on your printing device. Electrostatic and thermal types require special paper, but neither are suitable for business use. Dot matrix and daisy wheels allow you a wider choice. Continuous stationery, with pages linked together but perforated for repetitive work such as invoice is often used.

Printing:

Printing on computer papers will be done with the help of line printing press. Inks are applied to the press by which, the punching papers on surface dedicated with seven lines each in rows. The distance between two seven lines rows being concerned at about 1/5".

Even, the machine printed lines at a stack in continuous manner, lining should be complete upto both sides covering punching holes. Practically, the line printing are not forced for both sides of paper. Because there is no need of figure to be made in back side. Specially, the computer output dot matrix or line printers works only one side. Sometimes figures being drawn on the back side. But as a consideration of computer a paper printing only for one side.

There are today four major types of printing presses and printing systems for computer papers making lining letter press, offset. In letter press the image of lining to be reproduced is in relief. Ink is applied to the raised areas, and when a sheet of paper is pressed against then the film of ink is split, the image from the plate being left on the paper surface.

In offset lithography, a planographic process the image is in the same plane is the non-image areas. The printing of the image is from flat surface which is chemically treated so that ink is accepted in the image areas and repelled in the non-image areas.

Punching:

Computer papers are punched by five to eight tracks rows of dies striking against a steel matrix with a corresponding number of holes while the paper passes between the dies and matrix. The dies are activated by a mechanism under the control of computer output signals. Mechanisms used for the punching operation differ mainly in the movement of the dies and or the steel matrix. Although patents have been granted for poaches that have no moving parts because they are activated by Compression (air pressure waves) and operate at a speed of 1000 chps, no such devices are know to be on production.

The design of computer paper punches is complicated by the need. Punching was done on both sides of the paper. To examine the paper immediately after punching in small round shape. This means that the paper has to be punched in a horizontal plane, with the chads, or chips, from the punching being ejected upward.

Perforating:

is often done during a printing operation by a sharp steel rule just enough higher than the type of penetrate the paper. The perforated line is also inked, of course, unless the printer goes to the trouble and expense of cutting away a section of this ink rollers. On cylinder press a perforating can be attached to the cylinder.

Perforating is also handles as a separate operation on machines that punch or drill rows of tiny holes. This is considered as a finishing operating.

Mounting and Finishing:

Mounting is a fairly simple operation in which the mounting papers may be the major item in the total cost. Special mounting presses apply glue to the paper poster and to the cardboard backing and then squeeze both together in a short of winger.

The number and type of paper stacks can be varied to obtain a range of finishes (machine finish a stack of intermediates papers may be included before the last section of drying and depending on the finish required. An imitation art finish may be obtained on the paper machine by applying a thin film of water to the paper as it enters the nip of one or more of the paper unit.

Measuring Sizes:

The depth of 12 inches (304.8 mm) should be accepted in licenses of the depth of A4 in all cases where continuous forms are not reported. In other cases, the depth of 12 inches should be regarded as a untrimmed size which could, if so desired, be trimmed to the depth of A4. Of overall widths (including the sprocket holes), the following preferred sizes have been recommended, 180, 250, 340, 400 and 450 mm. For special applications wider forms any be required.

Removal of the edges of the paper containing the sprockets holes on the above sizes could lead to trimmed form widths identical to 'A' dimensions wider forms may be required. These width recommendations are not related to paper sizes of for on line data teleprinters and other machines with non-adjustables, pin feed platens.

In an article written for the publication about five. A sizes that may be used for business forms are:-

INCHES	MILLIMETERS	
A_3	11.69 * 16.54	297 * 220
A_4	8.27 * 11.69	210 * 297
A_5	5.83 * 8.27	148 * 210
A_6	4.13 * 5.83	105 * 148
A_7	2.97 * 4.13	74 * 105

Almost all the writing machines in the free world space in sixth of an inch and tenth of an inch horizontally.

SUPPLIERS OF MACHINERIES

Complete Plant & Machinery Supplier

Sud & Waren (P) Limited
72, Sector - 6, Indl. Estate,
Faridabad - 121 006 (Haryana)
Phones: 91-129-242342, 242402, 245027, 245028
Fax: 91-129-241243

Raj Trading Corporation
C-92, New Ashok Nagar,
New Delhi - 110 092

Convertaid Engineers (P) Limited
Plot No - 1, Sanjay Memorial Indl. Estate,
Phase - II, Opp. YMCA, Faridabad - 121 006
(Haryana)
Phone: 0129-289607, 263160
Fax: 0129-283204

Continuous Printing Machines

Bandhu Systems Private Limited
56, Maruti Industrial Complex,
Sector-18, Gurgaon,
(Haryana)
Phone/fax: 8-340012

Sarvottam Appliances (P) Ltd.
98, Sector-25,
Ballabgarh. (Haryana)
Phone/fax: 8-232949

Printpack Machinery Limited
41-42, Link Road, Sector-28,
Faridabad - 121 003 (Haryana)
Phone/fax: 8-276849, 276289

PCM Engineering (P) Ltd.
B-170, D.D.A. Shed,
Okhla Indl. Area I,
New Delhi - 110 020
Phone/fax: 6811993

Offset Printing Press Machines

Amit International
B-47, Cox House,
Naraina Indl. Area, Phase-II,
New Delhi - 110 028
Phones : 570 4301, 570 4201
Fax : 011-224 9320

Diamond Engg. Works
6/12, DLF, Indl. Area,
Moti Nagar, New Delhi - 110 015
Phones : 541 4571, 541 8352

Aksis Engg. Works (P) Limited
139, Sector 25,
Ballabgarh, (Haryana)
Phone : 8-234942

Dominent Offset (P) Ltd.
Palam Road,
Gurgaon, (Haryana)
Phones : 340019, 341916, 341917, 341918, 340032
Fax : 0124-340131

Bharat Machine Tools
133-138, Sector 6,
Faridabad, (Haryana)
Phones : 8-241798, 241167

Fair Deal Engineers
89, Ramsaroop Colony,
Mujessar, Faridabad,
(Haryana)
Phones : 8-237143, 234314

Fair Deal Graphics
3 & 4, Dharam Kanta Road,
Mujessar, Faridabad.
(Haryana)

Venus Offset House
15A/1, Industrial Area, N.I.T.,
Faridabad, (Haryana)
Phones/fax : 8-236821

SUPPLIERS OF RAW MATERIALS

Papers:

Usha Paper & Board Industries
17, D.L.F. Industrial Area,
Mathura Road,
Faridabad, Haryana.

Sandeep Paper Mills (P) Limited
A-20, Sector-6, Noida Distt.
Ghaziabad. (U.P.)

Om Prakash Jitendra Kumar & Company
63, Darya Ganj,
New Delhi - 11 00 02.
Phone/fax : 326 96 80, 3271380

Narain Paper Mart
4034/3, Haryana Market,
Chawri Bazar,
Delhi - 11 00 06.
Phone/fax : 291 51 35.

Himgiri Paper Products
B-24, Indl. Area Lawrence Road,
New Delhi - 110035
Phone/fax : 718 9005

Ashok Kumar Mohinder Kumar
73, Swaran Park,
Mundka, New Delhi - 110 041
Phone/fax : 251 0037, 541 7011

Chetan Papers (P) Ltd.
A-6, Everest Building,
Tardeo Road, Mumbai - 400 034
Phone : 4943680
Fax : 91-022-4952546

Mahavir Traders
52, Dadiseth Agiary Lane,
Mumbai - 400 002
Phone : 201 6839, 208 8020
Fax : 91-022-2060459

Printing Ink:

Baluja Spectra
C-50 Okhla Indl. Area-II,
New Delhi - 110020
Phone/fax: 6835715, 6835722

Ajanta Ink Company
Basai Road, Gurgaon (Haryana)
Phone/fax: 8-330028

Art Printing Inks Company
104 Site-4, Indl. Area,
Sahibabad, Ghaziabad.
Phone/fax: 767882

Inks India (Delhi)
C-49, Sector-8,
Noida-201 301 (U.P.)
Phone/fax: 523801, 011-8-557270

Van Inks & Chemicals (P) Ltd.
B-150, Phase-II,
Noida-201 305 (U.P.)
Phone/fax: 567141, 011-8-521507

Packing Materials:

Sonar Packaging,
Plot 48, T.D.L.F.
Industrial Area,
Faridabad, Haryana.

Printing Plates & Other Chemicals:

Alpha Graphic
19, Police Court Lane,
Fort, Mumbai - 400 001
Phone: 261 4441/42, 261 0603, 261 5191
Fax: 91-022-262 5534

PLANT ECONOMICS OF
COMPUTER FORMS & SECURITY PRINTING PRESS

Rated Plant Capacity = 40 Boxes per Day Containing 1000 Sheets and Job Work for Railways, Banks etc.

COST OF LAND & BUILDING

(Total Land required 1000 sq. mtr.)	Rs.	15,85,000.00

LIST OF PLANT & MACHINERY

1. Single Colour Offset Printing Machine
2. Slitter, Rewinder
3. Semi-Automatic Cutting Machine
4. Stitching Machine
5. Numbering Machine (Single phase)
6. Herdelberg Cylinder Letter Press
7. Chandler Machine (Single phase)
8. Lamination Machine
9. Pack to Pack Collector

LIST OF RAW MATERIALS

1. Plates for printing
2. Printing Inks
3. Graphic Films
4. Miscellaneous Stores & Consumables
5. Computer Stationery

FIXED CAPITAL

Land & Building	Rs.	15,85,000.00
Plant & Machinery	Rs.	22,60,000.00
Other Fixed Assets	Rs.	4,00,000.00
TOTAL	**Rs.**	**42,45,000.00**

TOTAL WORKING CAPITAL/MONTH

1.	Raw Material	Rs.	1,50,000.00
2.	Salary & Wages	Rs.	1,16,375.00
3.	Utilities & Overheads	Rs.	57,500.00
	TOTAL	**Rs.**	**3,23,875.00**

TOTAL CAPITAL INVESTMENT

Total Fixed Capital	Rs.	42,45,000.00
Total Working Capital for 3 Months	Rs.	9,71,625.00
TOTAL	**Rs.**	**52,16,625.00**

TURNOVER/ANNUM

1. By printing computer forms for Railway, Banks etc. on Job Work
2. Earnings from job-work of different printing works
3. By selling computer forms 12,000 Boxes (1 Box = 1000 forms)

TOTAL **Rs. 71,40,000.00**

PROFIT = RECEIPTS - COST OF PRODUCTION
= 71,40,000.00 - 56,93,782.50
= 14,46,217.50

PROFIT SALES RATIO = Profit / Sales x 100 = **20.26 %**

RATE OF RETURN = Operating profit / T.C.I. x 100 = **27.72 %**

BREAK EVEN POINT (B.E.P) = 64.62 %

12

DESK TOP PUBLISHING & OFFSET PRINTING UNIT

INTRODUCTION

Printing as it is understood in the modern context had its beginning in Europe in 1439 when the technique of printing from movable metal types was developed by Johannes Gutenberg of Mainz, Germany. Printing of some crude sort done from movable types was believed to have been produced in Holland by coaster before Gutenberg. The Gutenberg's invention consisted essentially in making brass moulds and matrices by which type could be accurately aligned and cast in large numbers. The metal chosen for the type was an alloy of lead, tin and antimony. The technique of printing consisted in composing the type into words, lines and pages, inking the printing surface and printing sheets of paper in a manually operated press made of wood. The first book printed by Getenberg was a Bible, in the year 1456. The art of printing spread quickly all over Europe and by the fifteenth century about twenty million copies of over 40,000 different editions had been printed mainly on hand presses. In the beginning of seventeenth centuary more or less regular newspaper printed from movable types started appearing in Germany, Austria the Netherlands and Italy.

Since the turn of the nineteenth century there has been a phenomenal advancement in science and technology which radically changed the mechanism involved in composing and printing techniques. Developments such as application of power to printing press and later adoption of photographic techniques to printing processes, have enabled incredibly fast rate of reproduction in highly mechanized presses, quick and precise preparation of printing surfaces and tremendous improvement in quality of the printed material.

The printing processes now in common use are broadly classified into four groups according to the principles on which their printing - image carriers are based. The four process families are - relief printing (letter press and flexography) in which printing areas of the image carriers are raised above printing (lithography and collotype) in which the printing and non printing areas are in the same plane of the image corner; intaglio printing (gravure) in which the printing areas are sunken in the image carrier, non - printing areas are on its surface, and screen printing (stencil printing) in which the printing areas consist of open pores of the image carrier, the blocked pores - constitute the non - printing areas.

The revolution in desktop printing started in 1985. Though the technology is just three years old, already plenty of hardware and software options are available. Johann Gutenberg installed a successful printing press in the fifteenth century. Since then, publishers have been booking for a better, cheaper and faster way to get words and pictures on paper. It look years to make even the slightest improvement on the printing press, but DTP keeps advancing at an accelerated pace. Like any other computer system the three main components of DTP are hardware, software and printer. (We described later on these topics).

Book is a important source of knowledge. Increase in standard of living further leads to develop interest in studying. Not always true. With increase in industrialization, the demand for books has to increase.

To sum up, desk top publishing has come to stay. But its full potential and applications by only be realized by those conversant with the various packages available and prepared to study the combinations there of.

MARKETSURVEY

Development of any country depends much upon its literacy, to achieve socialism, equalitarinism welfare society rational and forward looking people to have society free from all sorts of prejudices orthodoxy etc. books plays a very important role. Future of any nation depends upon how much people are educated. During the freedom movement press played a very important role in mobilising the people, the developing a nationalist spirit and to expose the true nature of British rule, and most important press played very important role in destroying the British myths of invincibility.

Education earlier was confined to very limited number of people. Books were not available in good numbers. Government took drastic step in removing illitracy which also lead to proportional growth of press industry. Large number of universities, Colleges, Schools were established, which simultaneously resulted in rapid demand of books, journals, periodical etc. printing industries increased tremendously at the end of 1980, there were 54,000 printing presses in the country with an investment of Rs. 550 crores and which employed six lakhs people. Apart from this there are also thousands of small printing units, involve of in the job working printing. The printing requirement of the country will increase in literacy education and awareness to national happenings and current affairs.

There is tremendous consumption of booking resulting increasing number of printed book every year rapidly. Increase the capital income standard of living realization of importance of education, various governments scheme and programmes for removal of illitracy, various social organisation strevous efforts etc. all have contributed the improvement of education further industrialisation also requires the more consumption of printed material looking to all these, it is assumed that demand of for books periodical journals etc. will increase at an annual rate of 25 percent of in coming five years.

Government has sanctioned total capacity of 5675 printing machine which roughly amounts to 5155 lakh rupees. These includes mostly offset machines of single colour or multi-colours.

DTP SYSTEMS

Laser Printers and Digitizers:

Desk Top Publishing involves many components, but without good output devices, all the effort that goes into designing and laying out pages is wasted. Currently, the primary high-resolution output device in a desk top publishing 'operation is the laser printer. Most good looking documents that result from desk top publishing are more that just nicely formatted type.

Laser Printers and digitizers as much as computers and software - makes desk top publishing a personal rather than a strictly corporate or industrial endeavor.

Laser Printers:

A laser printers is essentially a photocopier. In fast, many such printers use the same technology that photocopiers do, a photo sensitive drum temporarily holds an electric charge in the shape of an image transferred to it by a computer-driven laser beam. the charge and the image carried within it are transferred to a sheet of paper as it rools across the drum. The paper then attracts the toner (plastic ground into a fine powder) and heat bonds the toner to the paper.

Digitizers: Producing Graphic Images:-

A digitiser transforms an image into digital information you can store in a computers memory or on a mass storage device. You can then transfer that information to abit-maped screen, where you can edit it repeatedly or to a high resolution output device such as a laser printer. Digitizers are of two sorts : Video and optical.

Video digitizers use the standard video signal produced by, typically, a video camera, but also by a VCR or even a television set that can emit a video signal. A video signal digitizer scans an image and turns each element of the image into a linary number. On a screen, each number translates into a different light intensity, known a gray scale. On a printer, the numbers translates into dot patterns called pseudo halftones. From a distance, these patterns look like continuous gray tones. Examples of video digitizers are Micro Imager, Macvision, Magic and Micron Eye.

SOFTWARE

Two main types of DTP software are : the page make-up program and the typesetting program. Such programs combine the conventional roles of the typesetter and the pasteup artist. Text can be typed, arranged in columns and blocks on a page. It is also possible to break up the text, add headlines, captions and subheads.

Some programs provide the facility of inserting graphics within and around the text. The graphics may be as simple as a box or a line, or as complex as aline drawing, schematic or digitized photograph.

Macintosh page make-up programs are : Ready Setgo, PageMaker and MacPublisher. They allow mixing of text and graphics freely and are compatible with other Mac programmes such as Mac Write, MacWord, MacDraw and MacPaint. Some of the IBM PC software packages are: Click Art Personal Publisher, Front Page, Harvard Professional Publisher, PageMaker, Ventura Publisher and Superpage II.

Typesetting software is for operating galleys which are cut to proper lengths to be pasted manually on to a page. For the IBM PC they are Do-it from Studio Software, Genesy's Rim Writer, and Softype from Softtest. Typesetting programs for macintosh include Deskset from G.O. Graphics and just Text from knowledge Engineering.

Typesetting programs offer more features and flexibility than page make-up software. Two most desirable features are kerning and letter space justification. Kerning is adjustment of space between each character and the latter is making the right and left margins flush on every line by adjusting the space between each character. Typesetting software is expensive and more difficult to use than a page make-up program.

PAGEMAKE-UPPROGRAMMES

Pagemaker:

Aldus Corp's Pagemaker for Mac got DTP off the ground. It has simple menu commands, WYSIWYG (what you see is what you get) displays, the ability to incorporate text and graphics from other programs and to output to high resolution printers and typesetters.

MacPublisher II:

This program divides the screen into many windows. The right hand of screen contains the page which cannot be moved, resized or scrolled. Lower left corner has dog-ear flaps which enable to flip through the pages of the publication. Documents up to 96 pages can be created but disc space and number of documents in an average publication make this limit about 30 pages.

The page window has three modes - mini, maxi and dummi. The dummi window shows entire page in reduced form. It simply shows the layout of text relative to other elements on the page. Editing is not possible in this mode, but blocks can be moved around to modify the layout.

The mini page displays actual text with other elements Word file into a blank window. Now, click on the window that contains the text required position the scissors over the layout, and the text will flow on to the page. If it is longer than the page or blocks, then it is placed in another column. Now column is treated as the part of original article, so changes made in the text automatically reflow through the columns.

MacPublisher II's transparent rulers are used to measure the text. It can be specified whether rulers should display inches, centimeters, points or lines the text is going to occupy when laid out on the page and printed.

Ventura Publisher:

Xerox Corp's package offers page composition software with sophisticated features which make it suitable for long documents as well as short flyers and newsletters publishing.

Though it is not easy to learn its power and ability to run on a PC XT makes it a solid investment for PC desktop publishers. It is based upon GEM operating system.

Style sheets help to define the font and the format of repeating elements such as body text and major heading. Format of entire document can be changed by modifying the style sheet. There are over 20 style sheets for specific documents such as letters, reports, books, newsletter, magazines, price lists and tables.

Ventura allows to control character spacing and line spacing in decimal increments. It will automatically number the chapters, and up to right levels of headings, as well as footnotes and figures. Minimum number of lines to be isolated in windows or orphans can be specified. Text can be imported in six different file formats.

This package offers colours for both text and graphics. But colour ink jet printers still do not offer the typeset quality printing of laser printers. Multicolour laser printers will enable Ventura to produce limited runs of colour publications.

OFFSETPRINTINGPRESS

Offset Press Operation

Offset presses are rotary in nature and use the principle that greases and water do not misc to deliver the desired impressions on paper.

The printing section of the press includes a plate cylinder, an impression cylinder a blanket cylinder, inking rollers, a moisture system and a plate adjustment (Registration), devices. In addition of course, it has a feeder system to more the paper into the press and a delivery system for the finished work.

That all material to be printed is one thinflat, and pliable plate is one of the virtues of the offset process. Make ready is no problem, and the plate is easily rapped around, the plate cylinder much in the fashion that anmimegraph stencil is applied.

Once the plate is on the press the operator must apply, the moisture (water plus an additive) to the surface of the plate. The water adheres to the non image area of the plate and is repelled in the image areas. When ink a grease, is applied it adders only to the image area and is repelled by the water wet portions. Because of the water grease action and its photographic nature, offset printing is considered a chemical process.

It is called an indirect process because impression are not made directly from the plate. The plate never touches the paper, instead it deposits the inked image on the blanket cylinder with each revolution. The paper receives the image from the blanket cylinder as the sheet or web goes through the press between the blanket and impression cylinders. The impression cylinders is simply the surface backing up the paper as the blanket squeezes against it serving the same function as the platen in a typewriter or the bed of a traditional flat bed press.

Each revolution of an offset press therefore consists of :

1. Application of greasy ink to the image areas of the plate.
2. Application of greasy ink to the image areas of the plate.
3. Transfer of the inks image to a rubber, blanketed cylinder.
4. Pickup of the paper by the feeding system of the press, which inserts the paper between the blanket and impression cylinders.
5. Deposit of the image from the blanket to the paper.
6. Delivery of the sheets or web of paper.

Although is may seem to be a lengthy series of details, it is accomplished instantaneously. Because offset presses operate on the rotary principle, they are capable of extremely high speed. IN general their speed, are basically determined by the efficiency of their feeding and deliver system the cylinders can rotate as fast as an electric motor can turn a drive a shaft.

The most frequent problem in connection with offset press operation is the maintenance of a proper balance of moisture and ink change in humidity sometimes, give pressure a change in humidity sometimes give pressure a great deal of difficulty in this regard.

Printing Methods:

Letterpress printing process is the largest in use in India. In the composing section, hand composition is still the most common, through larger establishments are changing to machine composition. Among the mechanical composing machines, monotype, linotype and intertype are in general use. Besides English type can be composed on the machines for almost all important Indian languages.

Offset printing is presently popular to big printing establishments in large cities like Delhi , Calcutta, Chennai and Mumbai etc. Scarcity of machines and materials for which the industry has to depend to a large extent on imports, and of trained personnel have stood in the way of growth of offset printing in India. The offset process, however, is now fast competing with the letterpress process in big printing centres like Mumbai and Calcutta where most of the printing is devoted to commercial and publicity needs of the industrial sector.

METHOD OF TYPE SETTING & PRINTING

Laying of the Type:

The compository composes the matter to be printed in the proper not known as sticks assigned for it or the spaces and letters are set in such a way as to meet of the requirement of the material to be printed. The size of the page is kept in mind which lying the type. Thus the composing is made machines the measure ordered for by the customer for printing.

Proof Making:

After setting the type in the required size a proof is made out and select the correctness of the matter and there after correction and carried out of any is the composed out made.

Printing:

The composed matter is then fitted is iron frame and fixed with the lock with the keep of gotters and guild lays. The chaises is then taken to the printing machines and accordingly the matter is printed out in the required number.

The process of lithography in the world has indeed been spectacular during the last two decades there is ample proof to bear out the fact expanding improved durability of offset plates accompanied by improved quality of printed products have made it suitable process for printing magazines. Single colours machines are now being replaced by multi colours only. Both the paper makers and the ink makers have worked hand with the lithograph or with the result that the print quality of the offset process has become infact equal if not superior to letter press printing in sharpness. The use of coated stock for multicolour work to emulate the letter press process is a common feature in all three countries.

In the process section, the camera have become precision equipments. Films are being used in greater quantities the introduction of dimensionally stable easter based film has same further increased off take of films, the orthodox view, however, is that in spite of all the measures taken to control the temperature and humidity films are still unreliable in point of dimensional stability and that the industry would therefore continue to use and proper plates for register work.

Making is now widely used for colour correction and is claimed to have considerably reduced time on hand retouching. Multi mark films represent the latest progress in the production of a single mask for all the colours. Colour scanners like the scannation are in operation for product continuous time colour corrected the negative in the more progressive firms in all the countries.

Step and repeat printing down machines are more commonly adopted for duplicating purposes. the arc lamp continues to be the most common light source. The 3 phases are lumps being the more modern version. The latest light source are the pulsed Xenon Lamps.

Principle of Offset:

It will be seen that an off set print is not taken from the printing plate direct to the paper or stock, but the first made on an intermediate surface and transferred for there to the paper. The usual method is to have a special cylinder on which is stretched and offset blanket.

As the print is reversed on the off-set blanket and again reversed when it is transferred on to the paper, it follows that the job which is to be printed off set appears the same on the machine plate as an the final print. It should also be noted that offset printing is done by both rotary and flat bed machine and therefore, the term offset is not synonymous with rotary, despite the decline of flathead.

It will also be a appreciated that the term direct method as used by the first off set tin printing was quite clear to then but is now confusion due to the wilder subsequent application of the offset process. As this was specialized printing group very largely isolated from other trade contacts, the terms which they used were their down concern, but it should be clearly understood that all metal sheet printing is off-set printing that the principle is the same as used now for printing on paper and that litho offset machines have developed from earlier this printing machines.

For all practical purposes offset printing is exclusively a lithographic process, the notable exception being the specialized letter press machine for the printing of this metal collapsible tube of such types as are used for both paste, shaving cream and the like.

PROCESS

Preparation of Copy:

Most of the firms maintained their own art and design department. Some of them are located on the factory premises. It is also a common practice of the trade to utilize outside agencies for the preparation art work. The standard of design submitted for reproduction is generally high. In the art department, the artist takes into consideration the technical details of the reproduction process and arranges the colours to be used in such a manner that a faithful reproduction is possible.

The use of phototype setting machines is of recent growth and we did not see much of it is Britain. In the American factories, however some firms were using photo setters. In Japan since the phototype setting machines, is similar and less expensive, phototype setters for composition are more common, particularly in big printing establishments.

Wherever a copy is received it is carefully scrutinized before it is actually sent into the works for processing. Some firms have a copy preparation department when the details are worked out. Normally an art department take on itself the task of (a) Scrutinizing type matter for reproduction by photography (b) Making off copy to suit the customers layout (c) Giving instructions regarding the percentage of enlargement or deduction and how they should for into the layout (d) Determining the number of colour (e) Grouping together of jobs of small matter.

Screens:

Both contact screens and the glass cross line screens are in use. The more progressive factories have however, started using contact screen because they give very much better results.

Colour Works:

Most of the four colour work is done with standard inks. There are, however, accessories when special shades of ink of a particular colour are required. In these cases, it is usual for the proofing section to mix inks from the standard inks. After the colour has been approved indications is given as to the ingredients used and the proportions of each. This enables the machine room or the ink making section to mix the ink for matching without the much difficulty.

Machine Room Layout:

The machine room should be extremely will laid out with wide many ways and plenty of space around the machines. The space ear marked for raw stock and printed stock is liberal mechanical devices are also provided for turning round huge stocks of one side printed paper.

Condition of Paper:

Every fun is in Japan executing high grade sheet fed offset printing work has installed have made paper conditioners. Steps are taken to ensure that no paper reaches the machine room unless it has been duly conditioned in the paper conditioning machine. For the purpose of improving the quality and increasing productivity, it will be advantageous for the printer in India to follow the Japanese method unless our paper makers are in a position to supply mill conditioned paper. Make ready time and running speed. It is generally recognised that the extra time taken with plate making department to ensure that the printing do work is absolutely accurate and the there are no positional errors, has greatly enabled made ready times being reduced. Good paper is one of the main influencing factors as far as the running a speed is concerned.

Damping Roller blankets:

The damper converting are generally of excellent moleskin. The sleeves are ordered to suit the damper of the roller and are put on the roller stocks effectively by means of drawing on machine. The inking rollers are generally of the vulcanized rubber type. It is the normal practice to use synthetic rubber blankets all over. For washing blanket proprietory washes are used.

Each machine is provided with sufficient no of damping and inking rollers as also space blankets for use in every emergency.

Flexibility of ester support is many times that required of photographic film support. The specific gravity of ester base film is stay submerged during tray processing. This avoids the difficulty of the film resin to the surface of the developing solutions with consequent uneven development.

Colour Separation:

Making has come to a acceptable universally and a number of variations one available. It has been admitted that as much as 70% of the retouching time is saved as a result of adoption of masking techniques.

Plate Graining:

With the increasing use of anodized aluminium plates presensitives plates and bi-metallize plates, its has the practice of lithographers in India to buy the plates ready from the plate suppliers. Consequently the graining dept. is recending in importance in lithographic printing units.

Machine used for graining are very large and are of the lifting and washing type. There are some which are suspended for the coiling. It is a common practice to wash both the machine toughs and the marble with copious supplies of water, with a view to ensure that the marbles that are used again are entirely free from any kind of grit of the graining material previously used. There is an increasing tendency to use steel balls of small size them marbles of large size. Abrasive used, for graining purpose very considerably and consists and consists generally of aluminium oxide, 200 to 240 mesh and very fine sand. After graining a plate is scrubbed carefully with hard brush under running water. The surface is wipped off by a squeezer and the plate thereafter is dried in an electric or gas stove.

Plate Making:

The need to control both humidity and temperative in this section has begun to be felt more and more and we found that the plate making department received particular attention in this matter even through.

SPECIFIC FOLDING METHODS

Cross Association:

This technique is employed on double-width news presses and similar machines where double folders are in use. The idea is to feed all of the webs into one folder so that the number of pages per copy is increased at the expense of the output of the other folder.

Balloon Folding:

This is a technique used on newspaper and similar machines for producing multiple sections of broadsheet newspapers at one pass through the press. It is quite commonly used on the Continent and North America, as well as producing some of our own Sunday supplements.

Collection:

Where the page size of the publication is smaller than the circumference of the printing cylinders, this will mean providing two, three, four or even more page positions around the cylinder, often with the same pages repeated several times. A simple example of this is normal newspaper situation in which each page is repeated around the cylinder 'two-set' with the result that two complete sets of plates are necessary.

The term 'collection' refers to a technique whereby the separate cut-off sections can be gathered together at the folder in order to obtain the maximum number of pages in a publication without multi-plating.

The pages will be cut at the normal length, in the usual manner, but every other set will be carried around a 'collection' cylinder and eventually mated with an alternative section to provide a double-size product at half the speed.

The system is at its simplest for conventional newspaper work where the main mechanical arrangement is that an additional set of needles is provided in the cutting cylinder, while one of the two sets of needles in the folding cylinder is removed. The 'collect' needles in the cutting cylinder then pierce the first section and take it around the cylinder until it arrives back at the cutting position again.

At this time the folding cylinder needles operate and pierce the second section as well as the first, before taking both sections to the cross-fold rollers.

3:2 folders:

Not all folders have the simple arrangement where the cutting cylinder circumference is the exact length of the cut-off product, with the folding cylinder being twice this circumference. It is often considered to be a mechanical advantage to have larger cylinders where possible, particularly if high speeds are anticipated, a considerable variation in the number of pages to be folded is probable, several sections are produced, and the page size is variable.

The simpler variation is the '3:2' folder which is used on some magazine and news machines. In this folder the cutting cylinder is twice the cut-off length of the product, therefore two cutting knives and boxes will be required, while the folding cylinder is three times the cut-off length, with the appropriate numbers of buffers, needles etc. Some of the advantages are fairly evident, i.e. twice the number of knives means longer blade life before replacement; similarly with buffers; larger cylinders means more efficient paper transport with less chance of distortion and buckling, particularly with larger products; higher speeds are attainable as the same circumferential speeds can be obtained at fewer r.p.m.

For multi-set magazine and tool book machines the 3:2 ration may refer to the proportions of the gripper and jaw cylinders respectively. The advantages of larger cylinders become even more applicable for collect work because of the additional copies to be carried around the cylinders and the exact timing of the intricate operations involved. For extra-large numbers of pages a 5:4 folder may be used, and if this is still insufficient then double-collection can be employed to produce a three-section product from the appropriate three or six-set printing cylinders.

ALTERNATIVE DELIVERIES

Folders are often provided with more than one delivery station, but the reasons for this may vary. It may be desirable to take the sections coming from a high-speed folder and deliver them at a steady rate to subsequent operations in the warehouse such as stacking gathering, trimming etc. Multiple deliveries can also be used where more than one section is being printed on the machine, so that by skilful imposition of the pages on the printing cylinders the different sections can be arranged to exit from their appropriate delivery outlets.

Where varying sizes and shapes of product are required at different times form the one folder, e.g.: straight-run for newspapers, quarter-page fold for magazines, or double parallel fold for book production, then the different end products may require alternative exits and suitable deliveries for each type of work.

SUPPLIERS OF RAW MATERIAL

Newsprint:

National Newsprint & Paper Mills Ltd.
Neponagar,
Madhya Pradesh.

Mysore Paper Mills Ltd.
16/4, Ali Saker road,
B.P. No. 112,
Bangalore - 560 052

Paper Suppliers :

Om Prakash Jitendra Kumar & Company
63, Darya Ganj,
New Delhi - 110 002
Ph. 326 9680, 327 1380

Narain Paper Mart
4034/3, Haryana Market,
Chawri Bazar,
Delhi - 110 006
Phone : 291 5135

Himgiri Paper Products
B-24, Indl. Area,
Lawrence Road,
New Delhi - 110 035
Phone : 718 9005

Printing Ink:

Baluja Spectra
C-50 Okhla Indl. Area-II,
New Delhi - 110 020
Phone/fax : 6835715, 6835722

Ajanta Ink Company
Basai Road, Gurgaon,
(Haryana)
Phone/fax : 8-330028

Art Printing Inks Company
104 Site-4, Indl. Area,
Sahibabad, Ghaziabad,
Phone/fax: 767882

Van Inks & Chemicals (P) Ltd.
B-150, Phase-II, Noida-201 305 (U.P.)
Phone/fax: 567141, 011-8-521507

Printing Material:

Dewan Chand & Sons
Chawri Bazar,
Delhi - 110006

Printer Stores
1525, Ist Floor,
A. Chand Marg,
Delhi - 110006

Suppliers of DTP System:

Zenith Electro Systems Pvt. Ltd.
106, Mittal Chambers,
Nariman Point,
Mumbai - 400021

Pearl Digital Systems
704, Rohit House,
Talstoy Marg,
New Delhi - 110001

Cameras:

National Instruments Ltd.,
1/1, Raja Subodh Chandra,
Mullick Road, Jadavpur,
Calcutta - 700032

New India Industries,
Jatalpur Road,
Baroad - 390005

LIST OF MANUFACTURERS OF PRINTING MACHINERY

Offset Printing Press Machines:

Amit International
B-47, Cox House,
Naraina Indl. Area,
Phase - II,
New Delhi - 110028
Phones : 570 4301, 570 4201
Fax : 011-224 9320

Diamond Engg. Works
6/12, DLF, Indl. Area,
Moti Nagar,
New Delhi - 110015
Phones : 541 4571, 541 8352

Aksis Engg. Works (P) Ltd.
139, Sector 25,
Ballabgarh,
(Haryana)
Phone : 8-234942

Dominent Offset P. Ltd.
Palam Road,
Gurgaon,
(Haryana)
Phones : 340019, 341916, 341917, 341918, 340032
Fax : 0124-340131

Bharat Machine Tools
133-138, Sector 6,
Faridabad,
(Haryana)
Phones : 8-241798, 241167

Fair Deal Engineers
89, Ramsaroop Colony,
Mujessar, Faridabad,
(Haryana)
Phones : 8-237143, 234314

PLANT ECONOMICS OF OFFSET PRINTING PRESS

Rated Plant Capacity = 40000.00 Nos./Day

COST OF LAND & BUILDING

(Total land area required 1000 sq. mtr)	Rs.	11,25,000.00

LIST OF PLANT & MACHINERY

1. H.M.T. Single Colour Complete with all Accessories
2. Reprographic Camera (Horizontal type) with all Accessories
3. Plate Making eqpt - light table,red lithographer's tape, goldenrod sheets, Scissors, Scribing Tools etc.
4. Computer PC/XT
5. Printer (Laser)
6. Mouse
7. Ventura
8. Air Conditioner
9. Paper Cutting Machine

LIST OF RAW MATERIALS

1. 2000 Rim Size of sheet require 23"x 36".
   Each Rim contents over 500 sheets white paper
2. Ink (For Offset Printing)
3. Phototypesetting Paper
4. Graphic Art Film
5. Rubber Blankets
6. Miscellaenous Chemical and Material

FIXED CAPITAL

Land & Building	Rs.	11,25,000.00
Plant & Machinery	Rs.	17,64,500.00
Other Fixed Assets	Rs.	2,50,000.00
TOTAL	**Rs.**	**31,39,500.00**

LIST OF RAW MATERIAL

1.	Raw Material	Rs.	5,33,000.00
2.	Salary & Wages	Rs.	71,875.00
3.	Utilities & Overheads	Rs.	19,400.00
	TOTAL	**Rs.**	**6,24,275.00**

TOTAL CAPITAL INVESTMENT

Total Fixed Capital	Rs.	31,39,500.00
Total Working Capital for 3 Months	Rs.	18,72,825.00
TOTAL	**Rs.**	**50,12,325.00**

TURNOVER/ANNUM

By sale of 1.2 crores of sheets **Rs. 1,08,00,000.00**

PROFIT = RECEIPTS - COST OF PRODUCTION
= 1,08,00,000.00 - 90,90,565.50
= 17,09,434.50

PROFIT SALES RATIO = Profit / Sales x 100 = **15.83 %**

RATE OF RETURN = Operating profit / T.C.I. x 100 = **34.10 %**

BREAK EVEN POINT (B.E.P) = 54.38 %

13

FLEXO & ROTO GRAVURE PRINTING

INTRODUCTION

The printing processes now in common use are broadly classified into groups according to the principles on which their printing image carriers are based. The four process families are relief printing (letter press and flexography) in which printing areas of the image carriers raised above the plane of the supporting material; planographic printing (lithography and collo- type) in which the printing and non-printing areas are in the same plane of the image carrier; intaglio printing (gravure) in which the printing areas are sunkem in the image carrier, non-printing areas are on its surface; and screen printing (stencil printing) in which the printing areas consist of open pores of the image carrier, the blocked pores constitute the non-printing areas.

Gravure printing with copper or steel engraved plates is very ancient. In olden days, the pictorials or lettering were cut or etched into the face of rigid plate of copper or steel. The whole surface then inked and wiped clean so that the ink was only retained in the incised or engraved lines. Printing was done by pressing paper against the inked plate.

The modern commercial derivations of the intaglio process are based on photography and photo mechanics. These are rotogravure and sheet-fed gravure. Of these the largest and the most important commercially is rotogravure which is used in news papers roto sections for some of the big edition magazines and for big commercial works.

Rotogravure employees an exquisitely polished copper cylinder as the printing surface and makes use of a screen to break-up the light and dark areas into small unshaded dots.

The text is usually first set in type. It is printed in white ink on a very shiny black paper. Negatives of any picture required are pasted up with the text in accordance with or determined layout. From this a transparent positive is obtained on a sensitized glass plate or film. The positive is turn printed photographically on a sheet of thin paper coated with sensitized gelatin, called 'carbon tissue'. After a suitable exposure has been made, the positive is replaced with a screen consisting of a network of transparent lines on a black background. The sensitized tissue is subjected to a strong light so that the lines of the screen are superimposed on the previously printed image and break up the entire surface into tiny squares.

The screen used in those process is reverse, i.e. the lines are transparent and the interversing squares are opaque. The sensitized gelatin becomes insoluble in water in proportion to the amount of light to which it has been exposed and the result is a printing image with a lattice work of lines rendered insoluble by light.

The tissue is dampened and laid over the highly finished surface of the copper cylinder with the sensitized side in contact with the metal. The tissue is then soaked with hot water; this allows the paper to be peeled off and any unexposed gelatin is dissolved. Parts of the gelatin that are not to be etched are protected with a special bitumen-based paint. Etching is done in acid by revolving the cylinder slowly whilst acid is poured over it. When etching is complete, the remaining gelatin is removed by washing, leaving on the copper cylinder an enormous number of cells of varying depths which serve to hold the ink during the printing. A shallow cell imparts thin film of ink whilst a deep cell gives a VERY thick film. Thus the varying shades of the subject are translated in terms of varying shades of depths of cells in the metal surface. For longer life the copper cylinder is sometimes chromium plated.

The etched cylinder is designed for running on a web-fed rotogravure machine. The cylinder revolves in a trough of a ink, the ink floods over the surface of the cylinder and is at once scraped clear by a thin blade called 'doctor'. This blade of cylinder length keeps the surface free of ink, but leaves the cells full.

The reel paper runs between the printing cylinder and smaller rubber cylinder which exerts enough pressure to redraw the ink from the cells and impress it on the paper. In a finished rotogravure print it is almost impossible to detect the halftones which show up clearly in letterpress., and that is why the process is well adapted to the reproduction of shaded subjects. Because of the time required for plate preparation and relatively high initial costs, rotogravure is essentially a large scale production process.

Sheet-fed gravure is a high quality picture printing method. It is a slower process compared to rotogravure and is used for every moderate runs. It differs from rotogravure mainly in the facts that printing image is usually etched into a thin flexible copper plate which clamped around a printing cylinder in much the same manner as an offset plate, and that printing is carried out on the sheet-fed presses.

The presses for this process have automatic sheet feeders and exist in varying numbers of printing units. Sheet-fed gravure is done on better grades of paper and coated stocks.

Plaster for printing on a rotary press must be thin and curved for mounting on the press cylinder. Wrap around plates can be used in gravure printing but most often the printing is from copper plated cylinders that have been etched and chromo-plated after the images have been transferred to them. The printing image is produced on these cylinders with carbon tissue lithographic transfer film or direct rating. All lithographic plates are wrap around plates.

METHODSOFPLATEMAKING

Printing image carriers of plates or cylinders can be produced in any or a combination of six different ways :-

1. **Manually :-** By the use of hand tools, engravers, knives etc. to produce image - carriers for the relief and intaglio.

2. **Mechanically :-** With the help of engraving and geometrical late ruling machines, pantographs etc. for the relief and intaglio processes but hand transferring and Benday machines can be used for lithographic plates.

3. **Electromechanically :**
4. **Electronically :**
5. **Electrostatically :**
6. **Photomechanically :**

GRAVUREPLATEMAKINGANDCYLINDERMAKING

The adoption of the crossline screen for photogravure printing initiated the modern commercial process. Modifications for multicolour printing have been made.

PRINTINGSURFACE:

Modern gravure printing is done principally from images etched in cylinder on web processes and is generally referred to as rotogravure. On sheet-fed presses the printing element is a thin copper plate, which is wrapped around the cylinder. Preparation of the printing surface is essentially the same for cylinders and for plates.

For monochrome printing by conventional gravure, bichromate sensitized carbon tissue or transfer film is contact-printed through a continuous-tone positive and then exposed a second time while in contact with a screen consisting of transparent lines and opaque square dots, 24 or 28 per cm (60 or 70 per in.) The ratio of line to dot width usually is 1 : 3. The exposed carbon tissue or transfer film is moistened and squeeged in contact with the clean copper surface. Warm water is applied and the paper for the carbon tissue or backing of the film is peeled off. The gelatin thus transferred to the copper surface is further developed with warm water to produce a gelatin relief resist. Etching is done with 35-43 wt. % ferric chloride solution (sp. gr. 1.34-1.45 (37-45$^{o\ be}$)). This solution etches the copper to different depths. Depending of the thickness of the gelatin resist in the different tone areas. Usually several solutions of different densities are used. The areas corresponding to screen lines remain unetched and provide lands., which support the doctor blade in printing. For long runs and to minimize wear, the etched cylinder or plate is chromium plated.

For multicolour printing the principal process involves a combination of halftone and continuous-tone positives for each colour. The halftone positive has a lateral dot formation, which is similar to conventional gravure in the shadows but with varying dot sizes in the middletone and highlights. The two positives are contact-printed successively, in register on to a sheet of carbon tissue and the gelatin is transferred to the copper cylinder. Development and etching are essentially the same as for conventional gravure.

LIMITATIONS:

The serious problem with gravure cylinder making has been the difficulty of reproducing identical cylinders from the same films due to difference in materials, etching solution, impurities in copper, environmental conditions and other factors. As a result, repress proofing has not been successful and corrections must be made on the cylinder which is expensive.

GRAVURE:

Not much gravure printing is from sheet-fed presses, which involves plates. By far the greatest amount of gravure printing is from cylinders on rolls of paper or film. The cylinders are removable and cylinders of different diameters can be used so that different print lengths can be accommodated from job to job, if necessary. This is desirable in packaging but not as necessary in magazine printing. The gravure printing unit consists of a printing cylinder and a impression cylinder, and an inking system. Ink is applied to the printing cylinder by an ink roll or spray and the excess is removed by a doctor blade and returned to the ink function.

Single-colour rotogravure printing yields excellent pictorial reproduction on a wide range of papers. Its reproduction type matter and line drawings leaves something to be desired., however because the screen somewhat reduces sharpness. Colour reproduction is done in three or four colours on multicolour presses. Gravure printing is applicable for catalogues, cartons, labels, and in the printing of cellophane, plastic films, foil and plastic laminates. It is the most practical process for the printing of gold, i.e. bronze, silver, i.e. aluminium and opaque whites.

USES AND APPLICATIONS

Gravure or intaglio printing finds applications in the production of newspaper, supplements, book review sections, feature magazine, catalogues, illustrated magazines, advertising literatures, calendars, greeting cards, wall papers, patterns in textiles, linoleum and oil cloth, labels and wrappers on aluminium foil, gassoline, cellophane, vinyl polymers, LDPE, HDPE, PP and similar other materials, security papers, paper money and stamps etc.

PRESENT MANUFACTURERS (USING ROTOGRAVURE MACHINES)

Arya Roto Prints
401, Main Bus Stand Road,
Vill. Badli, Delhi - 110 042
Phone/Fax : 7180888

Chawla Plastics
C-135, Mayapuri Indl. Area,
Phase-II, New Delhi - 110 064
Phone/Fax : 540 1533, 540 0162,

Ambica Enterprises
Plot No. 12, 16/2, Mathura Road,
Faridabad - 02 (Haryana)
Phone/Fax : 8-292391, 286426

Balaji Polymer
131-132, M.I.E., Bahadurgarh - 124 507
(Haryana) Phone/Fax : 8-313731

Gravure Cil India (P) Ltd.
A-27, Sector - 8, Noida - 201 301
Distt. Ghaziabad (U.P.)
Phone/Fax : 550046, 553023, 011-8-520985

FLEXOGRAPHICPRINTING

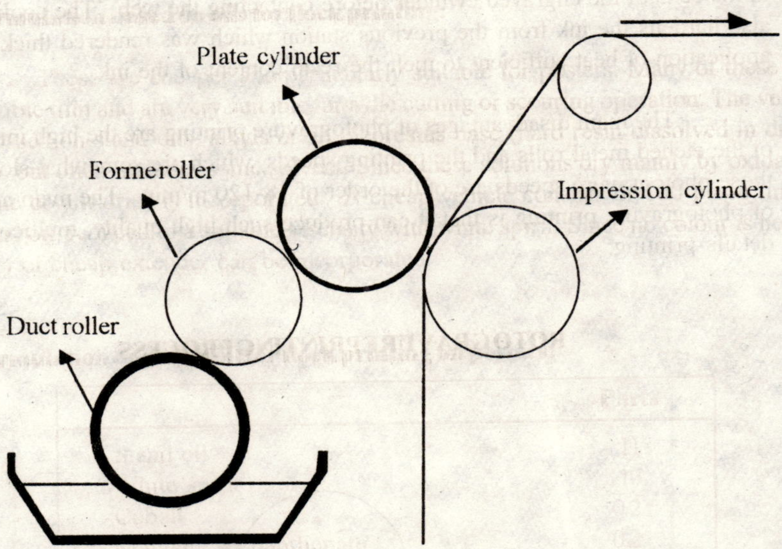

Members of Aniline Printing Unit

To summarise, therefore, flexographic printing has the advantages of high speed, relatively inexpensive of high speed, relatively inexpensive plates and short change over times but has the disadvantage of being unable to reproduce fine detail.

ROTOGRAVUREPRINTING

This process consists in inking an engraved printing roller which then transfers the ink directly on to the film. The engraved design is made up of a series of tiny cells of varying depth so that different amount of inks are picked up by parts of the roller. Excess ink is removed by a doctor blade. For all practical purposes photogravure printing is a continuous one tone process. For it is only in the light and some medium tones that the cell walls are visible after printing and then only under magnification. The size of the individual can be seen from the fact that the screen size used to produce the cells on the roller is about 60 lines per centimeter which means to total of 3600 cells to the square centimeters. Even finer screens are used for high definition work.

The principle of the process can be seen in the following figures with multi-colour work it is essential to dry between each colour application. After passing through a hot air blast, the film passes over a water cooled roller to prevent transference of heat from the drying chamber to the next printing unit, where an increase in temperature would cause the volatile ink to partially evaporate and dry in the cells of the engraved cylinder before contacting the web. The cooling roller also hardens the ink from the previous station which was rendered thickly by the application of heat sufficient to melt the resin content of the ink.

The main disadvantages of photogravure printing are the high initial costs of the etched metal rolls and the printing speeds, which are somewhat slower than those photogravure speeds are of the order of 18-120 m/min. The main advantage of photogravure printing is that it can produce such high quality, multicolour fine details printing.

ROTOGRAVUREPRINTINGPROCESS

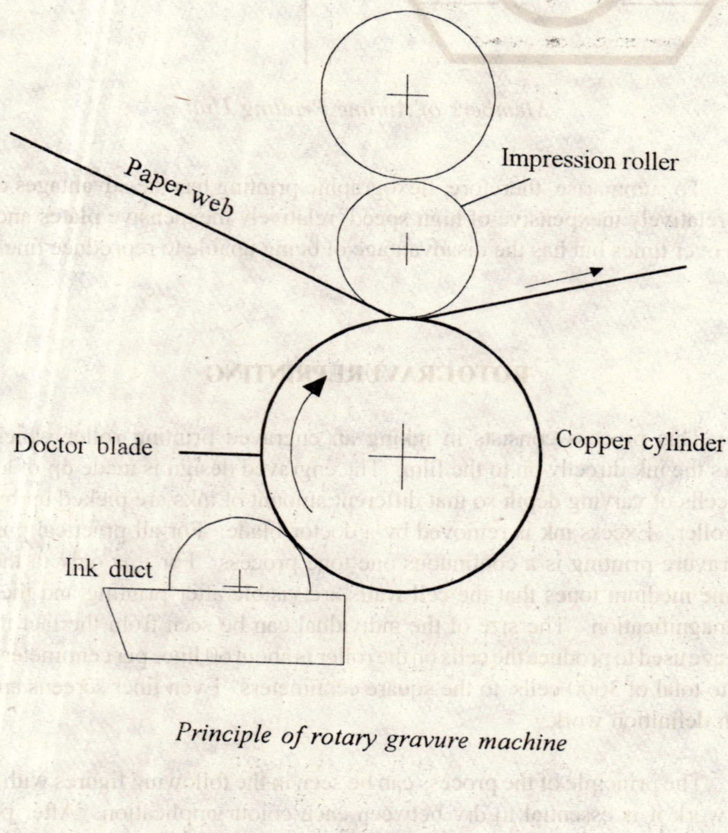

Principle of rotary gravure machine

Plate/Cylinder making Equipments:

1. Complete with Cameras
2. Enlargers
3. Contact printers
4. Arc lamp
5. Whirter
6. Graining Machine
7. Etching Machine
8. Expressure frame
9. Densito meter etc.

PLANT & MACHINERY SOURCES

Camera:

News Shot Products
507, Udyog Vihar, Phase-III,
Dundahera, Gurgaon-122 016
(Haryana)
Phone/Fax: 0124-341106, 341150

Roto Gravure & Flexo Graphic Printing Machine:

Anjana Machinery Mfrs. (P) Ltd.
206, Udyog Sadan, Sharma Estate,
Mumbai - 400 063
Phone/Fax: 873 0146

Calico Industrial Engineers
20A, Chakala Road, Andheri East,
Mumbai - 400 099
Phone: 832 8381-83
Fax: 834 5715

Tyagi Engineering Works
B-166, Hari Nagar,
New Delhi - 110 064
Phone: 540 1250
Fax: 91-11-513 5333

Frans Engineering Corporation
Plot No. 908, IIIrd Phase,
G.I.D.C., Vapi - 396195 Gujarat.
Phone: 31453
Fax: 07638-30668

Gum Tape Machinery:

Guru Nanak Industries
Plot No. CP-6 & 7, N.H.-5,
Railway Road, Faridabad - 121 001
(Haryana)
Phone: 212365, 216885

RAW MATERIAL SUPPLIERS

Rubber Blankets:

Kapoor Sales Corporation
2, Masilamani Road,
Balaji Nagar,
Chennai - 600 014
Phone : 826 7598
Fax : 828 4944

Volga Rubber Industries
76, Indl. Estate, Delhi Road.
Near Maruti, Gurgaon-122 015
(Haryana)
Phone : 0124-340348
Fax : 0124-342390

Printing Ink:

Baluja Spectra
C-50 Okhla Indl. Area-II,
New Delhi - 110 020
Phone/fax : 6835715, 6835722

Ajanta Ink Company
Basai Road, Gurgaon.
(Haryana)
Phone/fax : 8-330028

Art Printing Inks Company
104 Site-4, Indl. Area,
Sahibabad, Ghaziabad.
(U.P.)
Phone/fax : 767882

Inks India (Delhi)
C-49, Sector-8,
Noida-201 301
Distt. Ghaziabad. (U.P.)
Phone/fax: 523801, 011-8-557270

V an Inks & Chemicals (P) Ltd.
B-150, Phase-II,
Noida-201 305
Distt. Ghaziabad. (U.P.)
Phone/fax: 567141, 011-8-521507

Paper Suppliers :

Om Prakash Jitendra Kumar & Co.,
63, Darya Ganj,
New Delhi - 11 00 02.
Ph. 326 96 80, 3271380

Narain Paper Mart,
4034/3, Haryana Market,
Chawri Bazar,
Delhi - 11 00 06.
Ph. 291 51 35.

Himgiri Paper Products
B-24, Indl. Area Lawrence Road,
New Delhi - 110 035
Phone : 718 9005

Gum & Adhesive:

Bhiwadi Polymers Ltd.,
15, Najafgarh Road,
New Delhi - 110 015
Phone/Fax: 541 8552/011-542 1454

PLANT ECONOMICS OF FLEXO & ROTO GRAVURE PRINTING

Rated Plant Capacity = 93600.00 Mtr./Day

COST OF LAND & BUILDING

(Total land area required 1500 sq. mtr) Rs. 7,00,000.00

LIST OF PLANT & MACHINERY

1. Printing Machine:-6 color roto gravure printing machine 30" size working width complete with 2 H.P. blower
2. 5 H.P. driver 16 kwh heater & printing cylinder dia = 150 mm (fully automatic)
3. Slitting and rewinding machine 48" cap. with min= 80 mm slit & max in wind dia=45" with 5 H.P. drive
4. Roll to Roll making machine 48" capacity
5. Bidsmen lamination plant (complete plant)
6. Gum tape machinery plant (complete plant)
7. Rotary sheet cutter machine 48"
8. Small working tools/tackels and material handling
9. Composing machine complete with mono key boards mono casters and lines
10. Plate/Cylinder making equipments

LIST OF RAW MATERIALS

1. Metal plates
2. Rubber blankets
3. Inks and founts
4. Gum and adhesives etc.
5. Paper :- sunlit bond 11,000 rims
6. Thermoplastic films 25 mt.

FIXED CAPITAL

Land & Building	Rs.	7,00,000.00
Plant & Machinery	Rs.	21,85,001.00
Other Fixed Assets	Rs.	4,64,350.00
TOTAL	**Rs.**	**33,49,351.00**

TOTAL WORKING CAPITAL/MONTH

Raw Material	Rs.	15,87,500.00
Salary & Wages	Rs.	42,600.00
Utilities & Overheads	Rs.	1,23,000.00
TOTAL	**Rs.**	**17,53,100.00**

TOTAL CAPITAL INVESTMENT

Total Fixed Capital	Rs.	33,49,351.00
Total Working Capital for 3 Months	Rs.	52,59,300.00
TOTAL	**Rs.**	**86,08,651.00**

TURNOVER/ANNUM

By sale of printed straps for flexible packaging Rs. 2,81,00,000.00

PROFIT = RECEIPTS - COST OF PRODUCTION

= 2,81,00,000.00 - 2,30,39,671.66

= 50,60,328.34

PROFIT SALES RATIO = Profit / Sales x 100 = **18.01 %**

RATE OF RETURN = Operating Profit / T.C.I. x 100 = **58.53 %**

BREAK EVEN POINT (B.E.P.) = 35.08 %

14

FLOCK PRINTING ON PLASTIC AND METALLIC ITEMS

INTRODUCTION

Flock printing is done by using the screen printing process for printing an adhesive size and then dusting with cotton, silk or rayon flock. Screen printing prints using porous stencils or screens. It can be done on almost any surface and can be printed. It is used for art prints, posters, decalcomania transfers, greeting cards, menus programmes, covers, and wall paper.

Screen printing is important in the direct printing of textiles and for short run heat transfer printing. In addition it is particularly suited to the printing of leather metal glass, wood, ceramic materials and plastic goods, both flat and finished molded form. By kintiong an adhesive size and in dusting with cotton, silk or rayon flock, the finished design can be made to appear like felt or suede leather. For many of these applications there is no substitute for screen printing.

For some applications screen printing has distinct cost advantages for short runs because of the simplicity of the process and the equipment needed.

USES AND APPLICATIONS

Flock printing is particularly suited to the printing of leather metal, glass, wood, ceramic materials, and plastics, both flat and finished molded form. By printing an adhesive size and their dusting with cotton silk, or rayon flock the finished design can be made to appear like felt or suede leather to many of these applications there is no substitute for screen printing.

MANUFACTURINGPROCESS

The various steps involved in the process of Flock printing on various surfaces are given as under:

a. Preparation of Flock
b. Printing of the adhesive side on the base surface using the screen printing process.
c. Application of the flock on the resin-adhesive surface and dusting off the excess flock.

FlockPreparation:

Flock may be prepared from many synthetic fibers by cutting them accurately into machine. With cotton and wool fibers flock is usually prepared by grinding and lengths may be as short as 0.3 mm (0.013 in). The flock may be dyed or uncoloured. A suitable material is chosen to form the base for the flock and the base material and the flock may be composed or the same or different fibers. Surface plastic or steel goods. The base surface may be either coated with a suitable adhesive resin, or therein applied locally in a printed design. When printing is used a method which transfer a reasonably thick film gives the best results, e.g. flat screen printing on a small scale.

The resin adhesive used must be one which adheres firmly to the substrate being printed but equally so, must be capable of anchoring the flock firmly once it is attached. The resin film must be flexible have a soft handling texture and possess a good resistance to washing.

Screen Printing:

Screen printing is a relatively simple method of printing which can be carried out without the use of complicated and expenses equipments.

GeneralProcedure:

The silk gauze, the stretched on the frame, is painted with a sensitizing solution such as gelatin dichromate, and dried in the dark. The pattern to be produced is painted on transparent paper with a dense opaque ink, a separate painting and screen may be regarded as a piece of daylight photographic printing paper and the painted pattern as a negative or as it is more generally known, a positive. The positive is now placed in contact with the sensitized screen and exposed to light. The length of exposure will vary according to the actual distance from the source of light and the type of light used (electric or daylight). The exposed screen is now well washed, first in cold water to harden the insolubilised gelatin and then in warm water to remove the soluble gelatin. The screen is allowed to dry slowly. The layer of gelatin must be reinforced by the application to a lacquer which should be reasonably resistant to acids alkalis and organic solvents.

Details of Construction:

The screen frame, Screens Frames are usually made of either wood are metal. The wood must be smooth and well seasoned and only a soft wood with a low water absorbency, resistant to warping and to varying degrees of humidity and heat, is suitable.

Stretching of the Silk:

The screen gauze can be stretched over the frames either by hand or machine. To cover a screen by hand needs a great deal of care to enable the correct and even tension to be obtained. This is best achieved by ensuring that the warp and weft of the fabric are, throughout, parallel to the sides of the screen. Screens that have been loosely stretched or screens too tightly stretched give rise to inaccurate printing.

Sensitizing the Screen:

The majority of sensitizing solutions are based on gelatin or polyvinyl alcohol., sensitized with either ammonium or potassium dichromate, or a mixture of these dichromates. Any one of the following sensitizing solutions may be employed.

Sensitizing Solution 1 (Gelatin-dichromate)

A 125 parts gelatin dissolved at (50^0-60^0C)
552.5 parts water (120^0-140^0F) with the minimum of stirring

B 50 parts zinc oxide
200 parts water

C 13.5 parts ammonium dichromate
6.5 parts potassium dichromate

D 50 parts ammonia (sp.gr) (0.880)
2.5 parts 'Calsolene' Oil HS

Add B to A, then C, and finally D, and bulk to 1000 parts. Strain the mixture and treat the screen with this solution at 50^0C (120^0F) and allow to dry at room temperature in the dark or in an orange safe light. Bulk to 1000 parts. Strain the mixture and treat the screen with this solution at 50^0C (120^0F) and allow to dry at room temperature in the dark or in an orange safe light.

Preparing the Positive Design:

The original drawing is first examined to assess its suitability for the screen printing process. It may require adapting to screen printing, or putting into repeat where possible we repeat, frames of a standard size can be produced and the stops on the printing tables will not require frequent adjustment.

Transferring the Positive Design to the Silk:

The positive is laid flat on the dry sensitized silk and secured to the screen frame by, for example, adhesive tape. A glass plate of suitable dimensions is then laid on top of the positive and securely clamped to the screen frame by means of suitable clamps. To ensure good contact between the positive and the silk the hollow underside of the silk screen should be supported by means of a wooden block of such a size as to fit comfortably in the silk frame.

	Distance from light source	Time of exposure required
Strong sunlight	—	5 min.
Bright daylight	—	10 min.
Dull daylight	—	upto 2h
Mercury vapour lamp	450 mm (18 in)	15 min.
150 W lamp	450 mm (18 in)	3 h
300 W lamp	600 mm (24 in)	upto 2h

Hardening of the Exposed Design:

Screens based on a gelatin-dichromate sensitizing solution are often given a hardening treatment, although this is not absolutely necessary. The screens are treated in the cold for 10-15 min. in the following solution:

25 parts	Ammonium dichromate
50 parts	Chrome alum crystals
50 parts	Formaldehyde (40%) solution
bulked 100 parts	

The screens are washed well in cold water and allowed to dry slowly. Screens based on a polyvinyl alcohol-dichromate sensistising solution screen for 45-60 min in the following solution:

50 parts	Acetaldehyle
50 parts	Isobutyraldehyde or normal butyraledhyde
20 parts	Sulphuric acid 66° Be (168° TW) at a temperature of 15°-20°C (60°-70°F)
bulked to 100 parts	

Reinforcement of the Screen:

In the case of screens prepared from polyvinyl alcohol the hardening treatment just described is sufficient protection and further reinforcement of the screen is not absolutely essential. With screens prepared from gelatin, protection of the gelatin is obtained by application of lacquer. The gelatin-coated screens are coated with lacquer from the inside of the screen by either brushing or scraping. While the lacquer is still wet, the outside of the screen is rubbed the screen. If it is considered necessary to coat both sides of the screen with lacquer, this is carried out after drying by applying the lacquer from the reverse side of the screen. If the lacquer used is viscous, it may also be necessary to wipe out with a solvent. A screen lacquered on both sides, such as the one just mentioned, should be satisfactory for the normal wear and tear of screen printing provided the lacquer used is resistant to acids alkalis and such organic solvents as are used n printing pastes.

Screen Printing Tables:

The length of the table for works practice varies between 50-100m (55-110 yd.) in length. It is usually 0.75 m (30 in) high and approximately 1.2-1.6 m (48-62in) in width. The table is made of well seasoned wood, reinforced concrete or a combination of iron frames and irons tanks with wooden tops.

Squeegees:

Various types of squeegees are available. Some are made entirely of wood while others have wooden handles with rubber or metal plates inserted. The length of the squeegees is approximately 40 mm (1.5 in) shorter than the internal dimensions of the screen.

Multi Colour Printing:

Most important aspect of screen printing is that it lends itself extremely well to multi-colour printing. The designs come in such a wide variety of colours that it is difficult to lay down any specific or hard and fast rule as to which colour should be printed first. Any colour should be printed first. Screen printing permits the over the printing of a lighter or white colour over a dark background. While printing one colour over another, it is just likely that faint tinge of the first colour might be discernible in the second colour. It may sometimes be necessary to print a slightly, thicker layer of the second colour to obscure any tinge of the first colour. If the design is such that a shellac stencil will do, it becomes vital to prepare as many stencils as the colours to be printed. When the colours on the design do not overlap one another, it is possible to achieve three, four or even five or even five colour printing using just one or two stencils. Leaving a particular portion of screen open, blocking out other areas with gummed tapes, multi-colour screen printing is possible using just one or two stencils. On the other hand, when two or more colours are close to one another, cut the stencil for each colour in such a way that while printing, each colour impression will overlap the previous impression by about one mm. By this way, even if there is slight error of registration in the printing, no gaps will be visible between any two impressions. In photo stenciling also, if the colours ion the original design overlap one another, it is best to prepare separate positives for each colour. If the design is simple it is even possible to make separate stencils from a single positive. If the design is in same size and a simple type, make as many tracings from the design as the number of colours and use these tracings as separate positives for preparing the photo-stencils for each colour. It may be in any colour. But the colour scheme, as may be required, should be marked properly.

There is no need to take paper negatives to note certain letters or typeset lines in white over ad ark backgrounds. This may be indicated in the colour scheme on the overlay of the normal black and white artwork. In multi-colour printing, it is very necessary to choose the right shades of colours. There is always a slight variation of inks. So as to get an exact shade you are required to mix inks, and before printing, it must be tested that whether the right or exact colour required is ready.

Different surfaces available for printing:

In screen printing, you may print on any surface, any size or any shape. And surface means, walls, glass windows, on vehicles, machinery, furniture etc.

Mostly it is used extensively in textile and ceramic industries, as well as on bottles crockery etc.

The printing surface falls into one or two main classes porous, non-porous. Design printed on non-absorbent surfaces. Hard surfaces like glass or plastic sheets require a stiffer squeegee like glass or plastic sheets require a stiffer squeegee and stiffer ink too, since non-porous surfaces not absorb the ink too, since non-porous surfaces. Hard surfaces like glass or plastic sheets require a stiffer squeegee and stiffer ink too, since non-porous surfaces do not absorb the ink, therefore, stiffer ink has to be spread with more pressure while printing on each surface.

Paper-Card:

Screen printing process is employed successfully for printing on all kinds of paper. With screen printing, light colour appear purer and more brilliant when printed on coloured stock.

Tin-Plate:

Tin plates require a base coating of the background colour ion the design. This can be done by hand printing each piece individually with a brush and then left it to dry. Coating can also be done by a spray-gun.

Tin-plates are not so thick and therefore, do not need any considerable build-up. It is very essential that the underside of the screen fabric be reinforced for added protection.

Cellophane Sheets:

Due to flexibility of thin cellophane sheets, it is difficult to handle them and to register accurately against the guides.

Printing on Plastic Goods:

Screen printing can be satisfactorily done on plastic sheets and items. For this purpose SSPVC inks are generally used. Different types of figures can be printed on PVC shoes, toys and gift items with the help of screen printing. Traders name, brand name and other special design can be printed by this process.

The screen printer can keep in touch with the manufacturers of toys and gift items for printing job work.

Printing on cylindrical shaped goods:

The basic principle of printing on round objects is the same but some special equipment is needed for facilitating the printing job on the article. A flat screen is generally round object gets easily fixed on the equipments and moves with ball bearing based rolling pins. So that the screen presses evenly on the item.

The squeegee remains fixed at one place whereas the screen moves forwards and backwards on a rail to enable the important to form on the object being printed. Such machines and equipment are generally locally available manufactured for specific requirement.

FORMULATIONS

Formulation based on oils for flock printing:

These are cheaper and particularly suitable for posters. Many of these give flexible film and are very suitable for a die cutting or scouring operation. The vehicle is based on stand oils, alkyls or an oleoresins base (hard resin dissolved in drying oil), but often includes some solvent. Since these solutions dry mainly by oxidation, some cobalt drier is incorporated. A cheap vehicle consists of 100 passe tinseed stand oil, reduced to a suitable viscosity with white spirit. Since no colour is needed a lot of cheap extender can be incorporated.

Formulation based on oil for flock printing on posters:

	Parts
Stand oil	11
White spirit	10
Cobalt	0.2
Manganese napthenate	0.2

Such solutions printed at 50 microns on M.G. poster paper set in about half an hour dry in about 4 and hours. The media consists of the a hard drying-oil soluble synthetic resin cooked in dehydrated castor oil, refined or locked linseed oil, thinned with Kerosene or naptha solvent; white spirit turpentine substitute or aliphate hydrocarbon distillate are sufficiently volatile to ensure quick drying. A cheap synthetic vehicle can be made from lime hardened resin or sector gum dispersed in a limited amount of linseed oil;l white spirit can be used as suitable diluent.

Formulation based on Nitrocellulose for flock printing:

Nitrocellulose formulations can be used at consistencies varying from 4-50 paise depending on printing conditions. They are more expensive than oil based screen inks but posses several advantages oil based formulations give thick films (40-60 microns, 1.5-2.25 than). Nitrocellulose gives media of suitable viscosity, bent which have a low solids content, consequently although nitrocellulose, based formulations are printed at the normal thickness for the type of screen, the films are much thinner (25 microns, thou) after drying. Secondly nitrocellulose formulation are fast drying. The only limit to the drying speed is set by the necessity of the solution remaining sufficiently wet in the screen that the mesh is not logged. Thirdly the solutions can be made much more transparent largely, due to the reduced film thickness. Fourthly the vehicle is completely colourless. Fifthly the vehicle adheres better to non absorbent and difficult

Zinc Oxide:

Newage Industries
6/21, Begampur, Khatola,
Gurgaon (Haryana)
Phone/Fax: 8-324644, 321220

Pukhraj Zinc (P) Ltd.
2375, Modern Industrial Estate,
Bahadurgarh - 124 507
(Haryana)
Phone/Fax: 8-314082

Potassium Dichromate:

Crescent Chemcials
Sanjay Building No.5
Mittal Industrial Estate
M.V. Road, Andheri (E)
Mumbai-400059

Stand Oil:

Mulji Devshi and Company
Red Cross Road,
Dharmpur,
Rajasthan 396050

White Spirit/Solvents:

Arte Paints and Chemicals Industries
Mahavir Industrial Estate
Saki-Naka, Mumbai -400 010

Cobalt Napthenatte:

National Chemcials and Dyes Co.
P.B. 70, D-43/42 Sadanand Bazar,
Varanasi (U.P.)

P.V.C. Resin:

Ahmedabad Manufactuers and
Calico Printing Company Ltd.,
Calico Chemicals, Plastics and Fibres Division
Anik Chembur,
Mumbai - 400 074

Printing Accessories and Chemicals:

Rama Printers
Sadar Bazar,
Behind Sadar Thana,
Delhi - 110 006

ADDRESSES OF MACHINERY SUPPLIERS

Screen Printing Press:

Solar Machines Pvt. Ltd.,
22-D, Wadia Charties Bldg.
2nd Floor S.A. Brelivi Road,
Fort, Mumbai - 400 023

Mixers:

Telematric
C-1/404 Phase 4,
G.I.D.C., Uitahl,
Udyog Nagar 388121

Spray Gun:

Jost's Engg Co. Ltd.,
C-7 Industrial Estate,
Thane,
Mumbai - 400 604

Flock Making/Shredding Machine:

Steel Fabs and Company
G.T. Road.
Panipat - 132 103

PLANT ECONOMICS OF FLOCK PRINTING ON PLASTIC AND METALLIC ITEMS

Rated Plant Capacity = 45,00,000 prints on plastic and metallic items/Year.

COST OF LAND & BUILDING

(Total land area required 200 sq.mtr.)	Rs.	5,00,000.00

LIST OF PLANT & MACHINERY

1. Solar screen printing machine with optional attachment such as flat printing device multi colour regd.
2. Gun for spraying flock
3. Flock making machine shredding and flocking machine for synthetic, cotton silk and wool fibres
4. Reaction (Mixing-vessel with agitator and allied accessories along with heating arrngement
5. Air compressor
6. Miscellaneouus accessories and labs equipment

LIST OF RAW MATERIALS

1. Chemicals such as gelattine zinc oxide, Pottassium dichromate for sensitizing solution
2. Cheimcals such as stand oil, white sprit, cobalt napthenate, managanese napthenate ethylte
3. Screens for printing process
4. Flock of synthetic fibres, cotton, silk, wool etc.
5. Miscellaneous chemicals and tape for fixing jobs

FIXED CAPITAL

Land & Building	Rs.	5,00,000.00
Plant & Machinery	Rs.	3,07,000.00
Other Fixed Assets	Rs.	62,000.00
TOTAL	**Rs.**	**8,69,000.00**

TOTAL WORKING CAPITAL/MONTH

Raw Material	Rs.	81,000.00
Salary & Wages	Rs.	33,686.00
Utilities & Overheads	Rs.	33,900.00
TOTAL	**Rs.**	**1,48,586.00**

TOTAL CAPITAL INVESTMENT

Total Fixed Capital	Rs.	8,69,000.00
Total Working Capital for 3 Months	Rs.	4,45,758.00
TOTAL	**Rs.**	**13,14,758.00**

TURNOVER/ANNUM

By sales receipts by flock printing of 45,00,000 prints on plastic and metallic items

Rs. 27,00,000.00

PROFIT = RECEIPTS - COST OF PRODUCTION

= 27,00,000.00 - 21,77,204.76

= 5,22,795.24

PROFIT SALES RATIO = Profit / Sales x 100 = **19.36 %**

RATE OF RETURN = Operating Profit / T.C.I. x 100 = **39.51 %**

BREAK EVEN POINT (B.E.P.) = 57.35 %

15

GREETING CARDS BY OFFSET PRINTING

INTRODUCTION

Greeting is the expression of ones feeling towards kindlness, of other person. Greeting becomes the usual practice of human beings. These days we usually greets other person with the expression of good morning with a smile. Others ways of greeting the other person is with the shower of flower of glanding the person to be greeted, sometime we greet with presentation like toys, bunch of flower (boyquet) interesting books, pens etc.,

Besides above , we express our feeling with the greeting card. The invention of greeting card was from greek..

These greeting cards are the symbol of the expression of printed on the good quality paper with the picture of colourful flowers, scenery of gardens, parks, Mills tation, Historical buildings, Artistic view, and many other things like " *good Wishes*" "*Happy New Years*" "*Happy Christmas Day*" , & *Happy Birthday*" etc.,

These greetings cards are produced by two types of printing. some greeting cards are produced with Intoglio or Gravu printing process and most of Greeting cards today are produced on planographic or lithographcy process which these days known as offset printing process.

COMPARISON OF THE PRINTING PROCESSES

Lithographing is an idieal process for text and pretorial reproduction for short and medium runs that are sheet fed or web fed upto 10^6 impressions letter press printing is good for text matter, flexibility, broad, lettring, solid backgrounds and large expanse of colour from short to long runs. Gravuze printing is best for long run pictorial reproduction such as magazine , mail order catalogues and packaging. Research in these and other processes e.g. flexography and waterless lithography, could result in improvements that could change these use catagories radically. Other printing processes , e.g. ink-jet and electronic printing could be completive with lithography, letterpress, flexography or gravure printings.

CHARACTERISTICS OF OFFSET PRESS

The offset press is characterised by the following important advantages over other printing methods:

1. The rubber printing surface conform to irregularities in the paper surface. Less printing pressure is needed, and print quality is improved. Half tons of high quality can be printed on rough papers.

2. Paper does not come into contact with the metal printing plate. Therefore, the plate is les subjected to abrasive wear and can run much longer editions.

3. Speed of printing is increase. The offset of press improvements on printing speeds in shwon by the following statisties for offset presses:-

Press	Printing Speed, Impressions/Hour
Litho Hand - Proving Press	10-20
Litho Power-Proving Press	1200
Direct Rotary Press (Hand fed)	2000
Rotary Offset Press (Stream fed)	upto 15000
Web Offset Press (Roil-fed)	upto 60000

4. The image on an offset printing plate roads right instead of in reverse or wrong reading. This facilitates both and and chemical photomechancial preparation.

5. Less ink required for equal coverege. This reduces trapping problems and decrease the tendancy of the printed sheet to smudge and set off, ie. produce mirror image on the back, in the delivery pile. Also, drying is quicker.

PROCESSOFMANUFACTURE

The steps involves in the offset printing of greeting cards are as follows:-

Design and Layout
Image Generation
Copy Preparation of the Camera
Photography
Colour Scanning
Slripping and Platemaking
Offset Press Operation
Finishing

DESIGN&LAYOUT

All designers follow certain basic ideas in planning and laying out a printed piece. These ideas serve as a starting point and as guides rather than hard and fast rules. The five basic elements of design are balance , rhythm, contrast, proportion and unity. Two other factors, colours, and type style, also affect the design of the printed piece.

Balance Basically , there are two methods of achieving balance. formal balance has elements of equal weight placed on both sides of an imaginory vertical centre line on the page. Informal balance gives an illusion of equal weights on both sides of an imaginary vetical centre line. a design is balanced by use of colour or different wieght of type, by placement of the elements or by using ohter design principles. Different kinds of balance create different feelings.

Formal balance, for example, for example. Can give a feeling of performance, dignity, tradition, strength, security, or oder,. In formal balance on the other emphasize the novelty and originality.

Rythem:-

Rhythem is that element of design that directs the reader's eye in a certain direction over a printed pice. Placing the elements vertically leads the eye in a vertical direction, horizontal positioning directs the eye in a horizontal direction. When used property, rhythem relates the messages forcefully and directly. Improperly used, rhythem may move.

The readers too quickly to next message.

Contrast:-

Contrast creates interest in the printed piece by providing veriety in the design. The designer adds contrast by changing colours, shapes, weights, sizes and similar facter in by out. Contrast may also be achieved by varying the type style. Under-scoring, changing the type weight size or face, using capital or small letter , adding colour , reversing the type, using tints or bracketing the words are some of the variations possibles.

Proportions:-

How the parts of a page relates to one another and to the whole is called proportion. All our lifes we have been exposed to materials printed in good proportion. Since the time of the ancient greeks, the 3 to 5 ratio, sometimes called the " Golden Rectangle" has been used in design throughout the world because of its pleasing proportions, Generally printing pages are longer in one dimension than the other. Greeting cards, for example come in standard size of 3x5, 4x6, 5x7, in dus. a square shape (equal in height and width) is seldom used for printed materials because it is static and uninteresting.

Unity:-

Unity hold the design together through the use of similar shapes , similar type styles, or similar colours. All elements should look as if they belog together.

Colour:-

Colour usually adds interest to a printed price and makes a design more attractive. It also presents some new problems for the designer. Some colour look good together; others appear to clash or greate a disturbing feeling. Colours can also create moods. For example red orange, and yellow seems to be warm and exciting, while green and blue are considered cool and calm. A good designr will use there principles to advantage.

Type:-

The printed word is the heart of the message you want to communicate. The type style or the design of the teller choosen, helps communicate the message. Type can be classified in siz main styles, roman, sqare seriff, sans serif, seript, text, and occasional or speciality types.

LAYOUTPRINCIPLES

A layout is to the printer what a blue print is to be contractor. It describes in detail what is to be done to complete the printed job. There are there type of layouts. Thumbail rough, and comprehensive.

Thumbanail layout is the first step in designing a printed price. It is a rough , quick sketch generally not drawn to scale. It presents designers first ideas. The rough layout is the next step in design. The design is there more carefully refined and drawn to scale to be right for the job. After rough layout, comprehensive layout is done. It is done by using drafting instruments to prepare drafting istruments to prepare a comprehensive layout as close as possible to the final printed product or the same paper that will be used for the final printing or white cardboard.

Image Generations:-

Image generation or type setting type characteritics to make up words, sentence and paragraphs for the printed prices.

The two basics methods of producing type are hot type composition, using cast metal, and cold type decomposition, which includes direct impression and photosetting. Hot types includes direct impression and photosetting.

Hot types includes all cast metal type whether set by hand or malchine cold type reffers to all other methods of setting type by a direct impression such as typewriter type, hand assembled alphabets, and phtoprocessors. In recent years, typesetting has probably changed more than any other aspects of offset lithography. At present, a large number of offset units gets their phto-type done from service units.

COPYPREPARATION

Once the printed price is designed, the illustrations choosen, and the type set, all the elements can be put together in to a single composite, called a mechanical this process is called paste-up. After pasteup, it is hand over to proof reader. The make certain corrections and then it is again reset. The tools and materials required for paste up is the browing board, or T-square, clear plastic triagnles, 45^0 and 30^0 - 60^0 - 90^0, ruler or scalem, marked in both under and mm. Cutting tools, scissors, light blue non- reproducing pencils for marking guidelies, writting and drawing pencils, black pens with various sizes of points, grease penuts, clean, white or hard gum creasens marking tapes and transparent tape, conpass, french curves, opaque brushes, opague fluid and any special materials needed for a particular Machancial or paste up.

Photography:

Photography is a way of recording an image. This recorded image used to make a printing plate. Some plate making methods require negatives and other require positives.

Some are reverse reading on the emulsion side and some are straight on the reading, depending on the pointing process. the photographic materials can be continus tone, line , or half tone. Many of the materials and techniques used in process photography are similar to those in photography.

Colour Scanning:

To print a full colour price as the eye sees it, each colour must be filtrered out, Additive primery filters are used, the break white light into primary colours, red and blue. When added together, those three colours have the potential of creating any colour visible to the eye.

For example, when a red filter over a camera lense is place, a negative record of all the red light reflected from original. The result is a red filter separation negative in which the clear area are a true record of the other two additive colour (blue and green). When blue and green light are mixed, a colour called cyan results.

In the same way, a green filter will yeild a printer that records the additive primary colours red and blue. When red and blue lights are mixed, magneta results.

The blue filter works in the same way to produce a negative record of all the blue in the subject. The clar areas left, record the red and green colours, which when mixed, from yellow. This negative then become the yellow printer.

The three colours cyan, magnets and yellow are called the substractive primary colours because each represents the two additive primaries left afte one primary has beeb substracted from the white light. Cyan, magneto and yellow are the colours of process inks and used for process color reproduction .

Stripping and Plate Making:

When the photo conversion is produced, the assembeled negatives into a unit flat for stipping anmd then plate is made offset printing works.

Stripping:

Different techniques may be used for stripping. The important thing to remember is that the end results depend on the negatives being sassembled on the gold enrold sheet in the proper oposition., Many lithographers use the following method:

1. Place a gold sheet on the light table with the head of the sheet within at the top or towards the left.

2. Line up the making sheet with the T-sqare some masking sheets, particularly for small press come gridded with guidelines already drawn on them. Larger presses require the stipper to mark gripper margins centre lines, and other necessary guidelines. The follwing information is based on the use of gridded goldenrold sheets.

3. The tape is goldenrod sheet down along the top endge only ,

4. Locate the paper are to be printed on the masking sheet and mark the exact position of the image. The iamge area must not extend into the gripper matrgin or the making sheet because this area will nto print when the plate is burned.

5. Carefully side the negative, emulsion side down, under the masking sheet. Emulsion side down means that type copy will appear correctly: it will be right reading. On halftones you can determine the emulsion side of the negative by observing the texture of the surface. On most negatives the emulsion side will have slightly flat or dull finsih.On some halftones, however, this is not true. If scaratched on the emulsion side, a mark will show. You will have to scratch the negative in a non image non -printing are to determine the emusion side.

6. Place the negative in the proper position in the area marked on the goldenrod sheet. Align the negative with a T-square and triangle or follow the gridded lines on the goldenrod sheet.

7. Once the negative is aligned, hold the negative and goldenrod sheet down with onehand , and iwth the other hand cut foodball whapped holes in non image area,. Be careful not to cut through the negative. Apply red lighographer's tape over the holes, to hole the negative and goldenrod together.

Plate Making:

After the flat has been prepared, an offset plate is made from it for the press. Many different types of presentizd plates can be used for this operation. Most shops use a negative acting additive plate, which will be discussed here. Most of these plates are either metal or foil types.

The negative -acting additive plate is exposed in a plate maker. This platemaker is usually a vaccum frame to hold negative and plate in very tight contact and a source of high-intensity light. Because the light on a platemaker is so strong, it can damage eyes.

OFFSET PRESS OPERATION

Offset presses are rotary in nature and use the principle that gressts and water do not misc to deliver the desired impressions on paper.

The printing section of the press includes a plate cylinder, an impression cylinder a blanket cylinder, inking rollers, a moisture system and a plate adjustment (Registration) devices. In addition of course, it has a feeder system to move the paper into the press and a delivery system for the finished work.

That all material to be printed is on one thinflat, and pliable plate is one of the virtues of the offset proces. Make ready is no problem, and the plate is easily apped around, the plate cylinde much in the fashion that amimeggraph stencil is applied.

Once the plate is on the press the operator must apply, the moisture (water plus an additive) to the surface of the plate. The water adheres to the nonimage area of the plate and is repelled in the image areas. When ink a grease, is applied it adheres only to the image area and is repelled by the water wat portions. Because of the water grease action and its photographic nature, offset printing is considered a chemical process.

It is called an indirect process because impression are not made directly from the plate.the plate never touches the paper, instead it deposits the inked image on the blanket cylinder with each revolution.

The paper receives the image from the blenket cylender as the sheet or web goes through the press between the blanket and impression cylinders. The impression cylinders is simply the surface backing up the paper as the blanket squezes against it serving the same function as the platen in a typewriter or the bed of a traditional flat bed press.

Each revolution of an offset press therefore consists of:-

1. Application of greasy ink to the image areas of the plate.
2. Application of greasy ink to the image areas of the plate.
3. Trasfer of the ink image to a rubber, blanketted cylinder.
4. Pickup of the paper . by the feeding system of the press which inserts the paper between the blanket and impression cylinders.
5. Deposit of the image from the blanket to the paper.
6. Delivery of the sheets or web of paper.

Although is may seem to be a lengthy series of a lengthy series of details. It is accomplished instantenously. Because offset presses operates on the rotary principle, they are capable of extremely high speed. In general their speed, are basically determined by the efficiency of their feeding and deliver system the cylinders can rotate as fast as an electric motor can turn a drive a shaft.

The most frequent problem in connection with offset press operation is the maintenance of a proper balance of moisture and ink change in humidity sometimes, give pressure a change in humidity sometimes give pressure a great deal of difficult in this regard.

A cross section of an offset press indicating the various system.

Finishing:

As printed cards come from the press, they usually require further operations to prepare them for use. These operations may be cutting, folding, collating, binding packaging. etc.

Paper Weights and Sizes:

Paper is sold by the Kgs hundered kgs, or by tones (1000kgs). Some company sells the paper sell the paper by number of varying size.

The price of paper depends on the kind of paper, quality and economic conditions. They are purchased the market in dimension of 28" x 22" size, 26" x 16" size with varying in the weight by 75,80,85,90,95,100, 110,120,130,140 etc, gram per square meter other paper characteristics:-

In addition to size and weight , other characteristics mus tbe considered in the selection of paper. They include colour, strength, strench, and opacity. Colours even mill to mill, vary in whitners. so, it is better to order to company that produced the original.

Papers also vary in strength depending on how the fibers are interminglesd. This important for web fed offset. All pape rwill stretch a cetain amount. This is more important in finer printing. Paper capacity is related to the thickness of the sheet and the fillers that have been added when the paper was made. a lithanium compound is often added to increase the opacity. If the stock is to be printed a both sides, high opacity is important.

PLANT & MACHINERY SUPPLIERS

Offset Printing Machines:

Victor Engg. Works
C-1/357, GIDC Estate,
ODHAV Road, ODHAV,
Ahmedabad-382415 (Gujrat)

Amit International
B-47, Cox House, Naraina Indl. Area,
Phase - II, New Delhi - 110 028
Phone/fax: 570 4301, 570 4201/011-224 9320

Diamond Engg. Works
6/12, DLF, Indl. Area,
Moti Nagar, New Delhi - 110 015
Phones: 541 4571, 541 8352

Dominent Offset (P) Ltd.
Palam Road, Gurgaon.
Phone/fax: 340019, 341916, 341917, 341918, 340032/0124-340131

Bharat Machine Tools
133-138, Sector 6,
Faridabad.
Phones: 8-241798, 241167

Paper Cutter:

MSL Graphics
15, J.N. Heredia Marg,
Ballard Estate,
Mumbai - 400038
Telex:-262711-13

RAW MATERIAL SUPPLIERS ADDRESS

Offset Printing Ink Suppliers:

Baluja Spectra
C-50 Okhla Indl. Area-II,
New Delhi - 110 020
Phone/fax: 6835715, 6835722

Ajanta Ink Company
Basai Road, Gurgaon.
(Haryana) Phone/fax : 8-330028

Art Printing Inks Company
104 Site-4, Indl. Area,
Sahibabad, Ghaziabad.
Phone/fax: 767882

Inks India (Delhi)
C-49, Sector-8,
Noida-201 301 (U.P.)
Phone/fax: 523801, 011-8-557270

Van Inks & Chemicals (P) Ltd.
B-150, Phase-II,
Noida-201 305 (U.P.)
Phone/fax: 567141, 011-8-521507

Art Paper Suppliers:

Om Prakash Jitendra Kumar & Company
63, Darya Ganj,
New Delhi - 11 00 02.
Phones: 326 96 80, 3271380

Narain Paper Mart
4034/3, Haryana Market,
Chawri Bazar. Delhi - 11 00 06
Phone: 291 51 35

Himgiri Paper Products
B-24, Indl. Area Lawrence Road,
New Delhi - 110 035
Phone: 718 9005

PLANT ECONOMICS OF
GREETING CARDS BY OFFSET PRINTING

Rated Plant Capacity = 20,000.00 Nos./Day

COST OF LAND & BUILDING

(Total land area required 500 sq. mtr) Rs. 3,41,000.00

LIST OF PLANT & MACHINERY

1. Plate process 24x28 vaccum printer complete with all accessores
2. Single colour sheet bed offset press size 22x31 (560x790)complete with all accessories.
3. Miscellaneous equipments, light table, drawing board, T square, metal trianges, plastic clear trangles scissors.
4. Paper cutting machine(semi-automatic) Size 32" complete with all standard equipments.
5. Miscellaneous tools and jigs weihig balance etc. laboratory equipment

LIST OF RAW MATERIALS

1. Arts paper of dimension (26x22) 2250 kg.
2. Offset ink 200 kg.
3. Fount, 18 litre
4. De sensitisor, 18 litre
5. Blanket cleaning, 18 litre
6. Metal Plate (anodised aluninium) size 22x31 av. Life /plate 10000/- coppies
7. Paper, paper plates, sheets, for stripping, designing layout, typing etc.
8. Rubber Blanket
9. Miscellaneous like gum, tape pins etc.

FIXED CAPITAL

Land & Building	Rs.	3,41,000.00
Plant & Machinery	Rs.	9,00,000.00
Other Fixed Assets	Rs.	1,14,000.00
TOTAL	**Rs.**	**13,55,000.00**

TOTAL WORKING CAPITAL/MONTH

Raw Material	Rs.	2,45,343.00
Salary & Wages	Rs.	14,924.00
Utilities & Overheads	Rs.	35,000.00
TOTAL	**Rs.**	**2,95,267.00**

TOTAL CAPITAL INVESTMENT

Total Fixed Capital	Rs.	13,55,000.00
Total Working Capital for 3 Months	Rs.	8,85,801.00
TOTAL	**Rs.**	**22,40,801.00**

TURNOVER/ANNUM

By sale of Greeting Cards 3"x5" with one fold 500000 doz.

TOTAL **Rs. 60,00,000.00**

PROFIT = RECEIPTS - COST OF PRODUCTION

= 60,00,000.00 - 42,79,597.22

= 17,20,402.78

PROFIT SALES RATIO = Profit / Sales x 100 = **28.67 %**

RATE OF RETURN = Operating profit / T.C.I. x 100 = **76.28 %**

BREAK EVEN POINT (B.E.P.) = 36.18 %

16

HAND BLOCK PRINTING ON TEXTILES

INTRODUCTION

Hand block printing is a slow operation. The size of the block is limited by the weight that the printer can handle for long periods without undue fatigue. The pattern must invariably be fitted both across and along the cloth. Early mechanization device increased the block size to print a full fabric width and two or even the pattern repeats. Both the perrotine printing machine and the press block printing machines were of this type. Practically no working examples survive, the reciprocating system having given way to a rotary one. This involved the replacement of the flat block by a cylindrical roller. Furnishing this printer roller was an endless felt blanket to which the print paste was applied and excess scraped off. These machine were frequently called surface printing machines and were used with great success for printing high quality furnishing fabrics.

The printing method involves relatively light pressure and machines based on these principles have been evolved for " duplex printing" i.e. printing the fabric simultaneously on both sides. Another variation is one in which the print paste up take of the raised part of the wooden printing roller has been greatly increased by using poly urethane foam. A machine modified in this way is used for printing carpets.

A wide variety of technique evolved for the purpose of taking the artists original design and reproducing it more rapidly.

The artists now draws the original design on some convenient medium not necessarily a textile material, and the craftman uses this as a working diagram. The craftman then have to separate out the various colours in the design since practically all printing processes apply colors to the cloth the application stage, i.e. the pattern, must be unfit or in the correct register.

Three main possibilities exist and represent quite different form of printing on textiles.

1. To raise the design in relief on a flat (usually wooden) surface-block making.
2. To cut the design through a metal flat surface-flat plate engraving.
3. To cut the design through a flat metal or paper sheet stencil cutting.

USES & APPLICATION

It is used for printing on textile and other surface in different textures, design, pattern, tints etc. at a very economical cost.

MANUFACTURING PROCESS

The following sequences are involved in the hand block printing methods pertaining to textile fabric (cotton & synthetic).

Details of construction:

A separate block is required for each different colour in the finished design. The majority of blocks are made largely of wood, metal may be used to reinforce parts of the design such blocks are used to apply thickened dye stuff pastes at normal room temperature. Although a block may be about 40 mm (1.5 in) thick the cutting necessary to raise the design in relief seldom penetrates deeper than 5 mm (0.2 in.). Dry bonding together a layer of carefully selected fairly hard, close-grained wood, with cheaper woods economics are possible. The layer in the bonded wood are arranged so that the grain runs in the direction at right angle to each other. The size of the block may vary slightly to allow for a design to be fitted in and have a irregular outline to encompass the pattern area. Because the block must be fitted and transferred to the cloth repeatedly during the printing operation, its weight and therefore its average size, must be restricted dimensions greatly in excess of 500 mm X 500 mm X 40 mm (18 in X 18 in X 1.5 in) are unusual but may be required for special design.

To enable the printer to fix his block lays in correct register on the cloth, 'pitch pins' are often fixed round the block sides. These pins are arranged so as to coincide with certain well defined point in the pattern printed during the previous lay.

Printing is generally carried out on very heavily built tables, preferably with stone on concrete tops. The printer may work in a standing position but in the East Sitting cross-legged on the floor may be preferred alternative. The weight of the table varies accordingly, but it is used to cover the rigid surface with a resilient material.

First several thicknesses of blanket are carefully laid on the table, and the whole is then covered with a sheet of water proof fabric. The cloth to be printed is spread out on the table and kept in a place either by pinning it on to a back grey (i.e. back cloth), or by gumming it down directly on the water proof cover at is essential that no movement of the cloth occurs during the printing operation.

Gumming Down:

The cloth is wound round on a wooden tube, called a shell Gum Single paste is then placed at the end of the table and spread along it in as then a film as possible using a rubber squeegee. The role of cloth is unrolled along the table so gummed, and lightly pressed into place either by hand or by careful ironing.

The Tiering table:

The method adopted for applying printing paste to the block is practically universal. A long printing tables are in use consists of a shallow box of dimension 0.6 m X 0.9 m (2 ft. X 3 ft.) fitted on a table that can be wheeled up and down along side the printing table. In the box which is known as the swimming tub is placed . Some old semi fluid starch paste or other thickening paste and upon. This floats a wooden sided tray the bottom of which consists of a sheet of water proof fabric. On this is placed a piece of blanket or a sieve impregnated with the color paste to be printed.

The Printing Operation:

The block is carefully placed on the blanket so that it picks up an even layer of paste which is then transferred to the cloth, the block being struck by the handle of a small but heavy mallet or maul to effect even and through penetration. After each transfer of printing paste, the sieve is respelled evenly with colour by means of a small white wash brush called a tiering brush. By repeated transfer of the color paste to the cloth the whole piece is therefore gradually printed with one color.

The sieve is then removed, replaced by a clean one, and the second colour is applied in the same way, the process being repeated until all the different colors have been separately applied. the cloth is then removed from the table, dried and treated in the manner appropriate to the particular dyestuff used.

PROCESS FLOW SHEET

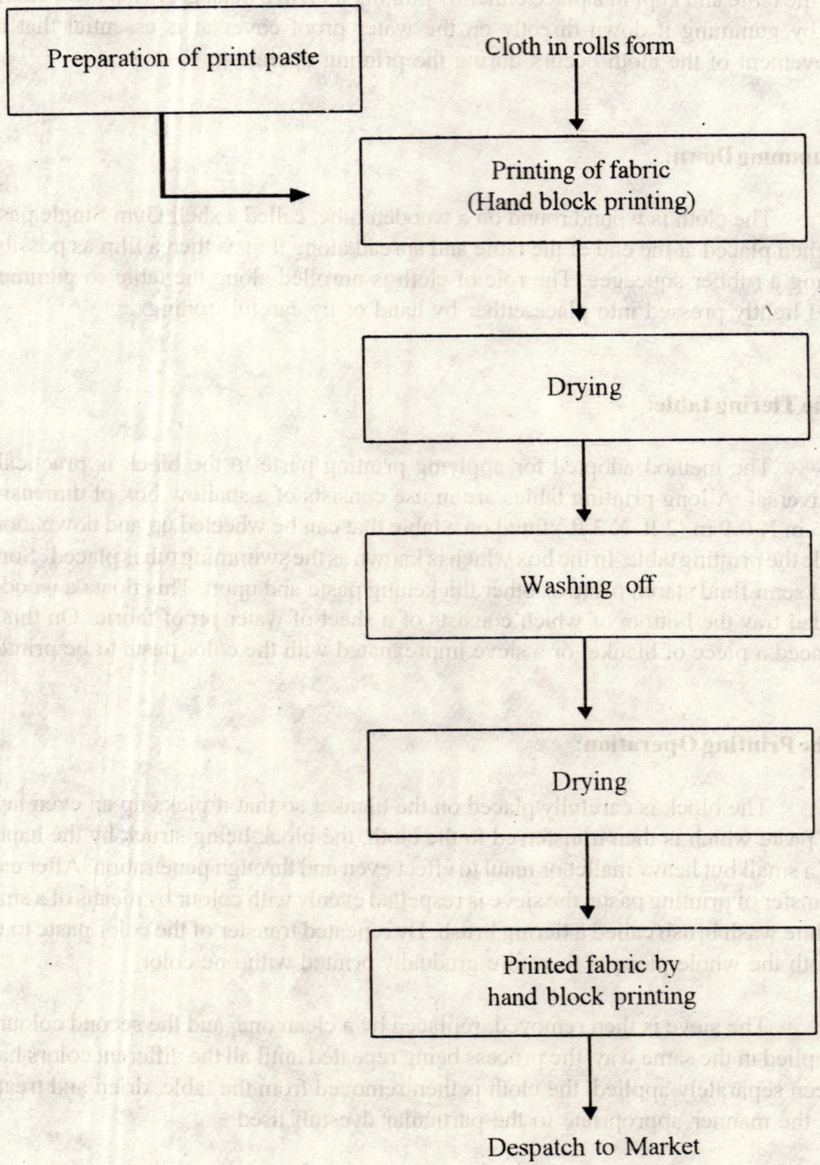

RAW MATERIALS SUPPLIER'S ADDRESSES

Cloth (Cotton & Synthetic):

Ahmedabad Cotton Mfg. Co. Ltd.
Out Side Sarang Pur Gate,
Ahmedabad-2 (Gujarat)

Bhilwara Synthetics Ltd.
26, Indl Area, Bhilwara - 311 001
Rajasthan

Textile pigments paste:

Colour-Chem Ltd.,
Registered Office: Ravindra Annexe,
194, Church Gate Reclamation,
Mumbai - 400 020

Sodium Alginate:

Cellulose Products of India Ltd.
National Chamber's ,
Office No. 4 & 5, 2nd Floor,
Near Dipali Theatre,
Ashram Road, Ahmedabad - 380 009
(Gujarat)

PLANT & MACHINERY SUPPLIERS

Storage Vessels:

Aeroquip Engineers (P) Ltd.
1325, Phase - III, GIDC. Vatva,
Ahmedabad - 382 445 (Gujarat)
Phone : 583 3021, 583 3075

Arko Industries
A-288, Wagle Industrial Estate,
Road No. 16/Z, Thane - 400 604 (M.S.)
Phone : 5321210 Fax : 022-5681141

PLANT ECONOMICS

Rated Plant Capacity = 100.00 Mts./Day

COST OF LAND & BUILDING

(Total land area required 4800 Sq. Ft.) Rental

LIST OF PLANT & MACHINERY

1. Wooden blocks of different design
2. Wooden printing roller's
3. Tiering table of dimension(2 ft X 3 ft.) with necessary arrangement
4. Pigment storage vessels (S.S.)
5. Miscellaneous viz. pitch pins, rubber squeegee etc.

LIST OF RAW MATERIALS

1. Cloth
2. Textile colour pigment paste of different colour
3. Miscellaneous consumables viz. thickening agents (sodium alginate) etc.

FIXED CAPITAL

Land & Building		Rental
Plant & Machinery	Rs.	12,500.00
Other Fixed Assets	Rs.	53,000.00
TOTAL	**Rs.**	**65,500.02**

TOTAL WORKING CAPITAL/MONTH

Raw Material	Rs.	1,23,000.00
Salary & Wages	Rs.	37,376.00
Utilities & Overheads	Rs.	10,800.00
TOTAL	**Rs.**	**1,71,176.00**

TOTAL CAPITAL INVESTMENT

Total Fixed Capital	Rs.	65,500.02
Total Working Capital for 3 Months	Rs.	5,13,528.00
TOTAL	**Rs.**	**5,79,028.02**

TURNOVER/ANNUM

By sale of Hand Block Printed cloth 30,000 mts. Rs. 24,00,000.00

PROFIT = RECEIPTS - COST OF PRODUCTION

= 2,53,009.96

PROFIT SALES RATIO = Profit / Sales x 100 = **10.54 %**

RATE OF RETURN = Operating Profit / T.C.I. x 100 = **43.70 %**

BREAK EVEN POINT (B.E.P.) = 57.19 %

17

LETTER PRESS PRINTING

INTRODUCTION

India has made much progress in the field of printing. Every kind of printing machinery is being manufactured in India. Thousands of workers are earning their livelihood by the grace of this industry. Margin of profit is very high in the field of printing industry. Some presses are being run by the foot in cottage of persons.

It is necessary to acknowledge people of daily happenings, the copies of matter is necessary to make and distribute. Making of copies can be done by many processes i.e. by type writers, cyclostyle, etc. But these processes or lacs of copies of any matter, only printing machine is explode. Generally to make copies of a matter within limited time is called printing technology.

Before some time printing was existing only upto extent of an art. But to recognize it as an art is not sufficient, it is a science too.

Now science has prevailed in printing technology also and rather to say it 'Printing Art' it will useful to say it 'Scientific Printing Technology.

Modern printing divided roughly into two classes. One is called the Letter Press. Letter press printing is made of the composition of types and setting of blocks with types of blocks along. Types can be composed with hand. When the matter is composed with hand, it is called hand composition.

Letter Press is a "relief process - that is the printing surface holding the image to be printed is raised above the non-printing background. This raised surface is inked by rollers and then pressed against the paper to make the impression. Because the background is lower than the printing area, it comes into contact with neither the inking rollers nor the paper, and so does not print.

In traditional letter press all the text is printed from metal type and the pictures from letter press blocks. These elements are assembled together imposed to create a "forme" inside a rigid frame(chase), which is placed in the press. The printing surface therefore may be made up of hundreds or thousands of different pieces of type, blocks and spacing. A development of letter presses uses : "stereo", or "electro" plates for each page or for the whole "forme", these are described.

CLASSIFICATION OF LETTERPRESS PRINTING MACHINES

The Machines used in the letterpress printing process are more in number than the number of machines used in other printing process. In this method the machines used range from hand operated machines to complicated automatic rotary machines. Keeping in view to the impressioning or printing surface, the Letterpress printing machines can be classified in three main groups.

1. Plane to Plane surface (Flat to flat)
   - (a) Hand Press
   - (b) Platen Machines

2. Plane to cylinder (Flat to cylinder)
   - (a) Stop cylinder machine
   - (b) Two revolution cylinder machine
   - (c) Swing cylinder machine
   - (d) Single revolution cylinder machine
   - (e) Reduced stop cylinder machine

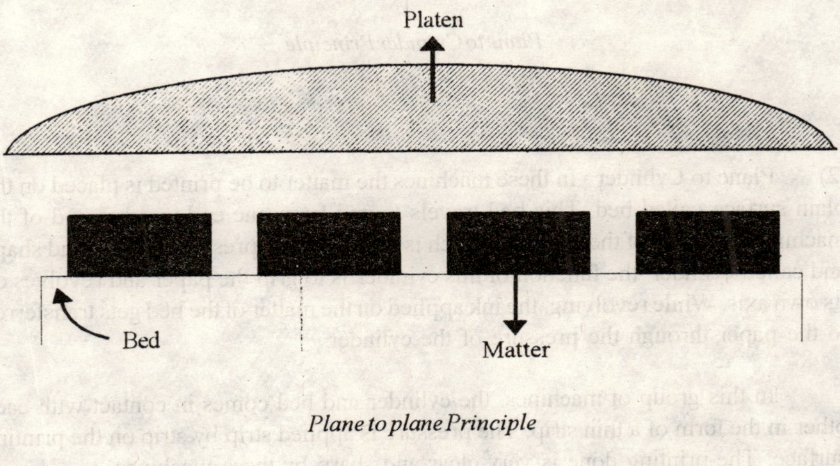

Plane to plane Principle

3. Cylinder to cylinder (Rotary machines)

(1) Plane to plane Surface : In this group of machines the printing surface and impressioning surface both are plane (flat). While printing, the plane surface comes in contact with each other. The whole matter comes under the pressure at the same time. A controlled pressure is required to transfer the ink from the matter (printing surface) to the paper clearly and correctly.

Before the invention of cylinder machines, all the machines used were based on this principle. The working of these machines is such that their size can not be made large. In these machines the matter surface and pressure surface may be either in vertical or horizontal stage. The works done by these machines are small in size and less in number. The machines of this group are small in size and their speed is slow. These machines are not suitable for high class colour, solid and book works.

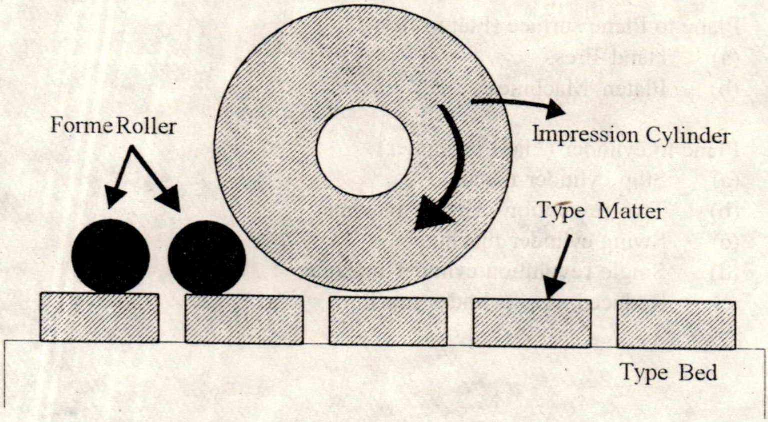

Plane to Cylinder Principle

(2) Plane to Cylinder : In these machines the matter to be printed is placed on the plain surface called bed. This bed travels to and from one end to other end of the machine. That part of the machine which is used to apply pressure, is in round shape and called cylinder. the function of this cylinder is to grip the paper and revolves on its own axis. While revolving, the ink applied on the matter of the bed gets transferred to the paper through the pressure of the cylinder.

In this group of machines, the cylinder and bed comes in contact with each other in the form of a thin strip. The pressure is applied strip by strip on the printing surface. The printing done is very clear and sharp by these machines.

This is the reason, why the printing done by cylinder machines is far better than platen machines. One reason for this is also that the pressure applied by cylinder machines is more and controlled, compared to the platen machines. High class printing works are done by this group of machines. Any type of book work and coloured printing is done efficiently with these machines. These are more popular in general printing industry. the speed of hand fed plane to cylinder machines is low. therefore printing in large numbers is done on automatic cylinder machines.

(3) Cylinder to Cylinder : In this group of machines, the printing, surface as well as the impression surface, both are cylindrical. The printing surface is prepared by duplicating process in round, shape. According to the letterpress printing process, the surface to be printed lies above the surface which is non-printed. This round plate is made according to the circumference of the plate cylinder. this round plate is fitted on to the plate cylinder. Pressure is now applied by means of the impression cylinder. the reel of paper for printing is placed in between these two cylinders.

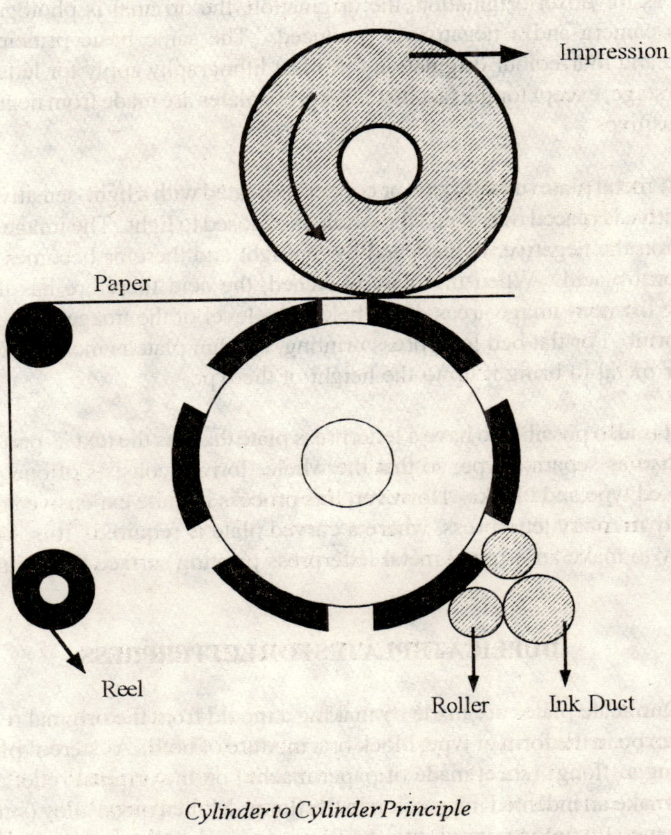

Cylinder to Cylinder Principle

In this type of cylinder machines, one end of the reel of paper is fixed in between the two cylinders. When both the cylinders start revolving on their axis, the reel of paper is pulled according to the speed of the cylinders. Printing is done by each revolution of the cylinder. the machines based on this principle are called rotary machines. the speed of these machines is comparatively very high. About 50 thousand news papers or having 64 pages each can be printed per hour by these machines. this is why these machines are used for printing news papers, magazines and books etc. High standard coloured printing is not done properly with these machines. Alongwith this, small sized and less number of jobs also cannot be done by this group of machines.

ORIGINATION FOR LETTERPRESS

In letterpress, pictures are printed from letterpress 'blocks' or plates which have a raised surface for the image area. Original plates are produced by etching. First, exactly as for offset origination, the origination, the original is photographed on a process camera and a negative is produced. The same basic principles of line, halftone and four-colour origination for offset lithography apply for letterpress upto the film stage, except for the fact that letterpress plates are made from negatives rather than positives.

A metal plate (usually zinc or copper) is coated with a light-sensitive emulsion; the negative is placed over it and the whole is exposed to light. The image area, which is clear on the negative, is hardened by the light and therefor becomes resistant to corrosion by acid. When the plate is etched, the acid therefore has the effect of bringing the non- image areas down below the level of the image area, so that they do not print. For flat bed letterpress printing, the thin plate is mounted on a base of wood or metal to bring it up to the height of the type.

It is also possible to have a letterpress plate that has the text as part of the plate rather than as separate type, so that the whole 'forme' consists of one plate rather than mixed type and blocks. However, hits process is quite expensive and normally used only in rotary letterpress, where a curved plate is required. It is, however, the only way to make an original metal letterpress printing surface from filmiest type.

DUPLICATE PLATES FOR LETTERPRESS

Duplicate plates are made by making a mould from the original relief surface which can be in the form of type, block or a mixture of both. A 'stereo' plate is made by placing a 'flong' (sheet made of paper mache) on the original relief and using a press to make an indented impression in the flong. Molten metal alloy (similar to that used for metal type) is poured into the flong, and when the metal solidifies it has a relief printing surface that is a duplicate of the original.

This method first came into use in the eighteenth century when all printing was from the original metal type. Long runs meant that the type wore out, so that the whole job had to be completely reset. By contrast, when stereos wore out, new plates could easily be made from the flongs.

Alternatively, stereos can be made from rubber or flexible plastic. Here the moulding material is usually thermosetting plastic (bakelite) and the plates are made from the moulds by the application of heat and pressure. These flexible rubber or plastic plates are still used for printing paperbacks on web-fed rotary presses, although offset is now taking over.

Another form of duplicate plate is called an 'electro'. The technique was developed particularly for fine-screen halftones, where a stereo cannot give a sufficiently precise result. The mould is made of plastic and its surface is sprayed with silver compound to make it electrically conductive; the mould is then placed in an electrolytic bath, so that a film of copper 'grows' on the recessed surface of the mould . The film is then removed from the mould and filled with molten metal alloy to strengthen it.

As a result of the demise of letterpress in most areas, there are now very few companies left making letterpress original or duplicate plates, and then only for specialized applications such as stereos for national newspapers.

Now a days, the frame is fixed on a flat bed, and paper is pressed into contact with type or a plate. Koeing made a cylinder press which was the copy of these used in the world of book-printing. In big presses which print dailies, rotary machines are set up. The production from several reels can be combined, collected at a plate where it is folded into the shape of a newspaper and delivered automatically at a remarkable speed.

Letterpress Characteristics :- Letterpress ink is dense and gives a strong black image. When type is printed on to a soft paper the 'squash' can be seen around each character, and this adds distinction to private-press work - when the right typeface is used: typefaces made up from fine lines print better on paper with a smooth surface using a lighter impression, as otherwise their fine detail is buried in the soft paper.

Letterpress blocks of photographs need a high-quality are paper to obtain the best results in either black-and white or colour, and the block themselves are very expensive compared with the equivalents used in other processes. This is because the zinc or copper used is itself expensive, and because the etching process is slow, with correction difficult to achieve.

Advantages and Disadvantages:- Except in the specialized areas mentioned above, letterpress, the dominant printing process until the mid-1960s, has largely given way to offset lithography. the disadvantages of letterpress are the high cost of the metal type and blocks: the fact that more expensive papers are required to achieve the kind of quality offset can achieve using cheaper ones; the relatively slow speed of most letterpress machines; and the fact that modern methods of origination are mainly photographic and do not lend themselves to the creation of a raised surface.

The advantages of the process are the denseness of the ink (not diluted by water or spirit as in offset or gravure) and the quality of the impression - 'excellent characteristics for high-quality private-press work. In the case of newspapers and paperbacks, letterpress survives where the origination process (for example, hot metal typesetting) lends itself to the production of a raised surface. Letterpress also wastes less paper than offset, as there are no problems of holding the balance between ink and water.

USES AND APPLICATION

The letterpress printing is used to print Newspapers, books, greetings, pictures drawing and so many other thing which is presently used by most of the people. Its application is very wide and it is needless to say the extent of its application.

Generally, this method of printing is more in use compared to the other methods, due to the reason that it is easy & simple, this was the method of printing which was invented in the beginning. Printing done by this method, the edges become sharp and a slight raise is found on the back side of the printed paper. This raise is called indentation.

B.I.S. SPECIFICATION

I.S. 11122 - Letter press printing plates & equipment.
I.S. 11122 - (Part - 1) - (1985) - Original printing plates size A4.
I.S. 11122 - (Part - 2) - (1984) - Flat material duplicate plates size A4.
I.S. 11122 - (Part - 3) - (1984) - Galleys size A4.
I.S. 11122 - (Part - 4) - (1984) - Jobbing chasis size A4.
I.S. 5046 - (1975) - Letter print ink, black, general purpose.
(Reaffirmed 1984)

PROCESS/TECHNIQUES

There are four main types of letter press printing machine. All combine the following elements, inking, printing, feeding and delivering.

There are several letter press printing methods, out of these.

1. The Platen press.
2. The flat bed cylinder press.
3. Rotary press
4. Belt press

Most printing processes require the paper to be either sheet fed or web fed.

In sheet-fed printing the paper, which is made in the form of reels (large rolls), is cut into sheets of a suitable size for the press being used. The 'feeder' section of the press picks up the sheets, usually with a combination of metal fingers and vacuum suckers, and feeds them through to be printed. The sheets then pass on to the delivery end of the press, still as flat sheets - folding or other finishing processes are a separate operation requiring other machinery.

With web-fed (also known as reel-fed) printing, the paper is supplied to the machine in the form of reels. The front end of the press has a reel stand, which holds the paper as it is unwound and fed though the press. The actual method of printing is the same as with a sheet-fed press, but printing can take place at much higher speeds because the machine is not slowed down by having to pick up and put down each sheet before printing the next.

Most web presses also incorporate some form of finishing facility after printing. Usually this folding, but it can also include various types of gluing, stitching and perforating to give special products for direct-mail and other purposes; here the folding section of the machine may have added equipment for gluing and perforating.

The advantages of web-fed printing are speed, the fact that folding can be done at the same time as printing, and that paper on reels is cheaper than paper in sheets. Web-fed presses therefor lend themselves to long runs.

The disadvantages, compared with sheet-fed printing, lie with the machines: web-fed presses involve a very high initial outlay, need more time before they are ready to start printing, and most produce only items of a fixed length. This last limitation arises from the fact that each length of paper going through the press to be brought into contact with the printing.

Surface (an impression) must be the same length as that printing surface. This length is known as the 'cut-off'; if the press are to be used to print a shorter printing image, it would require the same length of paper per impression. The printed sheets would then have to be cut down to size, with consequent wastage. Furthermore, web-fed presses waste more paper than sheet-fed paper in the make ready process, as their high speed means that more paper is spoiled before acceptable copies are produced.

An operation that applies to all printing process is 'make-ready; - that is , all the operations that take place prior to the first good copies being produced on a press. These operations include setting up the press to accept the size and thickness of paper being used, putting the printing plates on, putting the correct sort and colour of ink on the press, adjusting the folder (on a web-fed press), ensuring that the colour is of the right strength and that the image is in the right position - checking, in fact, that everything is correct prior to printing. Thus make-ready is a crucial area in printing, as the eventual cost of the job and the quality of the result depend on this part of the process. Obviously, while the press is being made ready it is not producing anything, and the high capital cost of equipment is not being recovered. Most modern printing techniques therefore aim to reduce the time and expense involved in make-ready.

The letter printing press methods are as follows :

The Platen Press:

The platen press consists of two plane surfaces : the forme constitutes one of these, the blank paper being placed on the opposite surface. The forme is inserted into the machine vertically and locked firmly into place. Ink is picked up by inking rollers from a revolving disc or drum above the machine, and these are then passed across the forme to charge it with ink. While the machine is open, the paper is inserted and the two flat surfaces, which re hinged at the bottom, are brought together under pressure by the press to make the impression (the printed sheet).

Such presses range from those where the paper is hand-fed and the power supplied by a food treadle to high-speed, electrically powered machines where the paper is fed in automatically by a vacuum feeder. On a platen press it is very easy to adjust the impression for different thicknesses of paper and board by altering the distance between the two surfaces, so the machine lends itself to a variety of types of work. Platen presses are normally small (up to A2) and used for jobbing work such as stationery, tickets and small leaflets. Most of this work can now be, and usually is, printed by the process of offset lithography, nevertheless, platen presses are still used for embossing, cutting and creasing and for hot-foil stamping.

The Flat-Bed Cylinder Press:

In this type of press, the flat-bed while the ink rollers and sheets of paper rotate over it alternately, the paper being held around a cylinder while it is being pressed on to the forme to make the impression.

These presses can print a sheet up to A0 size or even larger, and used to be used for printing more substantial work, such as books and magazines. However, most of this work is now produced using offset lithography and, apart from a few machines operated by private presses for fine book work, flat bed cylinder machines are today mainly used in commercial printing for cutting and creasing.

The Rotary Press:

Rotary presses print from a curved or flexible metal or plastic plate. The plate can be produced from a forme - by moulding from it and then making the plate from the mould - or photographically it is clamped to a cylinder which revolves against another cylinder carrying the paper. The plate cylinder first revolves against ink rollers and then makes an impression on the paper carried on the impression cylinder.

Rotary presses can be sheet fed or web-fed, and letterpress is still widely used with this latter kind of press, although even here offset and gravure processes are now-a-days often used instead Web-fed rotary letterpress is used for labels, business forms, computer stationery and national newspapers. The technique is used also for a large proportion of mass-market paperback books, with specialized presses printing by letter-press from plastic or, by flexography, rubber plates. Sheet-fed rotary letterpress presses are now rare.

The Beltpress:

The belt press is a version of the rotary press where flexible relief plates are mounted on two continuous belts the revolve against a web of paper. The belts vary in length depending on the number of pages in the book. The printed pages are cut and folded into four-page units, collated in order, and fed directly into a binding machine, so the process can turn reels of paper into bound books in one operation. However, the belt press can print in only one colour, and the binding has to be unseen.

These presses are used almost solely for book work, and the majority of the machines are made by Cameron, the company which invented this technique. The great advantages of belt presses are that they can produce virtually any size of book and lend themselves to short turns, down to two or three thousand copies, enabling the publisher to gear his runs closely to the demands of the market.

Printing Inks that are used in a Printing Press:-

1. Job black
2. High rate halftone black
3. Bond black
4. Book black
5. High class red ink that is used in quality printing
6. Priyon orange
7. Bronze blue
8. Millori blue
9. Purple lemon yellow
10. Process red
11. Yellow and Blue
12. Mixing white
13. Cover white etc.

CONSUMPTION OF INK IN DIFFERENT PAPERS

1.	Rough cartridge	88%
2.	Antique	80%
3.	Carton	80%
4.	News	72%
5.	Smoth cartridge	64%
6.	M.F.Pt.	56%
7.	Super calender	52%
8.	Imitation art	48%
9.	Art	40%

When ever a press owner gives quotations for printing a job he takes the above points into consideration.

The Lay of the lower case :

The plan of boxes of letters. When we put the proper type in the proper box or column, assigned for it, is called "the laying of the type".

The construction of the Type case has been so designed as to facilitate the compositor in composing and distribution. The spaces and letters are set in such as way as to facilitate the compositor according to the grouping and construction and order of letters and words. Sizes of the lower case boxes are made according to the use and the size of the letters.

The box of 'e' is made largest in the case because of English 'e' is used more than all the other letters, therefore, it is essential that its box may be made largest in size z,x,q,k,j are used in little quantities and occupy the boxes which are smaller in size.

Moreover there are may kinds of spaces but the thick space of other spaces are placed in such a box which is very nearest to the compositor.

It will be most appropriate if on the right of the 'e' box that is, the upper box of 'e' be divided into two parts so that the middle and thin spaces may be placed separately in the lower case.

Beginning of Work :

The compositor keeps the case on the right hand side of the frame and other helpful material space case or a letter-board on the left hand side of the case frame. A galley containing leads of the length required for the job is kept on the left side of the case frame .The composed type can be transferred into this galle from the composing stock.

How measure is made :

The width of a page is always in pica cms. or you may say twelve point without any consideration of the size of the type which is to be used. When books are composed, the measure may be any length in accordance with the size of the book. But when you used display type, it will be found more beneficial to make up the measure to the approxi-mate number of even cms, but there is an exception for a fifteen or twenty five cm measure. There is a reason behind it that spacing material sizes mostly increases in length by even two cms with the other odd measures and sizes fifteen and twenty five are counted as additional.

Method of the type setting:

Prepare yourself for composing red a few words of the copy and keep them into the mind and compose them into the stick. Search out the box for the first letter and pick up the letter for the box with the thumb and forefinger of the right hand. Now pick up the next letter, and place into the stick with the nick to the front. The whole process is done without looking again at the letter. Only the correct position of the nick is felt with the thumb or finger as the case may be. That is turning or twisting the right thumb and forefinger will give the correct position of the stick.

PROCESS OF AUTOMATIC LETTERPRESS PRINTING

The continuous automatic letter press printing is done by a belt press. In which two continuous belts .

1. By rollers to the first printing belt
2. Which is inked by inking rollers
3. This belt prints the first side of the paper. The printed paper passes by driers
4. Which dry the ink. the dried paper is turned over by turning bars.
5. So that the second side of the paper can be printed by the second belt.
6. Which is inked by the second set of inking rollers.
7. The paper now printed on both sides, is dried by driers
8. The paper is then slit
9. Folded by formers
10. Aand cut
11. The cut and foled paper passes along a conveyor belt to the collator
12. Where the sections are stacked in the correct order. The stacked sections
13. Are now ready for binding.

SOURCE OF RAW MATERIALS

Type:

Kamla Type Foundry,
Subji Mandi,
Ghantaghar,
Delhi - 110007

Standard type Foundry,
Chawri Bazar,
Delhi - 110 006

Laxmi type Foundary,
Machali Bazar,
Jama Masjid,
Delhi - 110 006

Printing Ink:

Baluja Spectra
C-50, Okhla Indl. Area-II,
New Delhi - 110 020
Phone/fax : 6835715, 6835722

Ajanta Ink Company
Basai Road, Gurgaon,
(Haryana)
Phone/fax : 8-330028

Art Printing Inks Company
104 Site-4, Indl. Area,
Sahibabad, Ghaziabad, (U.P.)
Phone/fax : 767882

Inks India (Delhi)
C-49, Sector-8,
Noida-201 301 (U.P.)
Phone/fax : 523801, 011-8-557270

Van Inks & Chemicals (P) Ltd.
B-150, Phase-II,
Noida-201 305 (U.P.)
Phone/fax : 567141, 011-8-521507

MACHINERY SUPPLIERS

Trading Machine:

Sodhi & Sons,
Bara Hindu Rao
Delhi - 110 006

Ecko Industries
Kishan Ganj Market,
Delhi - 110 007

Kishore Foundary Workshop,
159, Hussianpure,
Amritsar,
Punjab

Manuphai Sons & Company
16, Custom House Road,
Mumbai - 400 001

Printing Machine Mfrg. Company
Free Ghanj,
Chiman Lal Road,
Agra (U.P.)

Dadiala Engineering Works,
27, D.L.F. Industrial area,
Najafgarh Road,
New Delhi - 110 015

Asian Printing Machinery Co.
12, Ramjas Industrial Estate,
New Rohtak Road,
New Delhi - 110 005

Mach Engineering Pvt. Ltd.,
Plot No.4, Industrial Area,
NIT Faridabad - 121 001
(Haryana)
Phone: 81-24740

PLANT ECONOMICS OF LETTER PRESS PRINTING

Rated Plant Capacity = 2500.00 Pac./Day

COST OF LAND & BUILDING

(Total land area required 500 sq. mtr.) Rs. 2,42,500.00

LIST OF PLANT & MACHINERY

1. Automatic paper cutting machine complete with all accessories
2. Treadling printing machine (10"x15")(12"x18") complete with all accessories
3. Die punching machine (23"x36") complete with all accessories
4. Motor 1 HP
5. A. Stone for locking up the frame
   B. Quions huge and small with two different keys (2 doz.)
   C. Case racks (2 doz.)
   D. Galley racks (2 nos.)
   E. English & Hindi about 40 sets of cases
   F. Galley
      a. 15" x 18"
      b. 10" x 15"
      c. 11" x 18"
      d. 9" x 11"
   G. From 24 cm to 56 cm in breath galley 50 column
   H. Composing sticks (8" x 2") 20 nos.
   I. Composing sticks (6" x 2") 2 nos.
   J. Hand lead cutter
   K. Brush for cleaning the types.
6. Stitching machine & hand tools with motor
7. Numbering machine
8. Cylinder proof press floor size (60"x54") & (82"x 72")

LIST OF RAW MATERIALS

1. Paper 230 rim bundle 500 sheets of 16 kg.
2. Ink 100 kg.
3. Miscellaneous chemical and other items

FIXED CAPITAL

Land & Building	Rs.	2,42,500.00
Plant & Machinery	Rs.	95,000.00
Other Fixed Assets	Rs.	40,000.00
TOTAL	**Rs.**	**3,77,500.00**

TOTAL WORKING CAPITAL/MONTH

Raw Material	Rs.	79,000.00
Salary & Wages	Rs.	8,109.00
Utilities & Overheads	Rs.	4,050.00
TOTAL	**Rs.**	**91,159.00**

TOTAL CAPITAL INVESTMENT

Total Fixed Capital	Rs.	3,77,500.00
Total Working Capital for 3 Months	Rs.	2,73,477.00
TOTAL	**Rs.**	**6,50,977.00**

TURNOVER/ANNUM

1. Receipt through sale of 7,50,000 nos. packet
2. Job work printing 1200000 nos. impressions

TOTAL **Rs. 14,70,000.00**

PROFIT = RECEIPTS - COST OF PRODUCTION

= 14,70,000.00 - 12,65,208.44

= 2,04,791.56

PROFIT SALES RATIO = Profit / Sales x 100 = **13.81 %**

RATE OF RETURN = Operating Profit / T.C.I. x 100 = **31.21 %**

BREAKEVEN POINT (B.E.P.) = **53.22 %**

18

OFFSET PRINTING PRESS

INTRODUCTION

Book publishing started coming into its own only during the last four decades in the newly emerging countries of Asia , Africa, and Latin America. Before that they were primarily dependent on the colonial powers to fulfill the book read of their peoples, for both education and entertainment, in the developing world these are countries which do not have much publishing of their own, as well as those which have a developed and active publishing industries. But there is a great similarity in the problem facing all of them in the area of publishing. Low literacy is common features of all developing countries. In a sense publishers in there countries are serving only a small minority of their populations that is literate and can afford to buy books. A small readership means small editions and consequently high prices. A vicious circle, and this has adversely affected the education system and the intellectual life of the countries. However, cultural advancement does not entirely depend on books, but books are the most important tool of intellectual and cultural growth in developing countries which are in hurry to come into their own

"To establish an indigenous publishing house in an act of liberation and therefore a necessity because it breaks the control indeed, the monopoly which some countries have had over world literature for which reason, they have controlled the mind of Africa". This is the statement from the publishing progress in Nigeria, which reflects the mood and psche of most of the developing countries soon after independence.

The publishers have a special role to play in this respect as it is they, who, in practice, serve as custodians of the rights of authors, In India the federation of Indian publishers attaches special importance to the propagation and protection of copy right in the interests of publishers and the authors.

PUBLICATIONINDUSTRY

A publication industry should have various factors in the production of books, magazines and comics.

The publishers should be conversant with the publishing management techniques live objectives and priorities, planning publishing programmes , co-ordination among different departments in a publishing house, laison with authors, whole sellers, retailers, libraries and government departments, publishing concepts, basic progressional records, in come, break even point decision making. They should also know somehow, regarding capital requirement credit facilities, cash in flow, annual budgeting, fulfill and loss account and balance sheet.

Book , Magazine and Comics Manufacturing:

Publication industries depend on five basic factors :

1. Management
2. Labour
3. Equipments
4. Materials
5. Market

Management:

Book manufacture is by far the most complex and difficult from of printing requiring a high level of organizational skills. It is found that the managerial class in the top portion of India's printing industry to be sophisticated, hard working, resourceful, well-trained and educated, and fully cognizant of the problem it faces.

The publishers must have the talent to manage the publication successfully The publication should no be over manned and in sufficiently profit motivated to complete in real terms.

Labour:

Indian labour is abundant and remarkably low-prices by international standard, though excessively overmanning in the best run plants, are found .

However, balanced-making and fair pay may improve the standard of publication establishment, if these labors are skilled well efficient, resourceful, hardwarking and active.

Equipment:

Printing :- Small format one and two colour sheet fed offset press of obsolete design and capability are being manufactured in India and are the "new" norm to which old letter-press shops are convering . The same holds true for platen presses and single knife guillotines. None of this equipment, unfortunately, is suitable for book production, though it is being used for this purpose.

Single colour books should be printed on Camera on Belt, Web offset or sheet fed perfector presses. The perfectors, which simultaneously print one colour on both sides of the sheet, should be, for proper efficiency, 65 inch, or, at the very least, 54 inch. Inability to buy satisfactory offset paper of national origin in these formats (or any format, for that mater) , makes the importation of such equipment unlikely until and unless India faces up to its need to import book papers. Local paper supplied in reels often has as many as eight to ten splices in a reel, and in some of these the ends are not even pasted together. There is no way in which a Web press , Cameron or offset, can be used with any degree of efficiency under such conditions.

Binding:- There is no mechanical book binding in India. Most folding, gathering sewing and drawing on of covers is done by hand under totally archaic conditions.

Some, utilize cutting and stitching machine for cutting the pages and collecting and gathering by hand and then sticking by machine manually fed.

Materials:

Paper:- Paper is the medium of conveying of information to general public of publication industry. The quality of offset paper should be good appearance, modern cost to avoid the production problem course due to use of cheap and poor appearence of the paper. It is very benefited, if the quality of paper is good and attractive to the customers. The better quality paper has many advantages, as it attract the customers, durability for life long, resistance to water and moisture in the atmosphere, good fearing resistance, good in printing impression, etc.

Hence, the publications, however, constitute the sole source of a publishers livelihood and must be made at low enough cost and high enough quality to make them appearing to the public.

Film :- Film is an essential materials for offset printing. In future, when demand will groves, the film will be manufactured in India for high quality film, for publication. In the meantime, publishers are to be allowed to import it for book publications free of 200% duty.

Ink and Other Materials :- Materials such as inks, adhesives, photo polymers, binding cloth and board will, in a book market potentially as large as India's , be manufactured locally in increasing amounts and with gradually improving quality. This is inevitable. It is already happening with pre-sensitized offset print plates, In the meantime, however, book manufacturers or publishers must have continuing access to these materials from foreign source when the local product is of inadequate quality without the onus of a 200% duty.

Market:

The Indian market for books is large and growing. If books were manufactured more efficiently and with better quality the market would grow even faster. There is, further-more , an export market for decent quality books in which India does not participate at all. American and British book publishers buy substantial quantities of book manufacturing from Japan, Italy, Spain, Yugoslavia, Hong Kong, Singapore, and South Korea. Even Thailand is becoming a source. India would be able to participate to advantage in the world market if it were to develop its book manufacturing capabilities.

It is observed that Indian printers do not have large, aggressive sales staffs. Customers instead line up to place work with them. It is clear that whether in book manufacture or quality commercial printing, the demands and desires of the market far exceed current productive capacity.

PRINCIPLE OF OFFSET

It will be seen that an offset print is not taken from the printing plate direct to the paper or stock. But the first made on an intermediate surface and transferred for there to the paper. The usual method is to have a special cylinder on which is stretched and offset blanket. As the print is reversed on the offset blanket and again reversed when the transferred on to the paper, it follows that the job which is to be printed offset appears the same on the machine plate as an the final print. It should also be noted that offset printing is done by both rotary and plate bed machine and therefore, the term offset is not synom muous with rotary, despite the decline of flatbed.

It will also be appreciated that the term direct method as used by the first offset tin printers was quite clear to then but is now confusion due to the wilder subsequent application of the offset process. As this was specialized printing group very largely isolated from other trade contacts, the terms which they used were their down concern but it should be clearly understood that all metal sheet printing is offset printing that the principle is the same as used now for printing on paper and that litho offset machines have developed from earlier this printing machines.

PROCESS INVOLVED IN OFFSET PRINTING

Preparation of Copy :

Most of the firm maintained their own a stand design department. Some of them are located on the factory premises. It is also a common practice of the trade to utilize outside agencies for the preparation art work. The standard of design submitted for reproduction is generally high. In the art department, the artist takes into consideration the technical details of the reproduction process and arranges the colours to be used in each a manner that a faithfully reproduction is possible.

The use of phototype setting machines is of recent growth and we did not see much of it is Britain. In the America factories, however some firms were using photo sectors. In Japan since the phototype setting machines, is simpler and less expensive, phototype setters for composition are more common, particularly in big printing establishments.

Wherever a copy is received it is carefully scrutinized before it is actually sent into the works for processing. Some firms have a copy preparations department when the details are works out. Normally an art department take on itself the task of

(a) Sortinizing type matter for reproduction by photography
(b) Making off copy to suit the customers layout
(c) Giving instructions regarding the percentage of enlargement or reduction and how they should for into the layout
(d) Determining the number of colour
(e) Grouping together of jobs of small matter.

Screens :

Both contact screens and the glass cross line screens are in use. The more progressive factories, have however, started using contact screen because, they give very much better results.

METHOD OF TYPE SETTING & PRINTING

Laying of the Type:

The compository composes the matter to be printed in the proper not known as sticks assigned for it or the spaces and letters are set in such a way as to most of the requirement of the material to be printed. The size of the page is kept in mind which laying the type. Thus the composing is made machines the ordered for by the customer for printing.

Proof Making:

After setting the type in the required size a proof is made out and select the correctness of the matter and there after correction and carried out of any is the composed out made.

Printing:

The composed matter is then fitted in iron frame class of plastic called polyesters. Its unique physical properties have made of a natural choice for photo graphic film, support, The strength and toughness of easter support are extremely high. Easter support has approximately twice the strength of the cellulose triacetate support and about forth times the touchiness.

The most of the factory may not be fully air conditioned. The coating and printing down are done in different rooms in the longer work and the matter of lighting of the rooms we found the use of yellow fluorescent tubes.

Ample working space is provided around the whirelers, vacuum printing down frames and stop and repeat machines.

Equipments:

The majority of the wirelers used are of horizontal type. All the wireleers have electric heating elements, some with fans to blow air over the elements to dry the coating.

It is usual for a plate making department to be divided into sections for dealing with coating exposing for making ordinary plates and deep each plates stopping out, stepping in stencil and finishing.

Equipments for Proofing:

There are various type of proofing presses available now. The most modern of them have motorized cylinder and power. Operated incurs and dampers. The ordinary presses are semi automatic and have arrangement for hand damping and inking.

Coating Solution:

Various proprietory solution with casein as the base are manufactured and sold. It is claimed that a solution containing case in is superior to albumen in respect of sinceritory and enables better total reproduction. The casein coated plate must however be developed in alkaline solution since case in down not dissolve in plan water. It is further advocated that the developing ink for casein should be of very good quality and that there should be fast surface treatment.

Sizes of Papers:

16"	x	26"	=	41	x	66	cms.
17"	x	27"	=	43	x	68.5	”
17½ "	x	22½"	=	44.5	x	57	”
18"	x	22"	=	45.5	x	56	”
18"	x	23"	=	45.5	x	58.5	”
20"	x	30"	=	51	x	76	”
22"	x	28"	=	56	x	71	”
22"	x	30"	=	56	x	76	”
23"	x	36"	=	58.5	x	91	”
25"	x	30"	=	63.5	x	76	”
28"	x	34"	=	71	x	86.5	”
29"	x	44"	=	73.5	x	112	”
29"	x	45"	=	73.5	x	114.5	”
30"	x	40"	=	76	x	101.5	”
36"	x	46"	=	91.5	x	117	’

PRESENT MANUFACTURERS (USING OFFSET PRINTING PRESS)

Central Electric Press,
A-12/1, Naraina Indl. Area,
Phase I, New Delhi - 110 028
Phone : 291 0143

Capital Press,
1163/8, Naiwala,
Karol Bagh,
New Delhi - 110 005
Phone : 572 1099

Bhumica Printing Services,
B-32, NDSE - I,
New Delhi - 110 049
Phone : 462 4398

Kumar Offset Press
251/8, Padam Nagar,
Kishan Ganj, Delhi - 110 007
Phone : 528850

Goel Offset Works
A-60/1, G.T. Karnal Road,
Delhi - 110 033

SUPPLIERS OF OFFSET PRINTING PRESS MACHINERY

The Printers House Limited
10, Scindia House,
New Delhi - 110 001
Phone : 331 3071-72-73

Bandhu,
8 - B, Bahadur Shah Zafar Marg,
New Delhi - 110 002
Phone : 3311 286

Manugraphic Limited
304, Akashdeep Building,
26, Barakhamba Road,
New Delhi - 110 001
Phone : 331 47 68

Banubhai Sons & Company
Manuu Mansion,
16, Shahid Bhagat Singh Road,
Mumbai - 400 023
Phone : 286 4353

Amit International
B-47, Cox House,
Naraina Indl. Area,
Phase - II, New Delhi - 110 028
Phones : 570 4301, 570 4201
Fax : 011-224 9320

Diamond Engg. Works
6/12, DLF, Indl. Area,
Moti Nagar,
New Delhi - 110 015
Phones : 541 4571, 541 8352

Aksis Engg. Works (P) Ltd.
139, Sector 25,
Ballabgarh,
(Haryana)
Phone : 8-234942

Dominent Offset P. Ltd.
Palam Road,
Gurgaon, (Haryana)
Phones : 340019, 341916, 341917, 341918, 340032
Fax : 0124-340131

Bharat Machine Tools
133-138, Sector 6,
Faridabad,
(Haryana)
Phones : 8-241798, 241167

Fair Deal Engineers
89, Ramsaroop Colony,
Mujessar, Faridabad,
(Haryana)
Phones : 8-237143, 234314

RAW MATERIAL SUPPLIERS

Printing Ink :

Baluja Spectra
C-50 Okhla Indl. Area-II,
New Delhi - 110 020
Phone/fax : 6835715, 6835722

Ajanta Ink Company
Basai Road, Gurgaon.
(Haryana) Phone/fax : 8-330028

Art Printing Inks Company
104 Site-4, Indl. Area,
Sahibabad, Ghaziabad, (U.P.)
Phone/fax : 767882

Inks India (Delhi)
C-49, Sector-8, Noida-201 301,
Distt. Ghaziabad, (U.P.)
Phone/fax : 523801, 011-8-557270

Van Inks & Chemicals (P) Ltd.
B-150, Phase-II, Noida-201 305,
Distt. Ghaziabad, (U.P.)
Phone/fax : 567141, 011-8-521507

Paper Suppliers :

Om Prakash Jitendra Kumar & Company
63, Darya Ganj,
New Delhi - 110 002
Phones : 326 9680, 327 1380

Narain Paper Mart,
4034/3, Haryana Market,
Chawri Bazar, Delhi - 110 006
Phone : 291 5135

Himgiri Paper Products
B-24, Indl. Area Lawrence Road,
New Delhi - 110 035
Phone : 718 9005

PLANT ECONOMICS OF PUBLISHING & PRINTING (OFFSET UNIT)

Rated Plant Capacity = 6800.00 Magazine/Day

COST OF LAND & BUILDING

(Total land area required 2000 sq.mtr.)	Rs.	31,00,000.00

LIST OF PLANT & MACHINERY

1. Sheet Fed Offset, single colour printing machine, size 19"x26".
2. Offset Printing (single color), machine Size 23"x36".
3. Cutting Machine
4. Stitching Machine
5. Tools & Tackles, Jigs & Fixtures

LIST OF RAW MATERIALS

Magazines:-

1. For Magazine of 100 Pages/Months Printing Paper Size 22"x32"/8 637 Rims
2. Printing Ink (Black+Coloured)
3. Printing Paper for Tile Pages, 25 Rims
4. Printing Ink for Title Pages
5. Matter Writing Cost
6. Photo Composing
7. Processing Black & White Pages (Negative + Positive)
8. Processing of Color Pages (Negative + Positives for 8 Pages)
9. Processing of Title Pages

Comics:-

10. For Comics of 15000 Copies Single Pattern: Printing Ink
11. Printing Paper Size 17"x26" 504 Rims
12. Printing Paper for Title Pages 32 Rims
13. Artist on Contract
14. Plate Making Cost
15. Processing Cost
16. Other Consumable like Oil & Lubricants

FIXED CAPITAL

Land & Building	Rs.	31,00,000.00
Plant & Machinery	Rs.	15,75,000.00
Other Fixed Assets	Rs.	3,06,000.00
TOTAL	**Rs.**	**49,81,000.00**

TOTAL WORKING CAPITAL/MONTH

Raw Material	Rs.	5,05,900.00
Salary & Wages	Rs.	85,750.00
Utilities & Overheads	Rs.	95,000.00
TOTAL	**Rs.**	**6,86,650.00**

TOTAL CAPITAL INVESTMENT

Total Fixed Capital	Rs.	49,81,000.00
Total Working Capital for 3 Months	Rs.	20,59,950.00
TOTAL	**Rs.**	**70,40,950.00**

TURNOVER/ANNUM

1. By sale of 6,00,000 Copies of magazines
2. By sale of 14,40,000 copies of Comics.
3. Receipt from Advertisement

TOTAL **Rs. 1,38,90,000.00**

PROFIT = RECEIPTS - COST OF PRODUCTION

= 1,38,90,000.00 - 1,03,15,059.00

= 35,74,941.00

PROFIT SALES RATIO = Profit / Sales x 100 = **25.74 %**

RATE OF RETURN = Operating profit / T.C.I. x 100 = **50.77 %**

BREAK EVEN POINT (B.E.P) = 45.15 %

19

OFFSET SECURITY PRINTING PRESS

INTRODUCTION

Printing is important in the line of education (books, magazines), sociology (wedding cards and greeting cards, birth day cards, politics posters etc). Every day more and more people are adopting this phenomena and carrying is now an internal .part of every organisation and business house.

Characteristics of Offset Press:

The offset press is characterised by the following important advantages over other printing methods.

1. The rubber printiong surface conform to irregularities in the paper surface. Less printing pressure is needed, and print quality is improved. Half tone of high quality can be printed on rough papers.

2. Paper does not come into contact with the metal printing plate. Therefore, the plate is less subjected to abrasive wear and can run much longer editions.

3. Speed of printing is increased.

Press	Printing speed, impressions/Hour
Litho hand-providing press	10-20
Litho power-providing press	1200
Direct rotary press (hand fed)	2000
Rotary offset press (stream fed)	up to 15,000
Web offset press (roll-fed)	up to 60,000

4. The image on an offset printing plate reads right inrtoad of in reverse or wrong reading. This facilitate both hand and chemical photomechanical preparation.

5. Less ink is required for equal coverage. This reduces trapping problems and decreases the tendency of the printed sheet to mudge and set off, ie., produce mirror image on the back, in the delivery pile. Also drying is quicker.

INKANDPAPER

Fine quality printing can be accomplished only by using the correct combination of paper and ink. Today inks are specially formulated for the printing. Only offset ink made specially for lihtographic presses should be used on an offset press.

Ingredients of Ink The ingredients of ink are similar to those of paint.

1) Vehicles
2) Pigments
3) Driers or modifiers.

i) **Vehicles:-** The vehicle is the fluid part of the ink. It carriers the pigment or colour to the paper and holds it there. The most common type of vehicle is heat treated linseed oil, sometimes called lithovarnish. Today alkalyd resin oils are more commonly used. They provide higher glass and more resistance to rubbing off ink on hands or clothes.

ii) **Pigments:-** Pigments are the solid coloring matter of inks. Pigments are available in thousands of colours as well as black and white, they are visible part of ink. They also determine many of the characteistics of a particular type of ink. For example, pigments help determine capacity, transparency, and resistance to light, heat and chemicals. They also determine whether a particular ink will bleed in water, oil, alcohol, or grease. Because of all these variables, the pigment will determine to a considerable extent how a particular ink can be used. It will determine, for example, whether or not a particular ink may be used for offset printing or if it may be used to print food or soap wrappers.

There are two categories of pigments

1) Inorgnic
2) Organic

(iii) **Driers :-** The drier in ink acts as catalyst to speed up the oxidation of the vehicle, most driers are manganese or cobalt compunds. The manufacturer generally mixes in the proper amount of drier for a particular ink. Not enough drier will cause the ink to dry very slowly or not at all. Too much drier will cause the ink to dry on the press. Because the drier, the vehicle, and the pigments all combine to influence the drying of a particular ink, the manufacturer determines the proper amount of the right type of drier.

Special modifiers are also available to speed up the drying of ink. Heat set-inks use heat to vaporize the vehicle as the paper passes through a heating chamber. Moisture-sets inks dry when exposed to steam or a fine mist of water. Ultraviolet inks dry by exposures to ultraviolet light or to sunlight.

Ink Handling: Ink is availiable in containers of various types and sizes. A small job-shop or a school will probably purchase ink in one-pound cans or in tubes. Some companies are now packaging ink in tubes that are used with a special dispenser thast resembles a caulking gun. This is probably an economical way to purchase small quanities of ink because it does not dry out as rapidly as in cans.

If you use one pound cans always remember to relace the lids tightly to prevent oxidation of the unused ink. When you open a new can of ink, it is a good idea to apply a thin film of oil to the inside of the lid to prevent it from sticking to can. Always replace the paper covering on the ink before replacing the lid to prevent oxidizing and formation of a skin on the top fo the ink. Keep the ink level in the can, dont dig down. To do so increases the surface area exposed to air and caused waster.

OFFSETPRINTINGPRESS

Offset's emergence as a behemoth of the printing industry is one of the significant current developments that mark post 1950 as an era of competition and change for graphic communication.

The increasing importance of one method of printing is of course, not the only consequently current development in the graphics of communication. You need only to pick up occasional copies of weekly news magazines to read of new marvels of the printing process type being set be computers at rates several times that of hand operators trade marks being electrostatically printed on the yokes of eggs without crushing or other wise distributing then photocopies of pictures and words being sent great distance by telephone and other equally remarkable achievements.

These rapid changes have been called an information explosion and a communication revolution. Regardless of the name given to then they obviously exampligy, the need that now exists for a greater bread the and depth of knowledge about techniques of producing printed materials. Anyone who plans a career to use any system skillfully. His finished product must also meet higher standards than even before and must be produced more quickly. To be successful today, any printed material newspaper, magazine, broker, poster, newsletter, must be prepared with a talent, finess, and speed never before demanded with such urgency.

PHOTO OFFSET PRINTING

Photo-offset printing, of increasing intered to everyone in the filed of communication, differs from letter press because it is i) photographic ii) Planographic (printing is done for a flat surface), iii) Chemical is natrual rather than mechanical iv) Usually indirect rather than direct, each of the above can have an effect on editorial, as well as on mechanical procedures.

For examples, the fact, that it relies on photography for the proportion of copy prior to actual press operation means offset can employ several systems of type complosition. Anything that cn be photographed can serve as copy, for offset lithography. Hence a typewriter or similar machine can be composing machine material so composed is generally called 'cold type' because it did not have to be cast form molten metal. Why this feature is preferable for same editorials operation should be obvious, instead of being done by a skilled craftsman at some printers shop. Type for offset may be composed in a publication office. As type writer like machines become better adapted for such work this feature becomes increasingly significant.

Combined with its photographic characteristics the planographic natrual of offset has a direct bearing on the use of copy he is not concerned if line illustrations are an the same sheet with type material. Therefore, such illustrations can be used in quantity with no resultant effect on cost.

PRINCIPLE OF OFFSET

It will be seen that an offset print is not taken from the printing plate direct to the paper or stock. But the first made on an intermediate surface and transferred there to the paper. The usual method is to have a special cylinder on which is stretched and offset blanket.

As the print is reversed on the offset blanket and again reversed when the transferred on to the paper, it follows that the job which is to be printed offset appears the same on the machine plate as an the final print. It should also be noted that offset printing is done by both rotary and plate bed machine and therefore, the term offset is not synom muous with rotary, despite the decline of flatbed.

It will also be appreciated that the term - direct method, as used by the first offset tin printers was quite clear to them, but is now confusion due to the wilder subsequent application of the offset process. As this was specialized printing group very largely isolated from other trade contacts, the terms which they used were their down concern but it should be clearly understood that all metal sheet printing is offset printing that the principle is the same as used now for printing on paper and that litho offset machines have developed from earlier this printing machines.

For all practical purpose offset printing is exclusively a lithographic process, the notable exception being the specialized letter process machine of the printing of this metal collapsible tube of such types as are used for tooth paste, shaving cream and the like.

Process :

Preparation of Copy:

Most of the firms maintained their own art and design department. Some of them are located on the factory premises. It is also a common practice of the trade to utilize outside agencies for the preparation art work. The standard of design submitted for reproduction is generally high. In the art department, the artist takes into consideration the technical detalils of the reproduction process and arranges the colours to be used in such a manner that a faithful reproduction is possible.

The use of phototype setting machines is of recent growth and we did not see much of it is Britain. In the American factories, however some firms were using photo settors. In Japan since the phototype setting machines, is similar and less expensive, phototype setters for composition are more common, partiuclarly in big printing establishments.

Whereever a copy is received it is carefully scrutinized before it is actually sent into the works for processing. Some firms have a copy preparation department when the details are worked out. Normally in art department take on itself the task of a) Scrutinizing type matter for reprocution by photography b) Making off copy to suit the customers layout c) Giving instruction regarding the percentage of enlargement or deduction and how they should for into the layout d) Determining the number of colour e) Grouping together of jobs of small matter.

Screens :

Both contact screens and the glass cross line screens are in use. The more progressive factories, have however, started using contact screen because, they give very much better results.

MANUFACTURINGPROCESS

The step involves in the offset printing of security broctures like Cheque-Books, Lottery tickets etc. are as under:

1. Design and Layout
2. Image Generation
3. Copy Preparation for the Camera
4. Photography
5. Colour Scanning
6. Stripping and Platemaking
7. Offset Press Operation
8. Finishing

DESIGNANDLAYOUT

All designers follow certain basic ideas in planning and laying out a printed piece. These ideas serve as a starting point and as guides. The five basic elements of design are balance, rhythm, contrast, proportion and unity. Two other factors, colour and type style, also effect the design of the printed piece.

Balance:- Basically, there are two methods of achieving balance. Formal balance has elements of equal weight placed on both sides of an imaginary vertical centre line on the page. Informal balance gives an illusion of equal weights on both sides of an imaginary vertical centre line.

Rhythm:- Rhythm is the element of design that directs the reader's eye in a certain direction over a printed piece.

The reader too quickly to the next message.

Contrast:- Contrast creates interest in the printed piece by providing variety in the design. The designer adds contrast by changing colours, shapes, weights, sizes and similar factor in byout.

Colour:-

Colour usually adds interest to a printed piece and makes a design more attractive.

Layout Principles:

A layout is to the printer what a blue print is to the contractor.

IMAGEGENERATION

Image generation or type setting is the setting type characteristics to make up words or sentences for the printed pieces.

COPYPREPARATION

Once the printed piece is designed the illustrations choosen, and the type set, all the elements can be put together into a single composite.

PHOTOGRAPHY

Photography is a way of recording an image. This recorded image is used to make a printing plate. Some plate making methods require negatives and others require positives. Some are reverse reading on the emulsion side and some are straight on the reading, depending on the printing process.

COLOURSCANNING

To print a full colour piece as the eye sees it, each colour must be filtered out, additive primery filters are used. They break white light into primary colors, red to blue. When added together, these three colors have the potential of creating any colour visible to the eye.

STRIPPINGANDPLATEMAKING

When the photo conversion is produced, the assembled negatives into a unit flat for stripping and then plate is made for offset printing works.

Stripping:-

Different techniques may be used for stripping.

The important thing to remember is that the end results depend on the negatives being assembled on the golden rod sheet in the proper position. Many lithographers use the following method.

1. Place a golden rod sheet on the light table with the hed of the sheet wither at the top or toward the left.

2. Line up the masking sheet with the T-square. some maskin sheets, particularly for small press, come gridded (with guidelines already drawn on them). Larger preses require the stripper to mark gripper margins, center lines, and other necessary guidelines. The following information is based on the use of gridded goldenrod sheets.

3. Tape the golden rod sheet down along the top edge only

4. Locate the paper area to be printed on the masking sheet and mark the exact position of the image. The image area must not extend into the gripper margin of the masking sheet because this area will not print when the plate is burned.

5. Carefully side the negative, emulsion side down, under the masking sheet. Emulsion side down means that type copy will appear correctly; it will be right reading. On halftones you can determine the emulsion side of the negative by observing the texture of the surface. On most negative the emulsion side will have slightly flat or dull finish. On some halftones, however, this is not true. If scratched on the emulsion side, a mark will show. You will have to scratch the negative in a non image or non-printing area to determine the emulsion side.

6. Place the negative in the proper position in the area marked on the folden rod sheet. Align the negative with a T-square and triangle or follow the gridded lines on the folden rod sheet.

7. Once the negative is aligned, hold the negative and goldenrod sheet down with onehand, and with the other hand out football shaped holes in non image areas. Be careful not to out through the negative. Apply red lithographer's negative and goldenrod together.

SAFETYNOTE:-

Always be careful when using sharp cutting tools such as a stripping knife.

8. Remove that ape from the top edge of the masking sheet. Turn over the negative and masking sheet together, making sure not to separate that two.

9. Tape each of the four corners of the negative to the masking sheet with lithographer's tape. Keep the tape at least 1/4 inch from the image area.

10. Once the negative is secured, turn the flat over so that goldenrod sheet is on top. Cut away the masking sheet over the image area. The opening is called a window. use enough pressure to cut only the foldenrod sheet; do not cut through the negative.

Inspect the flat to make sure the entire image area is open. Do not worry about the area still covered; it will not transfer to the printing plate

11. Paint out all of the unwanted clear areas with opaquing fluid. Opaquing is normally done on the base side of the film because the opaquing solution contains some water which could swell the emulsion. Almost all negatives have pinholes caused by dust on the film either in manufacturing or in the darkroom. If these pin-holes are not opaqured, they will appear on the printing plate and print on the finished copy. Errors made is opaquing can be removed with a damp rag.

12. After opaquing, clean the brush in water an tightly stopper the bottle of fluid. The flat is now ready for platemaking. At this point scribing may be done or register marks may be included. Soribing means adding lins to an already developed negative by removing emulsion with a sharp instrument. For straight, even lines, a T-square or triangle is usually used.

For printing more than one color or superimposing letters over a halftone, it may be necessary to make two flats. Both flats, then must be stripped in the same position. This is called register. To insure proper registration, the flats are usually punched before assembly of the negatives. Register pins are then used on the stripping table to insure correct placement of both flats. You may also use fine, little register marks (target lines) to insure proper placement of the flats.

When you assemble a flat that has both line and halftone negatives on it, you normally strip up the line negative first. Then the halftone negative is placed in a window previously prepared and photographed.

Plate Making:

After the flat has been prepared, an offset plate is made from it for the press. Many different types of presententized plates can be used for this operation. Most shops use a negative acting additive plate, which will be discussed here.

Most of these plates are either metal or foil types.

The negative-acting additive plate is exposed in a platemaker. This platemaker is usually a vacuum frame to hold negative and plate in very tight contact and a source of high-intensity light. Because the light on a platemaker is so strong, it can damage eyes.

SAFETY NOTE:- Not to stare at an unshielded plate burner light.

To make a negative-acting additive offset plate:

1. Open the vacuum frame and check the glass for dirt or other foreign material. Clean if necessary.

2. Plate an unexposed plate, presensitized side up, on the vacuum - frame bed.

3. Position the flat, emulsion side down. Adjust the top and side edges so that the flat and the plate are in proper alignment.

4. Close the vacuum frame carefully so as not to move the flat and the plate.

5. Turn on the vacuum pump. Check to see that the flat and plate are in proper alignment and that the pump has reached maximum vacuum.

6. Set the timer and expose the plate. The exposure time depends on the type of plate, the type of light source, and the distance between lamp and plate. Check plate manufacturer's recommendations for exposure of a given plate. During exposure, light passes through the closer areas of the negative and causes as chemical change in the plate coating.

Note: when using a double sided plate, expose both sides of the plate before developing.

7. After exposure, turn off the vacuum, open the vacuum frame, and remove the plate.

8. Place the plate on a clean, flat surface, either a developing sink or a flat table top.

9. Pour a small amount of process gum into the plate. Rub if lightly with a sponge or soft pad. The process gum removes the unhardened plate coating. Move the sponge or pad in a figure eight motion across the plate, making sure. You cover the whole plate. Do not allow the plate to dry.

10. Once all the unwanted emulsion has been removed, pour a very small amount of developer on the plate. With light pressure and a circular or gigure eight motion apply the developer. Again be sure you cover the whole plate surface. If the second side has been exposed, develop it in the same manner as the first side.

11. Wash or wipe the plate with clean water to remove all the excess developer.

12. Apply a small amount of process gum to buff the plate. Buff it dry with a chesse cloth or similar material. The process gum will protect the non image area of the plate from oxidation and from fingerprints. When you use two separate flats to burn the same side of the plate, remember to expose all the flats before you process.

There are four categories of other presensitized offset plates that may be used in a shop. A negative-acting plate may be additive, as just described or substractive.

The whole surface of a substractive plate has been coated by the manufacturer with a lacquer emulsion. The image is then hardened on the plate and the developer removes the emulsion from all non image areas.

Instead of negatives, positives can also be used to make plates. These plates are desensitized where light strikes and will not take the developing lacquer in these areas. Positive-acting plates come in additive and in subtractive forms. With additive plates, the developing lacquer is added to the image area; with substractive plates the whole plate is covered with the lacquer emulsion. Developing then remove lacquer in the areas struck by light.

Some plates are made directly on the camera. They are called camera direct plates and are made of metal, paper, or plastic. To make a camera direct plate, place the copy on the camera board so the image is protected through the camera lens to light-sensitive material. The image can be enlarged or reduced with the copy camera lens. Expose and process the plate. If it is not to go directly to the press, store the plate according to the manufacturer's recommendations.

PLANT AND MACHINERIES SUPPLIERS

Offset Printing Press Machines:

Amit International
B-47, Cox House,
Naraina Indl. Area,
Phase - II,
New Delhi - 110028
Phones : 570 4301, 570 4201
Fax : 011-224 9320

Diamond Engg. Works
6/12, DLF, Indl. Area,
Moti Nagar,
New Delhi - 110015
Phones : 541 4571, 541 8352

Aksis Engg. Works (P) Ltd.
139, Sector 25,
Ballabgarh.
(Haryana)
Phone : 8-234942

Dominent Offset P. Ltd.
Palam Road,
Gurgaon.
(Haryana)
Phones : 340019, 341916, 341917, 341918, 340032
Fax : 0124-340131

Bharat Machine Tools
133-138, Sector 6,
Faridabad.
(Haryana)
Phones : 8-241798, 241167

Fair Deal Engineers
89, Ramsaroop Colony,
Mujessar, Faridabad.
(Haryana)
Phones : 8-237143, 234314

Cameras:

National Instruments Ltd.,
1/1, Raj Subodh Chandra,
Mullick Road,
Jadavpur,
Calcutta - 700 032.

New India Industries,
Jatalpur Road,m
Baroda - 390 005.

Suppliers of Offset Printing Press:

Manugraphic ltd.,
Manu Mansion,
16, Shahid Bhagatsingh Road,
Mumbai - 400 023
Ph:286 43 53/286 44 09/286 47 36.

New Delhi;

304, Akash Deep Building,
26 Bara Khamba Road,
NewDelhi-110001
Ph: 331 47 68/331 06 55.

Plate Making & Process Equipments;

International Sales Enterprises,
D-77, Sector-2,
NOIDA,
Distt: Ghaziabad.
(U.P.).

Amal Electrocrafts
A/5, Shri Ram Indl. Estate,
Wadala, Mumbai.
Phone : 412 7458

RAW MATERIAL SUPPLIERS

Printing Materials:

Printer Stores,
1525, Ist Floor,
A. Chand Marg,
Delhi - 110 006

Dickinson & Co. Ltd.,
7, Kumpta Street,
Balard Estate,
Mumbai - 400 001

Sumaco Industries (Regd.)
Cheel Mandi, Inside Mohan Singh Gate,
Amritsar (Punjab).

Printing Ink:

Baluja Spectra
C-50 Okhla Indl. Area-II,
New Delhi - 110 020
Phone/fax : 6835715, 6835722

Ajanta Ink Company
Basai Road, Gurgaon.
(Haryana)
Phone/fax : 8-330028

Art Printing Inks Company
104 Site-4, Indl. Area,
Sahibabad, Ghaziabad. (U.P.)
Phone/fax : 767882

Inks India (Delhi)
C-49, Sector-8,
Noida-201 301 (U.P.)
Phone/fax : 523801, 011-8-557270

Van Inks & Chemicals (P) Ltd.
B-150, Phase-II,
Noida-201 305 (U.P.)
Phone/fax : 567141, 011-8-521507

Graphic Film:

Konishiroku Photo Ind. Co. Ltd.,
Shinjuku Nomura Building No.26-2,
Nishishinjuku-1 Chome,
Shinjuku-ku, Tokyo 163,
JAPAN

Fotoplate
B-57, G.T. Karnal Road,
Indl. Area, Delhi - 110 033
Phone/Fax: 721 3474

Plates:

Polychrome,
GMBHD-3360,
OSTERODE AM HERZ,
West Germany

Fuji Offset Plates Manufacturing P. Ltd.,
2, Jalan Rajah, 05-26/28,
Golden Wall Flatted Factory,
Singapore - 1232

Ask Advertising Aids (P) Ltd.
88, DSIDC Shed,
Okhla Indl. Area - I,
New Delhi - 110 020
Phone/Fax: 681 6824, 681 9487

PLANT ECONOMICS OF OFFSET SECURITY PRINTING PRESS

Rated Plant Capacity = 22.40 Lkh./Day

COST OF LAND & BUILDING

(Total land area required 1000 sq. mtr)	Rs.	11,85,000.00

LIST OF PLANT & MACHINERY

1. Four Colour Offset Printing Machine
2. Single colour printing machine
3. Semi-Automatic cutting machine
4. Stitching machine
5. Numbering machine (single phase)
6. Herdelberg Cylinder Letter press
7. Chandler machine (Single phase)
8. Lamination machine

LIST OF RAW MATERIALS

1. Plants for Offset Printing
2. Printing Inks
3. Graphic Films
4. Miscellaneous Stores & Consumables

FIXED CAPITAL

Land & Building	Rs.	11,85,000.00
Plant & Machinery	Rs.	61,37,000.00
Other Fixed Assets	Rs.	26,00,000.00
TOTAL	**Rs.**	**99,22,000.00**

TOTAL WORKING CAPITAL/MONTH

Raw Material	Rs.	2,20,000.00
Salary & Wages	Rs.	1,23,931.50
Utilities & Overheads	Rs.	1,49,500.00
TOTAL	**Rs.**	**4,93,431.50**

TOTAL CAPITAL INVESTMENT

Total Fixed Capital	Rs.	99,22,000.00
Total Working Capital for 3 Months	Rs.	14,80,294.50
TOTAL	**Rs.**	**1,14,02,294.50**

TURNOVER/ANNUM

1. By selling of Lottery Tickets Printed in 4 colours - 40000 x 2 x 28 x 300 = 6720 Lakh No.
2. Earnings from job-work of different printing works

TOTAL **Rs. 1,29,74,000.00**

PROFIT = RECEIPTS - COST OF PRODUCTION
= 1,29,74,000.00 - 1,00,97,649.79
= 28,76,350.21

PROFIT SALES RATIO = Profit / Sales x 100 = **22.17 %**

RATE OF RETURN = Operating Profit / T.C.I. x 100 = **25.23 %**

BREAK EVEN POINT (B.E.P.) = 64.56 %

20

ROTO GRAVURE PRINTING

INTRODUCTION

The printing processes now in common use are broadly classified into groups according to the principles on which their printing image carriers are based. The four process families are relief printing (letter press and flexography) in which printing areas of the image carriers raised above the plane of the supporting material; planographic printing (lithography and collo- type) in which the printing and non-printing areas are in the same plane of the image carrier; intaglio printing (gravure) in which the printing areas are sunkem in the image carrier, non-printing areas are on its surface; and screen printing (stencil printing) in which the printing areas consist of open pores of the image carrier, the blocked pores constitute the non-printing areas.

Gravure printing with copper or steel engraved plates is very ancient. In olden days, the pictorials or lettering were cut or ethed into the face of rigid plate of copper or steel. The whole surface then inked and wiped clean so that the ink was only retained in the incised or engraved lines. printing was done by pressing paper against the inked plate.

The modern commercial derivations of the intaglio process are based on photography and photomechanics. These are rotogravure and sheet-fed gravure. Of these the largest and the most important commercially is rotogravure which is used in news papers rotosections for some of the big edition magazines and for big commercial works.

Rotogravure employees an exquisitely polished copper cylinder as the printing surface and makes use of a screen to break-up the light and dark areas into small unshaded dots.

The text is usually first set in type. It is printed in white ink on a very shiny black paper. Negatives of any picture required are pasted up with the text in accordance with or determined layout. From this a transparent positive is obtained on a sensitized glass plate or film. The positive is turn printed photographically on a sheet of thin paper coated with sensitized gelatin, called 'carbon tissue'. After a suitable exposure has been made, the positive is replaced with a screen consisting of a network of transparent lines on a black background. The sensitized tissue is subjected to a strong light so that the lines of the screen are superimposed on the previously printed image and break up the entire surface into tiny squares.

The screen used in those process is reverse, i.e. the lines are transparent and the interversing squares are opaque. The sensitized gelatin becomes insoluble in water in proportion to the amount of light to which it has been exposed and the result is a printing image with a lattice work of lines rendered insoluble by light.

The tissue is dampened and laid over the highly finished surface of the copper cylinder with the sensitized side in contact with the metal. The tissue is then soaked with hot water; this allows the paper to be peeled off and any unexposed gelatin is dissolved. Parts of the gelatin that are not to be etched are protected with a special bitumen-based paint. Etching is done in acid by revolving the cylinder slowly whilst acid is poured over it. When etching is complete, the remaining gelatin is removed by washing, leaving on the copper cylinder an enormous number of cells of varying depths which serve to hold the ink during the printing. A shallow chell imparts thin film of ink whilst a deep cell gives a VERY thick film. Thus the varying shades of the subject are translated in terms of varying shades of depths of cells in the metal surface. For longer life the copper cylinder is sometimes chromium plated.

The etched cylinder is designed for running on a web-fed rotogravure machine. The cylinder revolves in a trough of a ink, the ink floods over the surface of the cylinder and is at once scraped clear by a thin blade called 'doctor'. This blade of cylinder length keeps the surface free of ink, but leaces the cells full.

The reel paper runs between the printing cylinder and smaller rubber cylinder which exerts enough pressure to redraw the ink from the cells and impress it on the paper. In a finished rotogravure print it is almost impossible to detect the halftones which show up clearly in letterpress., and that is why the process is well adapted to the reproduction of shaded subjects. Because of the time required for plate preparation and relatively high initial costs, rotogravure is essentially a large scale production process.

Sheet-fed gravure is a high quality picture printing method. It is a slower process compared to rotogravure and is used for every moderate runs. It differs from rotogravure mainly in the facts that printing image is usually etched into a thin flexible copper plate which clamped around a printing cylinder in much the same manner as an offset plate, and that printing is carried out on the sheet-fed presses.

The presses for this process have automatic sheet feeders and exist in varying numbers of printing units. Sheet-fed gravure is done on better grades of paper and coated stocks.

Plaster for printing on a rotary press must be thin and curved for mounting on the press cylinder. Wrap around plates can be used in gravure printing but most often the printing is from copper plated cylinders that have been etched and chromo-plated after the images have been transferred to them. The printing image is produced on these cylinders with carbon tissue lithographic transfer film or direct erating. All lithographic plates are wrap around plates.

METHODSOFPLATEMAKING

Printing image carriers of plates or cylinders can be produced in any or a combination of six different ways :-

1. **Manually :-** By the use of hand tools, engravers, knives etc. to produce image - carriers for the relief and intaglio.

2. **Mechanically :-** With the help of engraving and geometrical late ruling machines, pantographs etc. for the relief and intaglio processes but hand transferring and Benday machines can be used for lithographic plates.

3. **Electromechanically:**
4. **Electromically:**
5. **Electrostatically:**
6. **Photomechanically:**

GRAVUREPLATEMAKINGANDCYLINDERMAKING

The adaption of the crossline screen for photogravure printing initiated the modern commercial process. Modifications for multicolour printing have been made.

PRINTINGSURFACE:

Modern gravure printing is done principally from images etched in cylinder on web processes and is generally referred to as rotogravure. On sheet-fed presses the printing element is a thin copper plate, which is wrapped around the cylinder. Preparation of the printing surface is essentially the same for cylinders and for plates.

For monochrome printing by conventional gravure, bichromate sensitized carbon tissue or transfer film is contact-printed through a continuous-tone positive and then exposed a second time while in contact with a screen consisting of transparent lines and opaque square dots, 24 or 28 per cm (60 or 70 per in.) The ratio of line to dot width usually is 1 : 3. The exposed carbon tissue or trnsfer film is moistened and aqueeged in contact with the clean copper surface. Warm water is applied and the paper forthe carbon tissue or backing of the film is peeled off. The gelatin thus transferred to the copper surface is further developed with warm water to produce a gelatin relief resist. Etching is done with 35-43 wt % ferric chloride solution (sp gr 1.34-1.45 (37-45$^{o\ be}$)). This solution etches the copper to different depths. depending of the thickness of the gelatin resist in the different tone areas. Usually several solutions of different densities are used. The areas corresponding to screen lines remain unetched and provide lands., which support the doctor blade in printing. For long runs and to minimize wear, the etched cylinder or plate is chromium plated.

For multicolour printing the principal process involves a combination of halftone and continuous-tone positives for each colour. The halftone positive has a lateral dot formation, which is similar to conventional gravure in the shadows but with varying dot sizes in the middletone and highlights. The two positives are contact-printed successively, in register on to a sheet of carbon tissue and the gelatin is transferred to the copper cylinder. Development and etching are essentially the same as for conventional gravure.

LIMITATIONS:

The serious problem with gravure cylinder making has been the difficulty of reproducing identical cylinders from the same films due to difference in materials, etching solution, impurities in copper, environmental conditions and other factors. As a result, repress proofing has not been successful and corrections must be made on the cylinder which is expensive.

GRAVURE:

Not much gravure printing is from sheet-fed presses, which involves plates. By far the greatest amount of gravure printing is from cylinders on rolls of paper or film. The cylinders are removable and cylinders of different diameters can be used so that different print lengths can be accommodated from job to job, if necessary. This is desirable in packaging but not as necessary in magazine printing. The gravure printing unit consists of a printing cylinder and a impression cylinder, and an inking system. Ink is applied to the printing cylinder by an ink roll or spray and the excess is removed by a doctor blade and returned to the ink function.

Single-colour rotogravure printing yields excellent pictorial reproduction on a wide range of papers. Its reproduction type matter and line drawings leaves something to be desired., however because the screen somewhat reduces sharpness. Colour reproduction is done in three or four colours on multicolour presses. Gravure printing is applicable for catalogues, cartons, lables, and in the printing of cellophene, plastic films, foil and plastic laminates. It is the most practical process for the printing of gold, i.e. bronze, silver, i.e. aluminium and opaque whites.

USES AND APPLICATIONS

Gravure or intaglio printing finds applications in the production of newspaper, supplements, book review sections, feature magazine, catalogues, illustrated magazines, advertising literatures, calendars, greeting cards, wall papers, patterns in textiles, linoleum and oil cloth, lables and wrappers on aluminium foil, gassoline, cellophane, vinyl polymers, LDPE, HDPE, PP and similar other materials, security papers, paper money and stamps etc.

PRESENT MANUFACTURERS (USING ROTOGRAVURE MACHINES)

Arya Roto Prints
401, Main Bus Stand Road,
Vill. Badli, Delhi - 110 042
Phone/Fax : 7180888

Chawla Plastics
C-135, Mayapuri Indl. Area,
Phase-II, New Delhi - 110 064
Phone/Fax : 540 1533, 5400162,

Ambica Enterprises
Plot No. 12, 16/2, Mathura Road,
Faridabad - 02 (Haryana)
Phone/Fax : 8-292391, 286426

Balaji Polymer
131-132, M.I.E., Bahadurgarh - 124 507
(Haryana) Phone/Fax : 8-313731

Gravure Cil India (P) Ltd.
A-27, Sector - 8, Noida - 201 301
Distt. Ghaziabad (U.P.)
Phone/Fax : 550046, 553023, 011-8-520985

Plate/Cylinder making Equipments:

1. Complete with Cameras
2. Enlargers
3. Contact printers
4. Arc lamp
5. Whirter
6. Graining Machine
7. Etching Machine
8. Expressure frame
9. Densito meter etc.

Camera:

News Shot Products
507, Udyog Vihar, Phase-III,
Dundahera, Gurgaon-122 016
(Haryana)
Phone/Fax: 0124-341106, 341150

Roto Gravure Printing Machine :

Anjana Machinery Mfrs. (P) Ltd.
206, Udyog Sadan, Sharma Estate,
Mumbai - 400 063
Phone/Fax: 873 0146

Calico Industrial Engineers
20A, Chakala Road, Andheri East,
Mumbai - 400 099
Phone: 832 8381-83
Fax: 834 5715

Tyagi Engineering Works
B-166, Hari Nagar,
New Delhi - 110 064
Phone: 540 1250
Fax: 91-11-513 5333

Frans Engineering Corporation
Plot No. 908, IIIrd Phase,
G.I.D.C., Vapi - 396195
Gujarat.
Phone: 31453
Fax: 07638-30668

Gum Tape Machinery:

Guru Nanak Industries
Plot No. CP-6 & 7, N.H.-5,
Railway Road, Faridabad - 121 001
(Haryana)
Phone: 212365, 216885

RAW MATERIAL SUPPLIERS

Rubber Blankets:

Kapoor Sales Corporation
2, Masilamani Road,
Balaji Nagar,
Chennai - 600 014
Phone: 826 7598
Fax: 828 4944

Volga Rubber Industries
76, Indl. Estate, Delhi Road,
Near Maruti, Gurgaon-122 015
(Haryana)
Phone: 0124-340348
Fax: 0124-342390

Printing Ink:

Baluja Spectra
C-50 Okhla Indl. Area-II,
New Delhi - 110 020
Phone/fax: 6835715, 6835722

Ajanta Ink Company
Basai Road, Gurgaon.
(Haryana)
Phone/fax: 8-330028

Art Printing Inks Company
104 Site-4, Indl. Area,
Sahibabad, Ghaziabad.
(U.P.)
Phone/fax: 767882

Inks India (Delhi)
C-49, Sector-8,
Noida-201 301
Distt. Ghaziabad. (U.P.)
Phone/fax: 523801, 011-8-557270

Van Inks & Chemicals (P) Ltd.
B-150, Phase-II,
Noida-201 305
Distt. Ghaziabad. (U.P.)
Phone/fax: 567141, 011-8-521507

Paper Suppliers :

Om Prakash Jitendra Kumar & Co.,
63, Darya Ganj,
New Delhi - 11 00 02.
Ph. 326 96 80, 3271380

Narain Paper Mart,
4034/3, Haryana Market,
Chawri Bazar,
Delhi - 11 00 06.
Ph. 291 51 35.

Himgiri Paper Products
B-24, Indl. Area Lawrence Road,
New Delhi - 110035
Phone: 718 9005

Gum & Adhesive:

Bhiwadi Polymers Ltd.,
15, Najafgarh Road,
New Delhi - 110015
Phone/Fax: 541 8552/011-542 1454

PLANT ECONOMICS OF ROTO GRAVURE PRINTING

Rated Plant Capacity = 93600.00 Mtr./Day

COST OF LAND & BUILDING

(Total land area required 1500 sq. mtr) Rs. 7,00,000.00

LIST OF PLANT & MACHINERY

1. PRINTING M/C :-6 color roto gravure printing machine 30" size working width complete with 2 H.P. blower
2. 5 H.P. driver 16 kwh heater & printing cylinder dia = 150 mm (fully automatic)
3. Slitting and rewinding machine 48" cap. with min= 80 mm slit & max in wind dia=45" with 5 H.P. drive
4. Roll to Roll making machine 48" capacity
5. Bidsmen lamination plant (complete plant)
6. Gum tape machinery plant (complete plant)
7. Rotary sheet cutter m/c 48"
8. Small working tools/tackels and material handling
9. Composing machine complete with mono key boards mono casters and lines
10. Plate/Cylinder making equipments (for detail see 'Annexure P')

LIST OF RAW MATERIALS

1. Metal plates
2. Rubber blankets
3. Inks and founts
4. Gum and adhesives etc.
5. Paper :- sunlit bond 11,000 rims
6. Thermoplastic films 25 mt.

FIXED CAPITAL

Land & Building	Rs. 7,00,000.00
Plant & Machinery	Rs. 21,85,001.00
Other Fixed Assets	Rs. 4,64,350.00
TOTAL	**Rs. 33,49,351.00**

TOTAL WORKING CAPITAL/MONTH

Raw Material	Rs. 15,87,500.00
Salary & Wages	Rs. 42,600.00
Utilities & Overheads	Rs. 1,23,000.00
TOTAL	**Rs. 17,53,100.00**

TOTAL CAPITAL INVESTMENT

Total Fixed Capital	Rs. 33,49,351.00
Total Working Capital for 3 Months	Rs. 52,59,300.00
TOTAL	**Rs. 86,08,651.00**

TURNOVER/ANNUM

By sale of printed straps for flexible packaging Rs. 2,81,00,000.00

PROFIT = RECEIPTS - COST OF PRODUCTION

= 2,81,00,000.00 - 2,30,39,671.66

= 50,60,328.34

PROFIT SALES RATIO = Profit / Sales x 100 = **18.01 %**

RATE OF RETURN = Operating Profit / T.C.I. x 100 = **58.53 %**

BREAK EVEN POINT (B.E.P.) = 35.08 %

21
SCREEN PRINTING

INTRODUCTION

The idea of printing is very old indeed— if you interpret the word printing rather generously, it is the oldest form of writing. The continuing changes in the technology of reproducting the written words(and the picture) have had very profound effects on the surrounding society.

Writing was first invented approximately 5000 years ago. It was invented in a number of places all at roughly the same time. What concession there was between these locations is still a mystery. There are those who believe that writing in Egypt, in Mesopotamia (the fertile plain of the Tigris and Euphrates rivers, now in Iraq) and in the Indus civilization at Mohenjo-Daro and Harappa shows a connection between the three centres. Certainly we know that the idea of writing may have been passed between them. But the three areas developed quite different systems.

The writing that the Indus civilization produced comes down to us in the form of seals. You had a piece of stone-steatite—which was carved with the writing and then when you wanted to use it you pressed it onto soft clay. That, in my book, is printing. Five thousand years ago, the main principles of printing were known and understood: the seal had to be carved backwards, so that when pressed into the clay it would come out the right way round, and the sealcarver had to understand the idea of the negative: that the depressions in the seal would come out as high point in the result and vice versa.

Most of all, they had a system which would reproduce the same text every time it was used- it's the oldest form of mass-production and as I said, it shows that the idea of printing was inherent in writing in Hindustan at least, from the very earliest times.

USES AND APPLICATION

Designed for finest registration and precise printing on flat objects, Silo auto flat screen printing is ideally suited for printing on transparent plastics/acrylics boards, sticker, ceramic, transfer paper/and other speciality papers.

Screen printing process is used for printing displays, posters signs, instrument dials, wall papers textile etc.

SCREEN PRINTING PROCESS

This printing process essentially consists of the transfer of print paste through a stencil to the substrate to be printed. The stencil is made of polyamide or polyester (also metal frame. The pattern or design is produced in the stencil or screen by coating those posts that should not transfer the print paste with an imprevious material.

The design is transferred to a film and the film placed on the bolting cloth, which is coated with light. Sensitive material. After light exposure, the unexposed parts, having been protected by the light imprevious areas of the film, are removed by rinsing and thus the pattern is created on the screen. To with stand the mechanical stress of prolonged printing the light sensitive coating has to be very strong or has to be reinforced with suitable screen lacquer.

For hand printing or silk screening, the fabric to be printed is stretched over long tables, which are covered with a blanket of layers of felt and back grey or felt and rubber-coated material. The screen is placed on the textile material and the print paste is scraped across the screen by means of a squeegee, penetrating through the open areas in the screen on the textile. Then the screen in lifted and move along the table by hand or in a carriage to the next print position. A screen is used to deposit only one colour and for multi-colour designs as many screens as there are colours in the design are necessary. It is important that the textile material does not move or shift during the printing process, therefore it is pinned to the back grey or glued to the blanket.

The printing table with vacuum has plane with a tolerance minus or plus 0.02 mm. The machine incorporate many salient features including micrometer/dial gauge to ensure finest registration. SWJ2 bearing steel shaft of slide bars for steady and smooth operation and long life, brake dutch system electronic adjustment of printing stroke back synchronous “off contact” device designed for protecting the object from darksome and sticky condition control of squeegee and scrapper to match printing design and ink quality.

In the stencil or screen printing process, a stencil representing the non printing areas is applied to a silk, nylon or stainless steel fine mesh screen to which ink with the consistency of paint is applied and transferred to the surface to be printed by scraping with a rubber squeegee. This process is used for printing displays, posters sign, instrument dials, wall papers, textile etc.

Screen:

Screen printing equipment can be very simple, consisting only of a table, screen frame, and squeegee. However, power-screen presses with mechanical feed and delivery are in common use and produce 450-3500 prints per hour, depending on the sheet size.

Screen Angles:

In printing processes, halftones are made in the usual way using either glass screens or contact screens, as described in Halftone Photography. In colour reproduction, however, the angles of the halftone for each colour must be changed in order to avoid objectionable patterns or moire. When two screen patterns of the same ruling are placed over each other, an interference or beat pattern forms and varies in spacing, depending on the angle between the screens. Three are first-, second-, and third-order patterns, depending on the number of overprinting colours. The pattern is minimized when the angle between colours is 30°. With conventional crossline screens, in minimized when the angle between colours is 30°. With conventional cross line screens. In which the patterns repeat every 90°, there are only three possible positions at which 30° angles can be maintained between colours. This is ideal for three-colour printing.

In four-colour printing, however, either two colours must be printed at the same angle or one colour is printed at an intermediate angle. Because the most objectionable patterns are generally caused when there are slight errors as small as 0.10°) between colours, the practice has been adopted of printing the yellow, which is a light and less noticeable colour, at 15° between two other colours, usually the magenta and cyan. The closer the colours are, the more severe is the moire pattern.

Trapping:

Screen-process printing is for especially printing on almost any surface and for fine art printing. The screen are mainly monofilament nylon, mono and multifilament polyester metallized polyesters and stainless steel mesh fabrics. Monofilament screens are available in size Ca 2.35-0.03 mm. (9 500 mesh) so that fine detail can be produced. The thickness of the ink deposit depends on ink viscosity printing speed. Screen printing is commonly used for art prints, decalls, nameplates, greeting cards and programme covers and is particularly well adopted for printing on fabrics, felt, leather, glass, ceramic and plastic materials.

Surface Plates:

Albumin Plates:- The following steps are involved in making an albumin plate:

(1) Counteretch the metal plate with a weak acid solution, e.g. 0.75 wt. % HCl, to make sure it is chemically clean
(2) Coat with bichromated albumin or casein coating on a whirled
(3) Expose to a negative
(4) Apply a developing ink
(5) Develop in water or a very dilute ammonia solution e.g., 29 mL NH_4OH to 3.8 L solution
(6) Apply a surface treatment, i.e., Cronak for zinc, Brunak for aluminium, to remove residual protein from the non printing areas
(7) Desensitize the plate with an etch
(8) Gum with a dilute solution of gum arabic (sp. gr. 1.06 (8° Be)

Diazo Presensitized and Wipe-On Plates. Diazo presensitized and wipe-on plates, which are additive plates, are much simplier to make and generally print cleaner than albumin plates, because the surface treatments used on them prior to coating are very water-receptive and inhibit tendency to scum. Presentized plates are already coated. Wipe-on plates are coated with a solution of the diazo resin by wiping the coating on with a sponge and drying it with a cloth or by applying the coating with a simple roller coater.

Photopolymer Plates:- Photopolymer plates of the cinnamic ester type have been used for lithography and they are available as wipe-on or presensitized plates. All are exposed to negatives. Since the coatings are water-insoluble, they must be developed n organic solvents. This can be done by one of three ways: wiping the solvents over the plate, using a vapour-degreasing machine, or using an emulsion of the solvent with the desensitizing agent for rendering the non-image areas water-receptive. The plates are desensitized with an etch and are gummed.

Printing Characteristics:- As with all bichromated coatings, albumin and casein plates were affected by temperature and relative humidity. Also, if not made properly or if a surface treatment was not used after development, they had a tendency to scum on the press. This is one of the main reasons why presensitized plates have replaced them. These plates are not affected much by relative humidity but can deteriorate if exposed for any length of time to temperatures exceeding 52°C. The additive-presensitized and wipe-on plates are not very resistant to abrasions on sheet-fed presses or ove[illegible] impressions on newspaper and other web presses The pre-lacquered, presentisitized plates are capable of longer runs. Photopolymer plates show good resistance to temperature and relative humidity and to abrasion on the press. They are capable of runs in excess of 2.5×10^5 and baked plates have run over 10^6 impressions.

Deep-Etch Plates:

With the introduction of positive photopolymer plates and baking, deep-etch plates are gradually becoming obsolete. There are several presensitized deep-etch plates, by far the majority of deep-etch plates are of grained aluminium with bichromated gum arabic coatings.

Most plates in Europe are made on anodized aluminium. The most popular deep-etch plate in the United States is the copperized aluminium plate, in which copper is deposited chemically on the image areas. The following steps are needed to make a deep-etch plate.

1. Counteretch the grained aluminium plate with a solution containing ca 12 ml. 85 wt % phosphoric acid and water to make 3.8 L solution.

2. Coat with bichromated gum arabic solution on a whirler. A typical coating formula is 2.8 L gum arabic solution (sp. gra 1.11(14°Be), 200 mL ammonium hydroxide, water to make 3.8L, pH of final solution = 8.5-95, sp. gr. 1.11 (ca 14°Be), average thickness of dried coating = 12-13 um.

3. Expose through positives.

4. Stage out, i.e; paint, all areas that did not expose but are not to print, such as dust specks, film edges, crop marks, etc., with a pigmented cellulose nitrate lacquer, which is alcohol-soluble.

5. Develop in a nearly saturated salt solution. Water cannot be used for development because the exposed coating is too soluble in water. The solubility differential between exposed and unexposed bichromated gum arabic is maximized in almost saturated salt solutions containing an organic acid. A typical formula for such a developer is 3.6 L 39 wt.% calcium chloride solution (sp. gr. 1.38 (40°Be)), 192 mL 85 wt. % lactic acid.

   The solution is applied over the plate with a plush pad until metal is bared in the printing area or until step (9) is reached on the GATE sensitivity guide. The developer is squeegeed off and two more fresh applications of developer are made for the same length of time or until step 6 is reached on the GATE sensitivity guide.

6. Deep etching is also done with a nearly saturated salt solution. A typical formula is : 2.6L 39wt.% calcium chloride (sp. gr. 1.38 (40°Be); 1.04L zinc chloride, 0.75L 48 wt.% ferric chloride (sp. gr. 1.53(50°Be), 37 mL wt.% hydrochloric acid. This solution is applied to the plate with a plush pad for 1-1.5 min and squeegeed off.

7. The alcohol wash removes the residue from deep-etching. Approximately four washes of anhydrous denatured ethyl alcohol or anhydrous isopropyl alcohol are used. The first wash removes the staging lacquer and vigorous rubbing with embossed paper wipes is recommended to remove iron that was deposited in the image area during deep-etching. In some plate making procedures, developer is applied for 2-3 min to remove the iron.

8. While the plate is wet with the last alcohol wash, copperizing solution is poured on the plate. The formula for such a solution follows : 950 mL 99wt.% isopropyl alcohol, 30 mL corpus chloride, 30 mL 37% hydrochloric acid. Copper deposition is complete in 5-7 min. The plate then is washed with two more applications of anhydrous alcohol.

9. When the plate is thoroughly dry, it is coated with a thin layer of ink-receptive, vinyl-type lacquer or epoxy, either of which has excellent non-blinding characteristics, i.e., neither wets with acid and gum on the press. After the lacquer is thoroughly dry, developing ink is applied, rubbed well, and dried.

10. The dried, lacquered, and linked plate is soaked for approx. 10 min in warm water (ca 38°C) to soften the gum stencil, after which it is scrubbed under running water to remove all visible traces of the stencil and its lacquer and ink coating.

11. An etch is applied to the plat and rubbed over it for ca. 1.5 min.

12. The etch is rinsed off the plate; it is squeegeed to remove most of the water and is placed on a flat table. A solution of gum arabic (sp. gr. 1.06 (8°Be) is applied over the whole plate and the plate is rubbed smooth until it is dry. Drying with a fan is continued to ensure removal of all moisture.

Deep-etch plates are very dependable and durable and have been used for the majority of medium to long run, quality lithographic jobs. They have also been used extensively for colour printing, for web offset, and for packaging printing.

Printing Inks - General Consideration:

Printing ink is a mixture of colouring matter dispersed or dissolved in a vehicle or carrier, which forms a fluid or paste which can be printed on a substrate and dried. The colorants used are generally pigments, toners, and dyes, or combinations of these materials, which are selected to provide colour contrast with the background on which the ink is printed. The vehicle used acts as a carrier for the colorant during the printing operation, and in most cases, serves to in the colorant to the substrate.

Rheology:

The rheology of inks is of the greatest importance. In a Newtonian liquid, any stress produces a flow, and the rate of flow is proportional to the stress. But inks are generally non-Newtonian and the most common terms used by the ink maker to describe rheology are : viscosity (resistance to flow); yield value (point at which a liquid starts to flow under strees); thixotropy (decreasing visosity with increasing agitation); and dilatancy (opposite of thixotropy). Mayonnaise is an example of a material having a high yield value but a low viscosity.

Colour:

Colour is the third common denominator for all types of ink formulation and may very well be the most important one because it has such a tremendous psychological impact on the ultimate consumer. Color appears in in three different dimensions referred to a shue, saturation or chroma, and value.

Printing Ink:

Baluja Spectra
C-50 Okhla Indl. Area-II,
New Delhi - 110 020
Phone/fax : 6835715, 6835722

Ajanta Ink Company
Basai Road, Gurgaon.
(Haryana)
Phone/fax : 8-330028

Art Printing Inks Company
104 Site-4, Indl. Area,
Sahibabad, Ghaziabad.
(U.P.)
Phone/fax : 767882

Inks India (Delhi)
C-49, Sector-8,
Noida-201 301. Distt. Ghaziabad.
(U.P.)
Phone/fax : 523801, 011-8-557270

Van Inks & Chemicals (P) Ltd.
B-150, Phase-II,
Noida-201 305. Distt. ghaziabad.
(U.P.)
Phone/fax : 567141, 011-8-521507

Grafica Display Co.,
86, Mathuradas Vasanji Road,
Near Darpan Cinema,
Andheri (E), Mumbai - 400 093

M. M. Jones,
Brackhursh Grescent,
Walsall West Midlands,
England W85 4 A.P.
Telephone Walsall (+44922) 33516
Telex 339674 (L.P.S.).

M.S.L. Graphics
Mahindra & Mahindra Ltd.,
15 J.N. Heredia Marg,
Mumbai - 400 038
Telephone : 262711-12-13

Ahuja Graphic Machinery Pvt. Ltd.,
Prabhadevi Industrial Estate,
Veer Savarkar Marg, Mumbai - 400 025
Phones : 422 8515

Storage Tank & Pressure Vessels:

Bhasker Enterprises
70/1/1, Mangolpur Kalan,
Delhi - 110 083

Manoj Consulting Engineers
D - 20, Sector - 6,
Noida - 201 301 (U.P.)

Goyal Engineering Works
40/10, Bawana Road
Samaipur, Delhi - 110 042
Phone : 729 3145

Mech-fab-Engineers
E - 8, Greater Kailash - II,
New Delhi - 110 048
Phone : 641 5548 (Factory at Noida, Ghaziabad)

PLANT ECONOMICS OF SCREEN PRINTING ON VARIOUS ITEMS

Rated Plant Capacity = 40000.00 Nos./Day

COST OF LAND & BUILDING

(Total land area required 320 sq. mtr.) Rs. 1,51,000.00

LIST OF PLANT & MACHINERY

1. Auto Flat Screen printer. The squeege speed is 900 imprints/hour and the thickness of print is 0-20 m.m
2. Miscellneous Machinery
3. Storage tank (for Storing ink,ditution etc.)

LIST OF RAW MATERIALS

1. Printing Ink
2. Screen
3. Miscellneous Raw materials

FIXED CAPITAL

Land & Building	Rs.	1,51,000.00
Plant & Machinery	Rs.	9,75,000.00
Other Fixed Assets	Rs.	65,000.00
TOTAL	**Rs.**	**11,91,000.00**

TOTAL WORKING CAPITAL/MONTH

Raw Material	Rs.	60,000.00
Salary & Wages	Rs.	11,562.50
Utilities & Overheads	Rs.	36,700.00
TOTAL	**Rs.**	**1,08,262.50**

TOTAL CAPITAL INVESTMENT

Total Fixed Capital	Rs.	11,91,000.00
Total Working Capital for 3 Months	Rs.	3,24,787.50
TOTAL	**Rs.**	**15,15,787.50**

TURNOVER/ANNUM

1. 3x10 Sticker per annum (Printing)
2. 4.5x10 Screen Printing on Plastic
3. 4.5x10 Screen Printing on ceramic utensils

TOTAL **Rs. 24,75,000.00**

PROFIT = RECEIPTS - COST OF PRODUCTION

= 24,75,000.00 - 18,86,153.25

= 5,88,846.75

PROFIT SALES RATIO = Profit / Sales x 100 = **23.79 %**

RATE OF RETURN = Operating Profit / T.C.I. x 100 = **38.60 %**

BREAK EVEN POINT (B.E.P.) = 58.16 %

22

SCREEN PRINTING ON PAPER/CARDS

INTRODUCTION

Like many areas in science and technology ,printing technology has undergone a process of revolution during the last 10 years. Not only has there been a radical improvement in the machineries but also in the various back-up service areas which makes the technological scenario of the printing industry equally exciting, sophisticated, if not little complex in nature.

This has been the result of the introduction of computer and electronic aided mechanisms have made into print technology and its related service areas. The magnitude of development in print technology has been quite phenomenal during the decade.

As the world is becoming faster in communication for the growing demand of corporate world, use of paper, visiting cards, greeting cards is increasing.

To meet the growing demand of printed paper, visiting cards, greeting cards a faster and accurate system was urgently needed. For this purpose computerised screen printing was introduced. The process of screen printing with computer has got many advantages like.

1. The reproducability of print, shade is very good.
2. Copying rate of prints is faster and can be varied.
3. The whole process is heat and clear compared to conventional screen printing.
4. Fine and complex prints can also be obtained with ease.
5. It saves labour.
6. It saves time at many-a-places in the process of printing.
7. Overall cost of production is low.

USES AND APPLICATIONS

The use of printed paper, visiting cards, greeting cards is even increasing. A system sophisticated with computer for screen printing on paper will be definitely useful. Printed paper, visiting cards, greeting cards are used at places well known to common people.

1. In corporate and administrative office.
2. In publicity of some article.
3. Greeting cards etc. for various occasion, festivals by people.

Better the quality and low cost of printing more the people will be attracted to use such facilities.

PRESENT MANUFACTURERS

Adographica
B-267, Okhla Phase I,
New Delhi - 110020
Phone : 684 1686

ABI Overseas Ltd.
G-76, Basement,
Kalkaji.
New Delhi - 110019
Phone : 646 1682

Cartolabs Enterprises
T 5, Bagrumpur,
Malviya Nagar,
New Delhi - 110017
Phone : 643 0124

Lynx Printers
4B, Tamoor Nagar,
New Friends Colony,
New Delhi - 11C 065
Phone : 683 7072

COMPUTERISED SCREEN PRINTING PROCESS

The computerised screen printing can be divided into two parts. First part is making image on computer and taking out "Print out" and the second part is taking out copies of the "print out" by screen printing machines.

Part One :-

There are three main steps in "print out" from computer

1. The personal computer in which text and/or graphics are entered or transferred into it from other sources, like importing of files (from floppy) from other frames. This is done by the acceptance of images via. scanners and digitisers

2. The complete desktop publishing system will support output to a variety of devices including a laser printer, using a Xerographic technique to output directly on plain paper.

The output device, typically a laser printer supporting a standard page description language should allow the printing of combined text and graphics.

3. Page layout or typesetting software allowing screen based cut-and -paste from a variety of software sources and lending full support to the page description.

Part Two :-

Screen printing process is employed successfully for printing on all kinds of paper. With screen printing light color appear paper and more brilliant when printed on colored stock. It is also possible to print on silver, gold, bronze and other metallic papers if the ink is mixed with appropriate binding varnishes to reduce its brittleness upon drying. Bright colour do not hold well and are liable to get scratched or chipped. If the paper is more porous like blotting it is recommended to use a stiffer ink. Like paper, there are many varieties of card which can be used for screen printing. There are two method available for it.

1. Hand Printing or Silk Printing.
2. Automatic Printing Machine.

Cut a window in the cardboard so that the glass sheet fits exactly in it. While printing place the glass sheet inside the cardboard. This way when the glass sheet is surrounded by a cardboard of more or less the same thickness, the squeegee can be pulled evenly and smoothly across the screen and over the glass sheet without the screen mesh coming in contact with the glass edge, thus avoiding any possibility of damage to the screen mesh. In case due to some reason it is not practical or desirable to cut a window in a thick sheet of cardboard, there is another device. Cut two 'L' shaped pieces of cardboard of the same thickness, so that when placed together they form a window. Of these two pieces, one piece say 'X' may be fixed to the printing table using gum tape the other piece, say 'Y' being left loose and movable. While printing keep the glass sheet in position, one edge touching the fixed piece of 'X,' place the loose piece of 'Y' against the other edge of the glass sheet before lowering the frame. After printing, the loose picce 'Y' should be moved aside to remove the printed glass sheet.

Some form of build-up is necessary while printing on any thick material with shape edges. The usual fitting of the screen frame, as for printing on paper, will not serve for printing on a thicker material. For this purpose, the height of the screen surface will have to be slightly raised so that when the frame is lowered, it will rest evenly and flat on the surface to be printed. Besides, the underside of the screen fabric should be reinforced with cellotape for additional protection.

FLOWSHEET

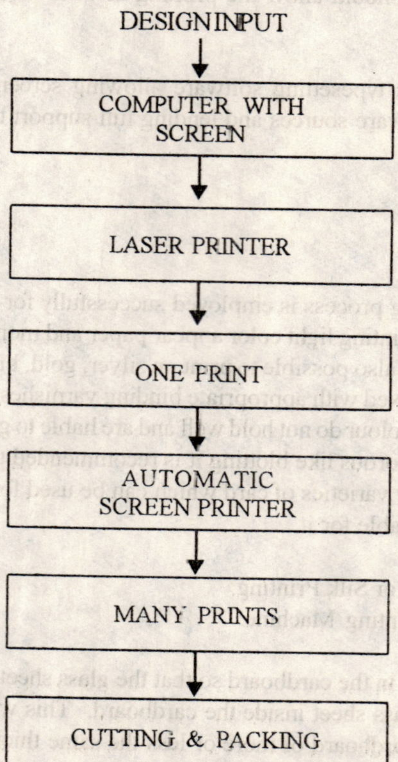

SUPPLIERS OF RAW MATERIALS

Papers :-

Om Prakash Jitendra Kumar & Company
63, Darya Ganj,
New Delhi - 110 002
Phones : 326 9680, 327 1380

Narain Paper Mart
4034/3, Haryana Market,
Chawri Bazar, Delhi - 110 006
Phone : 291 5135

Himgiri Paper Products
B-24, Indl. Area Lawrence Road,
New Delhi - 110 035
Phone : 718 9005

Inks - Toners etc. :-

Viram Dichen Corporation
281 - A, Samuel Street
Mumbai - 400 003
Phone : 329168

Kusum Enterprises
44 Gaya Building , 4th Floor,
109, Yusuf Mecharali Road,
Mumbai - 400 003
Phone : 345521

Printers Emporium
Connaught Circus,
New Delhi - 110 001

Khanna Printers Stores
Chata Bazar,
Mathura (U.P.)

Art Printing Inks Company
104, Site-4, Indl. Area,
Sahibabad, Ghaziabad, (U.P.)
Phone/fax : 767882

SUPPLIERS OF PLANT AND MACHINERY

Desk Top Publishing Systems :

Software Packages :-

A.T.E. Enterprises Limited (Marketed By)

Mumbai Telephone	:	287 2245, 636 6626, 636 7859
Delhi Telephone	:	371 2747, 371 2929
Bangalore Telephone	:	648760
Calcutta Telephone	:	287289
Chennai Telephone	:	75820
Coimbatore Telephone	:	33286

Solustan Electronics Systems Pvt. Ltd. (Developed By)
NIDC, Nr. Lambha,
Post Narol,
Ahemedabad - 382 405
Tel: 8335721, 832346

Gautam Gupta
PC Quest,
D-74 Panchsheel Enclave,
New-Delhi - 110017
Tel: 6433999, 6435999, 6413938

Inderjit Moulik
Sonata Software
36, Ganesh Chandra Avenue
Calcutta - 700 018
Tel. 279747/279749.

Hardware (Computer, Mouse, Printer etc) :-

Raba Contel (P) Ltd.
6 th Floor, Qutab Hotel,
New Mehrauli Road
New Delhi - 110016
Tel : 686 3901

Esskayjay's Kreation Pvt. Ltd.
7 B, Kiron Shankar Roy Road,
2nd Floor, Calcutta - 700001
Phone : 28 3903

Dealer :-

Team Computers Pvt. Ltd.
B - 12, Somdutt Chambers - 1
5, Bhikaji Cama Place,
New Delhi - 110 066
Ph : 609775, 674246

Screen Printing Machine :-

Lolita Manufacturing Works,
93-40, Katra Ganga Bishan,
Gaushalla Road, Krishanganj,
Delhi - 110 006 (Near D.C.M Ram Lila Maidan)

"Pricol " Automatic Screen Printing Machine
Premier Instruments & Controls Ltd.
Post Box No - 6331,
1087 Bec Avanashi Road,
Coimbatore - 641 037

Solar Machines Pvt. Ltd.
22 - D, Wadia Charities Buildings,
2nd Floor Brelvi Road,
Fort, Mumbai - 400 023

Ahuja Graphic Machinery Pvt. Ltd.
Prabhadevi Industrial Estate,
Veer Savarkar Marg,
Mumbai - 400 025
Phone : 422 8515

Inter Press Equipments & Machines Pvt. Ltd.
A - 16, Nariana Industrial Area - II
New Delhi - 110 028
Phone : 5704450/51/52

Print Link ,
Unit No. 31, Ist Floor,
Laxmi Industrial Estate,
Off Eastern Ceramics Ltd.,
Bangur Nagar, Goregaon (West),
Mumbai - 400 090
Phone : 672 7166

PLANT ECONOMICS OF SCREEN PRINTING ON PAPER/CARDS

Rated Plant Capacity = 10000.00 Nos./Day

COST OF LAND & BUILDING

(Total land area required 300 sq. mtr.)	Rs.	2,10,000.00

LIST OF PLANT & MACHINERY

1. Complete Desk Top Publishing System (including computer, laser printer, mouse, floppies etc.)
2. Automatic Screen Printing Machine
3. Symphony Air Condition Cooler for Computer
4. Miscellaneous

LIST OF RAW MATERIALS

1. Printing Ink
2. Screen
3. Paper For Visiting Cards, Greeting Cards And Other Type
4. Miscellaneous

FIXED CAPITAL

Land & Building	Rs.	2,10,000.00
Plant & Machinery	Rs.	2,82,000.00
Other Fixed Assets	Rs.	1,02,000.00
TOTAL	**Rs.**	**5,94,000.00**

TOTAL WORKING CAPITAL/MONTH

Raw Material	Rs.	1,30,000.00
Salary & Wages	Rs.	14,125.00
Utilities & Overheads	Rs.	7,620.00
TOTAL	**Rs.**	**1,51,745.00**

TOTAL CAPITAL INVESTMENT

Total Fixed Capital	Rs.	5,94,000.00
Total Working Capital for 3 Months	Rs.	4,55,235.00
TOTAL	**Rs.**	**10,49,235.00**

TURNOVER/ANNUM

1.	Paper Cost (Recovery)		
2.	Printing Charges(a) Visiting Cards		
	TOTAL	**Rs.**	**28,50,000.00**

PROFIT = RECEIPTS - COST OF PRODUCTION

= 28,50,000.00 - 21,17,516.70

= 7,32,483.30

PROFIT SALES RATIO = Profit / Sales x 100 = **25.70 %**

RATE OF RETURN = Operating profit / T.C.I. x 100 = **69.31 %**

BREAK EVEN POINT (B.E.P) = 36.05 %

23

SCREEN PRINTING ON TEXTILES

INTRODUCTION

Screen printing can be defined in proper terms as selectively blocking out a screen fabric, silk metal or synthetic; forcing a solution of cellulose ink through the open space by means of a roller for scrapping upper of paper, metal glass as the case may be which is to be placed in register as a base board table or special invention. The term silk-screen printing is therefore insufficient and inaccurate in addition to silk bolting cloth other material such as stainless steel, nylon terene, age constantly used now a days. In Europe the term serigraphing is currently derived from drawing on silk as the analogy of lithography. As it is very often difficult to distinguish a screen from a litho graphic print it is essential to consider the special characteristic of screen printing. Screen prints have a certain graphic solidity screen printed half tones are usually limited to between 45% to 65% screen on examination they reveal a character heaviness in the shadow areas and rather forced highlights, with a narrow range of middle tones. Typed matter down to eight points can be printed satisfactorily even during long runs, provided a letter design is suitable for reproduction by screen printing.

USES & APPLICATION

Screen printing is one of the important process having different application.

It is used in common for production of art prints, posters transfer papers, greeting cards, glass windows, diary covers electrical equipments, plastic and rubber sheet, and textile materials etc. Besides the above applications it can be used in textiles, fabric of cotton silk, Nylon, polyesters etc. The screen printing clothes are used for decorative or for wearing purposes. It has various applications.

Cotton:

In the case of very light cotton fabric it is sufficient to boil the material for 30-45 min in a solution containing 2 parts of 'Lissapol' ND and 5 parts of soda ash per 1000 parts of liquor. After this treatment the fabric is rinsed very thoroughly in water and dried.

To obtain the brightest shades on cotton, the material, if in the grey state, is bleached after scouring. This is done by working the material gently in a cold solution of 1.o° -1.4° Be (1.5°-2°) sodium hypochlorite solution for about 30 min and then washing thoroughly in cold water.

This should be followed by a treatment in weak acetic acid (0.1% solution) and, finally, by rinsing completely free of acid in cold water. Heavier cotton fabric require more severe treatment than this method. Industrially, this could consist of boiling for several hours under pressure in caustic soda in a closed vessel called a kiper. Alternatively, a shortened continuous operation using J-boxes to get the appropriate dwell times, and hydrogen or sodium peroxide as the active bleaching agent, would be used. These operations are not easily reproduced on a small scale.

Nylon & Terylene, Polyester Fibre:

A simple scour to remove yarn lubricants is given. The material is treated for 30 min at 70°C (160°F) in a solution containing 1.5 parts 'Lisspol' ND and 2 parts of soda ash per 1000 parts of liquor, well rinsed in water and dried. If required, an optical bleach may be given for nylon by applying 'Fluolite' XMF paste at the rate of 0.1-0.5% (calculated on the dry weight of material) at a temperature of 95°C (200°F) for 45 min.

This is followed by rinsing and drying in the normal manner. Two different types of optical bleaching agent are applicable to nylon and different types of optical bleaching agent are applicable to nylon and behave in manner analkogous to either acid or disperse dyes.

The acid dye type of fluorescent bleaching agent occupies the same dyeing site on the nylon as coloured acid used in printing this fibre. An excess of optical bleach present on the nylon may give lowered dye yields in printing. 'Fluolite' XMF behaves analogously to a disperse dye and thus does not affect the yield obtained from acid dyes.

Natural Silk:

When received in the state, silk contains both natural and adventitious impurities which must be removed before printing to ensure a smooth and even pattern. The main bulk of the natural gum present in raw silk is sericin which is a protein material which somewhat resembles gelatin in its general properties. Sericin is removed by a 'de-gumming' or 'boiling-off' operation. This consists of treating the fabric for 1-1.5 h at 95°C (205°F) in a solution of 10 parts olive oil soap per 1000 parts of water. This is followed by a through rinsing in warm and cold water and drying. If bleaching is required it is carried out after de-gumming, preferably using hydrogen peroxide with or without the addition of small amounts of sodium silicate. The colour of the fibre in wild silks is frequently a pale brown which cannot be completely removed even by bleaching.

Paste & Thickener:

Each printing method require a paste with special characteristics, frequently referred to as flow characteristics. For instance, a roller printing operation requires a paste that tends to flow from the engraved portions of the note onto the fabric. Where as screen printing operation require a paste that flow only under the direct pressure of the squeegee. For this reason, the choice of thick even is dependent not only on the type of dye stuff, but on the type of printing machine on which the printing is to be done & also on the type of fixation to be used.

FORMULATIONS

Rapid Fast Colours:- Rapid fast yellow G.G. powder (G.D.C)

80 gms
Rapid Fast Yellow G.G. Powder
30 gms
Caustic Soda 62°TW Warm water.
30 gms

Mix to a paste & add
310 gms of water
500 gms of starch tragacanth paste (neutral)
50 gms of neutral chromates solution.

1000 gum

Light Yellows:- (i) Part of above yellow
(ii) Part reduction paste for Rapid fast colours.

RAPIDOGEN PRINTING COLOURS

Dye stuff etc.	Grams.							
Rapidogen Yellow G	80							
" Orange G		80						
" Scarlet G			80					
" Red G				80				
" Red I.R.					80			
" Red R						80		
" Bordeaux R							80	
" Corinth R								80
Caustic Soda 32.5%	20	30	30	30	30	30	30	30
Methylated Spirit	30							
Monopol Brilliant Oil		30	30	30	30	30	30	30
Water (lulce warm)	150	150	150	150	150	150	150	150
Neutral Starch tragcant thickenin	500	500	500	500	500	500	500	500
Zinc oxide 1:1	50							
Neutral Chromate Solution	50							
Water (Cold)	170	210	210	210	210	210	160	230

1000 gm each by weight.

Dye Stuff etc.	Grams.								
Rapidogen PornithB	60								
" Violet B		45							
" Blue R			45						
" Blue B				45					
" Green B					60				
" Brown IR						80			
" Olive BrownIR							80		
" Brown IB								80	
" Brown IRR									80
Caustic Soda 32.5%	30	30	30	30	30	30	30	30	30
Methylated Spirit		30	30	30					
Monopol Brilliant Oil	30				30	30	30	30	30
Water (lulce warm)	150	150	150	150	150	150	150	150	150
Glyceine A.		30	50	50					
Neutal Starch tragcant thickenin	500	500	500	500	500	500	500	500	500
Uria			50	50	50				
Zinc Oxide 1:1		50	50						
Water (Cold)	230	145	115	145	130	210	210	210	210

1000 gm. each by weight

REDUCINGPASTEFORFOREGOINGCOLOURS

	A	B	C	D	E
	PARTS	PARTS	PARTS	PARTS	PARTS
Neutral Starch tragacanth thickning	600	600	600	600	600
Water	330	350	325	290	260
Caustic Soda	15	30	20	30	30
Methylated Spirit	20	-	-	30	-
Monopol Brilliant Oil	-	20	20	-	30
Glycine A	-	-	-	-	30
Neutral Chromate Solution	-	-	35	-	-
Uria	-	-	-	-	50
Zinc Oxide	35	-	-	50	-

1000 Parts each by weight

Part A :- for Rapidogen Yellow G
PartB:- for Rapidogen Orange G
" Scartlet R
" Red I R
" Cornith R
" Cornith IR
" Brown IR
PartC:- for Rapidogen Bordeaux Bb
PartD:- for Rapidogen Violet B
PartE:- for Rapidogen Blue R
for Rapidogen Blue B
for Rapidogen Green B

Part E is more expensive for light colours of all the above

Colours:- 1 Part of Rapidogen colour
2 Part of corresponding redusing paste.

The fore going colours, printed in unprepared cloth, were developed by acid-Blaming process. After printing and drying the goods were steamed in a rapid ager for 5 minutes in acetic-formic vapour and steam at 212°F, than washed, soaped and dried. It desired the colours may also be developed by following methods.

a. Wet developing process.

The printed and dried goods are parcel without previous steaming through a hot bath of

20 CC acetic acid 12°) TW
5 CC of formic acid 90%) Per Litre
25 gram Glaubers salt)

at 205°F and for 20 seconds and washed, soap's at the boil, washed and dried.

METHODS OF PREPARATION OF SCREEN

The Photographic (or Photochemical) Method

This method uses a silk, nylon or polyester gauze and has become the most important method for the preparation of screens. Fro some of the more intricate designs considerable experience and skill are required.

This method will now be discussed in detail, and reference to alternative methods will be found later.

General Procedure:

The silk gauze, stretched on the frame, is painted with s sensitizing solution such as gelatine dichromate, and dried in the dark. The pattern to be produced is painted on transparent paper with a dense opaque ink, a separate painting and screen being necessary for each colour of the desing. The coated screen may be regarded as a piece of daylight photographic printing paper and the painted pattern as a negative or as it is more generally known, a positive.

The positive is now placed in contact with the sensitized screen and exposed to light. The placed in contact with the sensitized screen and exposed to light. The length of exposure will vary according to the actualdistance from the length of exposure will vary according to the actual distance from the source of light and type of light used (electric or daylight). The exposed screen is now well washed, first in cold water to harden the insolubilised gelatine and then in warm water to remove the soluble gelatine. The screen is allowed to dry slowly. The layer of gelatine must be reinforced by the application of a lacquer which should be reasonably resistant to acids, alkalis and organic solvents.

Stretching Silk:

The screen gauze can be streched over the frames either by hand or machine. To cover a screen by hand needs a great deal of care to enable the correct and even tension to be obtained. This is best achieved by ensuring that the warp and weft of the fabric are, throughout, parallel to the sides of the screen. Screens that have been loosely stretched or screens too tightly stretched give rise to inaccurate printing.

Stretching the gauze by hand is carried out in the following manner. For illustration purpose the four corners on the screen frame can be labelled A,B,C,D, in a clockwise order. The fabric is cut larger than the frame to allow for gripping. Corner A is fastened either at the side or on the upper surface of the frame. On the upper surface the staples or tacks are placed about 20 mm (0.8in) from the outside edge of the frame. The fabric is stretched from A to B, ensuring that the threads of the gauze run parallel with the sides of the frame and keeping the gauze under tension, and it is fastened to the frame. The stapes or tacks must be close together. The fabric is then fastened at C, and again kept under tension with the threads parallel to the frame, while the whole side is attached. Pulling diagonally from B to D, the fabric is fastened at D. It is stretched tightly over the rounded edge of the frame between A and D and fastened along this side, the same procedure being followed for the last side from D to C.

The surplus fabric is trimmed and extra staples or tracks are inserted at each corner. The edges of the gauze, etc., may be covered with tape which is stuck down the glue, preferably of a waterproof type. The whole frame is painted with a lacquer to render it waterproof and easily washable. The screen is then washed thoroughly on both sides of the silk with warm water. This wetting out equalizes any laten tension in the gauze and removes impurities in the silk. After drying, the screen is ready for coating with the light-sensitive film.

Preparing the Positive Design:

The original drawing is first examined to assess its suitability for the screen printing process. It may require adapting to screen printing, or putting into repeat where possible without altering the character of the design. If the artist keeps to a standard repeat, frames of a standard size can be produced and the stops on the printing tables will not require frequent adjustment. Some designs, however, cannot be made to a standard repeat because of their nature. For every colour in a designs, however, cannot be made to a standard repeat because of their nature. For every colour in a design, a separate positive is required. These are produced on tracing paper which must be stable to moisture and temperature changes (if the material is unstable, distortions of the design occur, resulting in inaccurate fitting). For this purpose a smooth acetate film, frostated on one side and very stable, is suitable.

Transferring the Positive Design to the Silk:

The positive is laid flat on the dry sensitized silk and secured to the screen frame by, for example, adhesive tape. A glass plate of suitable dimensions is then laid on top of the positive and securely clamped to the screen frame by means of suitable clamps. To ensure goods contact between the positive and the silk hollow underside of the silk screen should be supported by means of a wooden block of such a size as to fit comfortably in the silk frame. This operation must be carried out in an orange safe light.

Hardening of the Exposed Design:

Screens based on a gelatine-dichromate sensitizing solution are often given a hardening treatment, although this is not absolutely necessary. The screens are treated in the cold for 10-15 min in the following solution;

Ammonium Dichromate	25 Parts
Chrome Alum Crystals	50 Parts
Formaldehyde (40%) Solution	50 Parts
	Bulked to 1000 Parts

The screens are washed well in cold water and allowed to dry slowly.

Screens based on a polyvinyl alcohol-dichromate sensitizing solution require a hardening treatment and this is carried out by immersing the screen for 45-60 min in the following solution:

50 Parts	Acetaldehyde
50 Parts	Isobutyraldehyde or Normal Butyraldehyde
20 Parts	Sulphuric Acid 66^0 Be (168^0w)
Bulked to 1000 Parts	at a temperature of 15^0 - 20^0C (60^0 - 70^0 F)

After rinsing and drying the screen is ready for use. If, after inspecting the screen it is found that certain parts of the motif are blocked, they can be cleared by brushing lightly over the screen with a 1:1 solution of lactic acid 80%.

Reinforcement of the Screen:

In the case of screens prepared from polyvinyl alcohol the hardening treatment just described is sufficient protection, and further reinforcement of the screen is not absolutely essential. With screens prepared from gelatin, protection of the gelatine is obtained by application of a lacquer. The gelatine-coated screens are coated with lacquer from the inside of the screen by either brushing or scrapping. While the lacquer is still wet, the outside of the screen is rubbed with a dry cloth, in order to remove the lacquer from the open places of the screen. If it is considered necessary to coat both sides of the screen with lacquer, this is carried out after drying by applying the lacquer from the reverse side of the screen. If the lacquer used is viscous, it may also be necessary to wipe out with a solvent. A screen lacquered on both sides, such as the one just mentioned, should be satisfactory for the normal wear and tear of screen printing provided the lacquer used is resistant to acids, alkalis and such organic solvents as are used in printing pastes.

The treated screen is dried and subsequently baked at a temperature of 120^0 - 150^0 C (250^0 - 300^0 F) for 3-5 min, the higher temperature requiring shorter time. The baked screen is coated in a similar manner on the reverse side, any excess being removed as before. After drying and rebaking, the screen is ready for use.

The Printing Operation

In using the screen, a suitable amount of print paste is poured into the well of the screen frame and transferred through on to the cloth underneath, by drawing it to and for across the screen with the squeegee, two to four passage generally being given. Before beginning to print with a screen it is advisable to wet out the screen first, by printing on to a piece of spare fabric or absorbent paper. A properly we-out screen ensures a good transfer of dyestuff paste to the fabric being printed in bulk. To avoid marking-off the screen printer does not carry out his printing in bulk. To avoid marking-off the screen printer does not carry out his printing in a continuous order, but prints in alternative positions, that is position 1 then misses a position to position 3, and on to position 5 and so on until the whole table length has been completed. The drying of the printed material is assisted by blowing hot air over the table or by heated tables, so that provided the printing pastes are not too hygroscopic and the material is not too light in weight (and consequently limited in absorbency), the material should then be dry; otherwise it is necessary to wait until the print is dry enough to avoid picking-up an marking-off. Printing is then continued in positions 2,4,6 etc. until the whole table is printed with the first colour. The same procedure is followed for the second and subsequent colours in the pattern.

SUPPLIERS OF PLANT & MACHINERY

Cranco Engineering Limited
Long Eaton, Nottingham (U.K.)

Macclesfield Engineering & Sheet Metal Co. Ltd.
Wind Mill Street, Macclesfield (U.K.)

George Hall (Sales) Ltd.
Hardman Street, Churchgate,
Stockport SK30HA (U.K.)

PRINTING ACCESSORIES SUPPLIERS & MANUFACTURES

Printers Emporium
Connaught Circus,
New Delhi-110001

Khanna Printers Stores
Chota Bazar,
Mathura (U.P.)

Screen Process Films

Ulano A.G.
8700, Kusnach, Zuricht,
Switzerland

Screen Printing Inks

Chemicoat
14, Rachika Nivas, Ist Floor,
M.V. Road, Andheri (East),
Mumbai -400069
Ph: 8342854, 8361465.

Screen Printing Auxillaries, Fabrics & Filter Fabrics

Nelson Traders,
9 Azad Shopping Centre, Goregaon (West),
Mumbai - 400062 Ph: 8724997.

SCREEN PRINTING MACHINE SUPPLIERS

Graphica Flextronica,
15/16, Navketan Industrial Estate,
M.C. Road, Andheri (East),
Mumbai - 400 093
Ph: 8327154.

Amit Engg. Works
9340, Katra Ganga Vishan,
Gaushala Marg, Kishanganj,
Delhi - 110 006
Phone : 354 4180

Lolita Manufacturing Works
9340, Katra Ganga Vishan,
Gaushala Marg, Kishanganj,
Delhi - 110 006
Phone : 752 1906

PLANT ECONOMICS OF SCREEN PRINTING ON TEXTILES

Rated Plant capacity = 5000.00 Mtr/Day

COST OF LAND & BUILDING

(Total Land required 1000 sq. mtr.)	Rs.	7,50,000.00

LIST OF PLANT & MACHINERY

1. Printing Screens with Various Designs
2. Printing Tables
3. Dye Mixing Machine
4. Washing & Treatments Tanks (R.C.C. work)
5. Baby Boiler 100 kg/m
6. Mangles and Rollers
7. Drying Machine Continuous Conveyor Type
8. Motors and Other mis/units like Mangles etc.
9. Exposure Cabinate
10. Screen Stretcher
11. Squeeges
12. Miscellaneous

LIST OF RAW MATERIALS

Chemicals: Dyes (Variable Proportions)

FIXED CAPITAL

Land & Building	Rs.	7,50,000.00
Plant & Machinery	Rs.	6,05,000.00
Other Fixed Assets	Rs.	85,000.00
TOTAL	**Rs.**	**14,40,000.00**

TOTAL WORKING CAPITAL/MONTH

Raw Material	Rs.	6,25,000.00
Salary & Wages	Rs.	64,747.00
Utilities & Overheads	Rs.	32,750.00
TOTAL	**Rs.**	**7,22,497.00**

TOTAL CAPITAL INVESTMENT

Total Fixed Capital	Rs.	14,40,000.00
Total Working Capital for 3 Months	Rs.	21,67,491.00
TOTAL	**Rs.**	**36,07,491.00**

TURNOVER/ANNUM

By screen printing 1500000 meters of cloth of width 1 meter	**Rs. 1,20,00,000.00**

PROFIT = RECEIPTS - COST OF PRODUCTION

= 1,20,00,000.00 - 96,54,332.02

= 23,45,667.98

PROFIT SALES RATIO = Profit / Sales x 100 = **19.55 %**

RATE OF RETURN = Operating profit / T.C.I. x 100 = **65.02 %**

BREAK EVEN POINT (B.E.P.) = 38.19 %

24

TABLE OFFSET & D.T.P.

INTRODUCTION

The revolution in desktop printing started in 1985. Though the technology is just 12 years old, already plenty of hardware and software options are available. Johann Gutenberg installed a successful printing press in the fifteenth century. Since then, publishers have been booking for a better, cheaper and faster way to get words and pictures on paper. It took years to make even the slightest improvement on the printing press, but DTP keeps advancing at an accelerated pace. Like any other computer system the three main components of DTP are hardware, software and printer.

Book is an important source of knowledge. Increase in standard of living further leads to develop interest in studying of course not always true. With increase in industrialization, the demand for books has to increase.

To sum up, desk top publishing has come to stay. But its full potential and applications can only be realised by those conversant with the various packages available and prepared to study the combinations there of.

DESKTOP PUBLISHING SYSTEMS

Laser Printers and Digitizers:

Desk Top Publishing involves many components, but without good output devices, all the effort that goes into designing and laying out pages is wasted. Currently, the primary high-resolution output device in a desk top publishing operation is the laser printer. Most good looking documents that result from desk top publishing are more than just nicely formatted type.

Laser Printers and digitizers as much as computers and software - makes desk top publishing a personal rather than a strictly corporate or industrial endeavor.

Laser Printers:

A laser printers is essentially a photocopier. In fast, many such printers use the same technology that photocopiers do, the photo sensitive drum temporarily holds an electric charge in the shape of an image transferred to it by a computer-driven laser beam. the charge and the image carried within it are transferred to a sheet of paper as it rolls across the drum. The paper then attracts the toner (plastic ground into a fine powder) and heat bonds the toner to the paper.

Digitizers : Producing Graphic Images:-

A digitiser transforms an image into digital information you can store in a computer memory or on a mass storage device.

SOFTWARE

Two main types of DTP software are : the page make-up program and the typsetting program. Such programs combine the conventional roles of the typesetter and the pasteup artist. Text can be typed, arranged in columns and blocks on a page. It is also possible to break up the text, add headlines, captions and subheads. Some programs provide the facility of inserting graphics within and around the text. The graphics may be as simple as a box or a line, or as complex as aline drawing, schematic or digitised photograph.

Macintosh page make-up programs are : Ready Setgo, PageMaker and MacPublisher. They allow mixing of text and graphics freely and are compatible with other Mac progrems such as Mac Write, MacWord, MacDraw and MacPaint.

PAGEMAKE-UPPROGRAMS

Page Maker:

Aldus Corp's Pagemaker for Mac got DTP off the ground. It has simple menu commands, WYSIWYG (what you see is what you get) displays, the ability to incorporate text and graphics from other programs and to output to high resolution printers and typesetters.

Page Maker permits working on a WYSIWYG view of a page in three different sizes - normal reduced and enlarged. Each view gives presentation of what appear at the laser printer.

A page is treated as a windowpane on the screen. Only a portion of the page is seen at a time. There are no scroll bars to move the page. To move to a different part of the page SHOE PAGE command is used. A miniature version of the page is displayed on the screen, with a dotted box within it. Place the box at the required spot, exit; the SHOW PAGE window, and the selected part of the page is now on the screen. Obviously, during heavy editing, the system will be very slow.

There are four blocks - text picture, solid and frame. Using text, a square block of 2.54 cm * 2.54 cm is created and can be resized to anything. Resizing requires grasping the lower right corner of the text block and tugging it. It is difficult to grab the right spot but some practice makes block manipulation scheme simple.

MacPublisher-II:

This program divides the screen into many windows. The right hand of screen contains the page which cannot be moved, resized or scrolled. Lower left corner has dog-ear flaps which enable to flip through the pages of the publication. Documents up to 96 pages can be created but disc space and number of documents in an average publication make this limit about 30 pages.

PFS:

ClickArt Personal Publisher. ClickArt has drop-down menus, dart text and graphics on a light screen background, mouse operations (optional), an I-beam text cursor, an arrow pointer and MacPaint like graphics tools.

The program lists most commands under the eight drop-down menus across the top of the screen. These commands are executed using a keyboard or mouse. Text can be typed directly from ASCII text files, and fonts can be selected for both of them.

Ventura Publisher:

Ventura allows to control character spacing and line spacing in decimal increments. It will automatically number the chapeters, and up to right levels of headings, as well as footnotes and figures. Minimum number of lines to be isolated in windows or orphans can be specified. Text can be imported in six different file formats.

PAGE DESCRIPTION LANGUAGES (PDL)

PDL enables a printer to construct a page grom a combination of text, fonts and graphics. The computer system can specify complete page images rather than small inked areas. The page is sent in the form of ASCII text and graphics 'Primitives' basic codes that describe the size and shape of graphic objects. PDL compiler in the laser printer intercepts this information, converts it into dots and processes it into an image ready for printing.

Post Script:

The most common PDL is post script. the computer talks to postscript with Engligh like commands. All programs that support a post script printer programs that support a post scrip printer drive will work with any post script compatible output device.

Interpress:

Interpress's files are in binary form. For debugging, binary codes can be translated into a more readily recognisable and readable form.

DDL:

DDL is the most recent PDL and includes most of the elements of the two other langaugues. It is programmable like post script and has document control features superior to those of tinerpress.

OFFSETPRINTINGPRESS
TABLEOFFSETPRINTINGM/CSPECIFICATION

Specification:

Plate Size	Punched 1/2" pinbar 381*254mm - 15"*10" strength edge upto381*254mm-15"*10"punched12.5mm368*250mm-14.5"*8*1/8"
Printing Area	330*341mm/13"*9.5"
Paper Sie-Maximum	368*257mm-14.5"*10*1/8"
Minimum	150*114mm-5*7/8*4.5"
Paper Substance	40-190 gsm(depended on quality)
Speed	3600-7200 impression per hour
Damping	Automatic Rotafount or intergated fount system
Electric Supply	220/240 V single phase 50 H. Full load running current 2 Amps. Other voltage and frquencies are available
Weight Apporox	120 Kgs/264 Ibs
Width	635mm25"
Height	610mm24"
Length (incl. delivary tray)	940mm37"
Cabinet Width	607 mm 23"
Height	660 mm 26"
Length	965 mm 38"

SPECIFICFOLDINGMETHODS

Cross Association:

This technique is employed on double-width news presses and similar machines where double folders are in use. The idea is to feed all of the webs into one folder so that the number of pages oer copy is increased at the expense of the output of the other folder.

The webs on one side of the press are first taken down the appropriate former and then transferred across to the draw rollers of the twin folder. The webs from both sides of the machine will now be together at this point and will progress together as for a normal production run. Where cross association is used to produce tabloid papers, this will result in a larger, one piece newspaper indistinguishable from the usual product apart from the extra pages. With broadsheets, however, the papers will be produced in two sections. The two sections will be alinged back-to-back, but folded in together as they pass through the cross fold rollers.

SUPPLIERS' ADDRESSES

Paper Suppliers :

Om Prakash Jitendra Kumar & Company
63, Darya Ganj,
New Delhi - 11 00 02.
Ph. 326 96 80, 3271380

Narain Paper Mart,
4034/3, Haryana Market,
Chawri Bazar, Delhi - 11 00 06.
Ph. 291 51 35.

Himgiri Paper Products
B-24, Indl. Area Lawrence Road,
New Delhi - 110035
Phone : 718 9005

Printing Ink:

Baluja Spectra
C-50 Okhla Indl. Area-II,
New Delhi - 110020
Phone/fax : 6835715, 6835722

Ajanta Ink Company
Basai Road, Gurgaon (Haryana)
Phone/fax : 8-330028

Art Printing Inks Company
104 Site-4, Indl. Area,
Sahibabad, Ghaziabad, (U.P.)
Phone/fax : 767882

Inks India (Delhi)
C-49, Sector-8,
Noida-201 301 (U.P.)
Phone/fax : 523801, 011-8-557270

Van Inks & Chemicals (P) Ltd.
B-150, Phase-II,
Noida-201 305 (U.P.)
Phone/fax : 567141, 011-8-521507

Printing Material:

Alcon Graphic
1693/121, Shanti Nagar,
Tri Nagar, New Delhi - 110 035
(Rubber Blankets)

Graphichan Sales
Bhupin Das Bhawan,
Krishna Mkt. Pahar Ganj,
Delhi - 110 055

Process Chemical Co.
Shanti Mohan House,
16, Ansari Road,
New Delhi - 110 002

SUPPLIERS OF DTP SYSTEM

Zenith Electro Systems Pvt. Ltd.,
106, Mittal Chambers,
Nariman Point,
Mumbai - 400 021.

Pearl Digital Systems,
704, Rohit House,
Talstoy Marg,
New Delhi - 110 001.

CMS Computers Pvt Ltd.,
201, Arcodia,
Nariman Point,
Mumbai - 400 021

DCM Data Products,
4th Floor, Vikrant Tower,
4, Rajendra Place,
New Delhi - 110 008.

Wipro Information Technology Ltd.,
5th Floor, s.B. Tower,
88, M.G. Road,
Bangalore - 560 001.

LIST OF MANUFACTURERS OF PRINTING MACHINERY

MOI Engineering Ltd.
612-A, Chiranjiv Towers,
43, Nehru Place,
New Delhi - 110 019
Phones : 6413093, 6450956

H.S. Enterprises
4852/24, Ansari Road,
Darya Ganj,
New Delhi - 110 002

J. Mahavir & Co. Pvt. Ltd.
3620-21, Netaji Subash Marg,
Darya Ganj,
New Delhi - 110 002

SID Mark Sales
186, Dr. Ambedkar Road,
Dadar, Mumbai.

Lakshmi Printers Store
3/3A, Asaf Ali Road
New Delhi - 110 002

PLANT ECONOMICS OF TABLE OFFSET & DTP

Rated Plant Capacity = 200.00 Pgs./Day

COST OF LAND & BUILDING

(Total land area required 22.69 sq. mtr) Rs. 46,500.00

LIST OF PLANT & MACHINERY

1. Table-Top offset printing M/C with all the accessories (Stand/StorageCabinet & Voltage Stabilizer)
2. Computer(PC/AT-486) with all the accessories & Power suppliers
3. Laser Printer
4. Dot- Matric Printer (132 column)
6. OA Scanner
7. Air Condition (cap 2 ton)
8. UPS (1 KVA) with batteries

LIST OF RAW MATERIALS

1. Plates - Paper Plates & Typing or Photocopying expenses for 125000 copies
2. Metal Plates
3. Inks & Solution
4. Rubber Blankets
5. Stationary
6. Floppy diskettes & misc.

FIXED CAPITAL

Land & Building	Rs.	46,500.00
Plant & Machinery	Rs.	5,62,000.00
Other Fixed Assets	Rs.	1,00,000.00
TOTAL	**Rs.**	**7,08,500.00**

TOTAL WORKING CAPITAL/MONTH

Raw Material	Rs.	10,430.00
Salary & Wages	Rs.	19,200.00
Utilities & Overheads	Rs.	6,500.00
TOTAL	**Rs.**	**36,130.00**

TOTAL CAPITAL INVESTMENT

Total Fixed Capital	Rs.	7,08,500.00
Total Working Capital for 3 Months	Rs.	1,08,390.00
TOTAL	**Rs.**	**8,16,890.00**

TURNOVER/ANNUM

1. By Printing 8,00,000 Sheets with paper plate
2. By Printing 7,00,000 Sheets with metal plate
3. By Composing 60,000 pages

TOTAL **Rs. 9,58,935.00**

PROFIT = RECEIPTS - COST OF PRODUCTION
= 9,58,935.00 - 7,22,892.20
= 2,36,042.80

PROFIT SALES RATIO = Profit / Sales x 100 = **24.62 %**

RATE OF RETURN = Operating profit / T.C.I x 100 = **28.65 %**

BREAK EVEN POINT (B.E.P) = 63.33 %

25
TIN PRINTING

INTRODUCTION

Tin printing & anodic aluminium are used as an industrial, metallic labels and are widely used on industrial machinery and domestic appliances for supplying the specifications, operating procedures and name of the manufacturer, Also name plates are seen on the houses & buildings. Most of the name plates are made from Brass, iron & S. Steel. Anodized aluminium have the advantage that it is unbreakable and ever shining.

Tin printing is used for decorating purposes. The term decorating is used here to include printed information & advertising matter. The designs are usually printed in multiples on to a sheet and subsequently stamped out and farmed into the shape of the article required. Anodizing of aluminium is the process by which the thick layer of aluminium oxide is made on the upper surface of the aluminium. Anodic oxidation or anodizing is on electrolytic process for thickening the naturally occuring film several hundred times. The anodic film is chemically stable and abrasion resistant.

This report will consist of tin printing & anodizing on aluminium.

USES AND SCOPE

As the name of the product suggests, tin printing inks are used to print the tin plates. Normally sheets are printed and after printing the sheet is processed into various articles.

The tin cartoons, boxes, collapsible tubes etc. are used widely for packing various products. For giving then attractive finish and charming appearance, they are printed in multicolour. For the purpose various tin printing inks are used.

The tin containers cartoons or cans are used in packing of biscuits, syrups, shoe polishes, tooth pastes, cigarettes etc. But due to the new introduction of plastic and P.V.C. packaging materials, the use of tin packaging materials has been reduced much. The reason is that the P.V.C and plastic containers are 10 times cheaper than tin with the fall of the demand of tin containers, the demand of tin printing ink will also fall and hence there is no much scope for this tin printing ink industry.

Formulation For Tin Printing:

There are numerous formulations which are frequently used in the preparation of tin printing ink. The various ingredients such as pigment, varnish, resin and solvent are generally procured from the market. The formulation for red colour tin printing ink is given below and it is used in the cost estimation of plant.

Red Tin Printing Ink:

Red colour pigment	17% by weight
Varnish	65% by weight
Resin	10% by weight
Solvent	8% by weight

The red pigment used here is Ferric oxide. Alkyd resins and solvent naphtha or benzene is used in the manufacture of tin printing ink.

The raw material requirement for the manufacture of red colour tin printing ink is given below :-

Basis :- 1000 kgs. of red colour ink

Red colour pigment	170 kgs.
Varnish of above Composition	650 kgs.
Alkyd resin	100 kgs.
Naphtha	80 kgs.

The above quantities can be changed by 10% to adjust the viscosity of the ink for lithographic printing.

Aluminium Etching Solutions:

Ingredients	Quantity
Ferric chloride	100 gms.
Alcohol 90%	200 gms.
Oxalic acid	1 gms.

Nearly all surface dirt can be removed. Greases can be removed with tricholoroethlene by immersion in liquid or vapour of spray grease.

MANUFACTURINGPROCESS

The process of tin printing has been divided into the following heads :-

1. Manufacture of Tin-printing ink
2. Printing on the tin containers

Manufacture of Tin Printing Ink:

The manufacture of tin printing ink is very simple. It involves mixing of all ingredients. First of all the alkyd resin is dissolved in the naphtha or benzene in a tank. This tank is made of mild steel with an agitator. The pigment is mixed with the varnish separately & simultaneously. Thus the prepared mixtures are then mixed together in a mixer. A thorough mixing is done & the viscosity is checked. If it is found to the desired value then the ink is packed in airtight containers. If resin and pigment is added to meet the requirement. Airtight containers used for packing are made of tin or plastic.

Printing on The Tin Sheet:

When the printing ink has been prepared, it is printed on tin sheet, for this purpose, the containers side on which the printing is alone should be cleaned properly so that no dirt is there. Now, the stencil which has already been prepared indicating design trade name and manufacturers name etc. whatever required it put on the tins, pressed hard and coating done. The coating may be repeated twice or thrice. This operation may be carried out by manual as well as mechanical. In the mechanical operation, the containers are moved by conveyor the stencil is fixed on the coating machine.

The sheets are kept in dryer for drying. The sun drying may also be done but dryer should be prepared for durability and long lasting.

Anodizing on aluminium Labels:

Raw material used for the manufacture of anodic aluminium items is aluminium sheet or foil of thickness varying from 0.5 mm to 1 mm. The aluminium sheets is available in the market in various thicknesses.

Prior to anodizing operation, the aluminium sheets are cut into desired sizes & cleaned with mechanical or chemical method, given in detail here with. The cleaned surface aluminium is now ready for anodizing process. Details are given herewith.

Mechanical Cleaning:

A feature of modern method is the rapidity, the saving of labour over the processes practical year ago. The several stages involve sand-blasting, grinding, emery nobing, these being the most important.

Chemical Cleaning:

The term chemical cleaning of aluminium covers a number of operations in which mechanical effects cannot be altogether excluded. For the most part, however, we are concerned with the removal mainly by the processes of chemical action of all those materials ordinarily present on the surface of metals subsequent to the process of manufacture and mechanical cleaning. These include many different operations intended for the removal of all greasy compounds and subsequently those films, which in many cases may have appreciable thickness, of oxides and other compounds definitely attached to the surface of the metal. Further the surface of the metal must not be unduly roughened in the process unless that is specially desired.

ANODIZING

The process of anodizing is one in which electric current is carried across an electrolyte and a substance is deposited at the anode.

The electrolytic is a medium that carried the current by means of 100 s. The ability of a solvent especially water, to ionise, substances dissolved in it i.e. to split them into components, that any positive and negative charges makes the electrolysis possible the electricity is carried across the electrolyte by the charged ions and products of electrolysis appears at the electrodes. This is a result of positively charged cathode while the negatively charged ions travel towards positively charged anode. The charges of the ions are then neutralized by the charges on the electrodes and the products of the electrolysis appear at the electrodes.

Chromic Acid Process:

Chromic Acid anodizing process uses chromic acid solution containing cromium oxide 3 to 10% by weight. A solution is made up by filling the tank about full of water dissolving the acid is the tank and then adding water to adjust to the desired level.

A chromic acid anodizing solution should not be used unless :

1. The pH. is between 0.5 and 1.0
2. The concentration of chlorides (as NaCl) is less than 0.02%.
3. The concentration of sulphate (as H_2SO_4) is less than 0..05%.
4. The total chromic acid concentrate as determined by PH and is less than 10% (when this percentage is exceeded, part of the bath is withdrawn and is replaced with fresh solution.

Hard Anodizing:

The primary different between the sulphuric acid and hard anodizing process are the temperature and current density at which anodizing is accomplished. Hard anodizing produces a considerable heavier coating that conventional anodizing for a given lengths of time.

The hard anodizing process employes a sulphuric acid bathes containing to 0.5% by weight. With as without additions. The operating temperature of the bath range from 32 to 50^{0}F and current density is between 20 to 30 amp. per sq. ft. This temperature causes the formation of soft and more porous other outer layers of the anodic coating. Excessive operating temperature results in dissolutions of coating, can burn and damage the work.

PLANT AND MACHINERY SUPPLIERS

Mixers:

Jayems Engineering Co. Ltd.,
139, M. Connaught Circus,
2nd Floor, New Delhi - 110 001
Phone : 332 4146, 332 3680

Bhiwadi Chemical (P) Ltd.,
DSIDC. 184, New Okhala Industrial Complex,
Phase - I, New Delhi - 110 020
Phone : 633 624

H.B. Mechanical & Engineering Works,
355/28, Tri Nagar, (Onkar Nagar -B),
Delhi - 110 035 Phone : 722 4505

Reddy Engineering Works,
8-9, DSIDC, Near SBI,
Raghbir Nagar, New Delhi - 110 027
Phone : 54 1 8080

Storage Tank & Pressure Vessels:

Bhasker Enterprises
70/1/1, Mangolpur Kalan,
Delhi - 110 083

Manoj Consulting Engineers
D - 20, Sector - 6,
Noida - 201 301, Distt. Ghaziabad.
(U.P.)

Goyal Engineering Works
40/10, Bawana Road,
Samaipur, Delhi - 110 042
Phone : 729 3145

Mech-fab-Engineers
E - 8, Greater Kailash - II,
New Delhi - 110 048
Phone : 641 5548
(Factory at Noida, Ghaziabad)

Anodizing Plant:

Aloz Pvt. Ltd.,
41, Haman Street,
Mumbai - 400 001

B. D. Gupta,
14/2, Old China Bazar Street,
Calcutta.

Tin Printing Machine:

Metal Printers,
28, IInd Floor, Haria Indl. Estate,
Majiwada, Thana - 400 601
Mumbai

Diamond Engineering Works,
308/3E, Shahzada Bagh,
Rohtak Road, Delhi.

Mart Metafab.,
A-3, Greater Kailash Encl. II,
New Delhi - 400 048

B.S. Tin Printers,
112-B, Co-operative Indl. Estate,
Vivkanand Nagar,
Kanpur - 208 002 (U. P.)

SUPPLIERS OF RAW MATERIALS

Pigment:

Associated Dyestuff Industries,
5/68, Industrial Estate,
Bapunagar, Ahmedabad - 23

Excel Impex Agencies,
210, Prasad Chambers,
Opera House, Mumbai - 400 004

Resin:

Associated Chemicals,
12-A, Mahendra Industrial Estate,
Behind Sion Fort, Sion East,
Mumbai - 400 004

Chomox Industrial Corporation,
Noble Chambers,
4th Floor, Parsi Bazar Street,
Fort, Mumbai - 400 001

Naphtha:

Hindustan Chemical Co.,
9, Lal bazar Street,
Merchantile Building,
Calcutta - 1

Sulphuric Acid:

Indian Ordnance Factories
Production Planning Office,
High Explosives Factory,
Kirkee, Poona - 411 003

Harshavardhan Chemicals and Minerals Ltd.
Antarvalia, Meghnagar,
District Jhabhua, M.P.

Aluminium Sheets:

Shahdara Aluminium Factory,
G.T. Karnal Road,
Delhi-110032

A.T. Goyal Metal Works Pvt. Ltd.,
1, Medl. Road,
Calcutta.

Alloy Castings Works,
42, BCD Govt, Indl. Estate,
Kandivli, Mumbai - 400 067

PLANT ECONOMICS OF TIN PRINTING

Rated Plant Capacity = Tin Printing on 1000 Plates and 100 Kgs. of Anodic Aluminium Items per Day

COST OF LAND & BUILDING

(Total land area required 500 sq. mtr.)	Rs.	2,50,000.00

LIST OF PLANT & MACHINERY

1. Tin printing machine mechanically operated
2. Anodizing plant including agitator
3. Storage tanks. Cap : 250 kgs.
4. Mixing tank with mixer Cap : 500 kgs
5. Pickling unit
6. Miscellaneous equipments & accessories

LIST OF RAW MATERIALS

1. **Section A:** Red colour pigment
2. Varnish
3. Alkyl resin
4. Naphtha
5. Packing material 1/2 kg. tin containers 2,000 nos. (tin plates)
6. **Section B:** Aluminium sheets
7. Sulphuric acid (98 %)
8. Other chemicals
9. Packing materials

FIXED CAPITAL

Land & Building	Rs.	2,50,000.00
Plant & Machinery	Rs.	1,89,000.00
Other Fixed Assets	Rs.	40,000.00
TOTAL	**Rs.**	**4,79,000.00**

TOTAL WORKING CAPITAL/MONTH

Raw Material	Rs.	1,29,260.00
Salary & Wages	Rs.	22,800.00
Utilities & Overheads	Rs.	8,700.00
TOTAL	**Rs.**	**1,60,760.00**

TOTAL CAPITAL INVESTMENT

Total Fixed Capital	Rs.	4,79,000.00
Total Working Capital for 3 Months	Rs.	4,82,280.00
TOTAL	**Rs.**	**9,61,280.00**

TURNOVER/ANNUM

By realization of printed 3,00,000 items

By sale of 30,000 kgs of anodic aluminium items

TOTAL **Rs. 25,05,000.00**

PROFIT = RECEIPTS - COST OF PRODUCTION

= 25,05,000.00 - 21,35,437.20

= 3,69,562.80

PROFIT SALES RATIO = Profit / Sales x 100 = **14.75 %**

RATE OF RETURN = Operating Profit / T.C.I. x 100 = **38.44 %**

BREAK EVEN POINT (B.E.P.) = 50.27 %

Part - 3

DIRECTORY SECTION

(INDIAN & OVERSEAS)

✓ MACHINERIES

✓ RAW MATERIALS

✓ TECHNOLOGIES

Aarkay Wrapping Machines Pvt. Ltd.

1, Hormuz, 131, A.K. Marg,
Mumbai - 400 036

Phone : 3670537,3675277
Fax : 91-22-3670217

Products : Shrink wrapping machines.

AB Kelva

P. O. Box 88-221-00 Lund
Sweden

Phone : +46-46-306000
Fax : +46-46-304913

Products : Web cleaners, diaphragm pumps, air brakes, air powered tension controls

ACIMGA - PUNTO ITALIA

-Italian Manufacturers Association of Machinery for the Graphic, Converting and Paper Industry

Corson Sempione, 4 Milan - Italy

Phone : 02-3495144
Fax : 02-3450647

Products : Promotion of Italian industry of printing & converting machinery manufacturers.

ACME Machinery Co. Pvt. Ltd.

B-3 Royal Industrial Estate,
Naigaum Cross Road, Wadala,
Mumbai - 400 031

Phone : 4146345,4146784
Fax : 4146928

Products : Carton pasting, punching, hydraulic paper cutting, corrugation, printer slotter box stitching & book stitching machines.

Acmevac Pumps and Engineering Pvt. Ltd.

Plot No. 1, Kashimira Industrial Estate,
Behind Kashimira Police Station,
Off. Western Express Highway, Mira,
Distt. Thane (M.S.)

Phone : 8112956,8115788
Fax : 022-8115788

Products: Vacuum pumps, Vacuum-pressure pumps, side channel blowers.

Ahuja Graphic Machinery Pvt. Ltd.

1st Floor, Prabhadevi Indl. Estate,
V.S. Marg, Mumbai - 400 025

Phone : 4222925,4228515,4300854
Fax : 4309195

Products : Rubber blankets, Underpackings, eye glasses, punches, inks, light tables, densitometers, creasing matrix, spray powders, p.s. plates, varnishes.

A.I.R. Engineering Co. Ltd.

A.I.R. Building, Congress Nagar,
Nagpur - 440 010 (M.S.)

Phone : 0712-523283,525123
Fax : 0712-526283

Products : Roll fed printing machine

Aksis Engineering Works (P) Ltd.

139, Sector-25,
Ballabgarh, Faridabad

Phone : 0129-283467,234942
Fax : +91-129-289264

Products : Tara-sheet fed offset (18"X25"), web-o stack-300 stacker, nippling machine (launching).

Amba Lamps Ltd.

10, Canada Close, Banbury, OX16 7RT
United Kingdom

Phone : 44-1295-272666
Fax : 44-1295-272611

Products : UV curing lamps, metal halide lamps, rapsid start lamps, ignitors, chokes, transformers.

Amit International

B-47, Cox House,
Naraina Industrial Area, Phase-II,
New Delhi - 110 028

Phone : 5704201,5704301
Fax : 2249320

Products : Adast dominant offset, programme cutting & hot foil stamping machine.

Andreotti Rotostar S.p.A.

Via Recinto, 4
03024 Ceprano (FR)

Phone : (0775)9161
Fax : (0775)950783

Products : In-and off-line laminating machines, printing presses.

Apple Computer International Limited

Suite 701, The Oberoi
Dr. Zafar Hussain Marg,
New Delhi - 110 003

Phone : 4363030 Ext. 701
Fax : 4362939

Products : Apple- Computers, printers, digital cameras, servers, laptops, softwares, publishing solutions, new technologies.

Arrow Coated Products Ltd.

432, Ansal Chamber-II
6, Bhikaji Cama Place,
New Delhi.

Phone : 6114348
Fax : 011-6115842, 6885149

Products : Printing machine, sign cutting machine, price marking guns etc.

Arvind Rub-Web Controls Limited

'Arvind', Jashodanagar Char Rasta,
N.H. No. 8, P.O. Vatva II,
Ahmedabad - 382 445 (Gujarat)

Phone : 5892367, 5892152, 5832270
Fax : 91-79-5830287

Products : Air expanding shaft, synthetic rubber rollars, web guiding system, rubber expander, polyband expander, quick lock, safety chucks.

Ashton Transmission Company

D-29, Hauz Khas,
New Delhi - 110 016

Phone : 668326, 663724, 660999
Fax : 011-6866386, 8522381

Products : Power transmission belts, conveyor belts, PU tubes/squeezes.

Asian Printing Machinery Co. (P) Ltd.

A-91/1, Naraina Industrial Area,
Phase-I, New Delhi.

Phone : 4363030 Ext. 701
Fax : 4362939

Products : Asian automatic offset printing machine, Asian DX 5215, Asian automatic offset printing machine, Asian DX 5205.

Associated Engineering Corporation & Associated Enterprises

298, Industrial Area, Opp. Mall Mandi,
Amritsar - 143 006 (Punjab)

Phone : 231343,233340(O),231821,232390(R)
Fax : 91-183-230540

Products : Sheet-fed offset, platen punching, fully auto paper guilotine, semi auto paper guilotine, film laminator, book, pamphlet & box stitcher, box making machinery.

Atlantic Zeiser Gmbh Co.

Bogenstn 6-8, 78576, Emmingen,
Germany

Phone : 0049-7465-2910
Fax : 0049-7465-291166

Products : CS-17 Numbering + imprinting machine, ALPHA-50 ink jet/micr - verifyer numbering machines & systems

Atlas Industrial Corporation

R-18, Navin Shahdara,
Delhi - 110 032

Phone : 2284311
Fax : 91-11-2284311

Products : Pad printing machines 1 & 2 colours. Semi-automatic screen printing machine for flats, substrates, round, curved, hollow, cylindrical or slightly conical objects. Semi-automatic metal label printing machine.

Aurelia S.p.A.

Via A. Volta - 16,
20093, Cologno Monzese (MI)

Phone : (02)253071
Fax : (02)25307235

Products : Sheet-fed and web offset machines.

Autopack Machines Pvt. Ltd.

101-C Poonam Chambers, Dr. A.B. Road,
Worli, Mumbai - 400 018

Phone : 4924800, 4925900, 4964926
Fax : 0091-22-4964926

Products : Powder dozing machine, Autofill, Cream Filler, Automatic Cream Filling, horizontal pillow-pack machine, automatic carton overwrapping machine.

Autoprint Machinery Manufacturers Pvt. Ltd

3E-3rd Floor, 'B' Block, CSR Pioneer Complex,
Avinashi Road, Coimbatore - 641 018

Phone : 214051, 214359
Fax : 0422-212130

Products : Autoprint 1510 mini offset printing machine, autoprint 1520 mini offset printing machine, accessories.

Balbro Manufacturing Co.

B-8, 1st Floor, Nehru Ground,
NIT, Faridabad (Haryana)

Phone : (0129) 215016

Products Vacuum/pressure pumps with flange mounted motor.

Baldev Mechanical Works

A-59, Sham Nagar,
New Delhi - 110 018

Phone 5438356

Products : Eccentric slotter (packaging machine), 4 bar rotary (packaging machine), single slotter (packaging machine).

Baldwin Technology / Misomex

65, Rowayton Avenue,
Rowyaton, CT 06853

Phone : 203-8387470
Fax : 203-8527040

Products : Cleaning systems, fountain solution and ink control systems, newspaper inserter equipment, dryers, and automated imposition and plate exposure equipment

Bandhu Group of Companies

8B, Bahadur Shah Zafar Marg,
New Delhi - 110001

Phone : 3316722,3731750,3715547
Fax : 3317947

Products : Web offset presses, form presses, cutting machines and peripherals.

Barco Pte. Ltd. (Barco Graphics)

20 A Lorong Ampas,
QS Building,
Singapore - 328430

Phone : 65-2562126
Fax : 65-256214

Bell Graphics

46/1, Velayutnam Road,
Sivakasi - 626123

Phone : (04560)21550
Fax : (04560)25861

Products : Embossing machine, fabric label printing machine, shrink tunnel.

Bharat Hydraulics

122, East Mohan Nagar,
Amritsar - 143006 (Punjab)

Phone : 230957
Fax : 0183-230957

Products : Hydraulic paper cutting machine & die punching machine.

CERUTTI Giovanni Officine Meccaniche S.p.A.

Via Adam 66, 15033,
Casale Monferrato (AL), Italy

Phone : +39-142-459411
Fax : +39-142-76350

Products : Rotogravure presses (with possibility of flexo combinations) for printing and in-line converting of a wide range of packaging materials. coaters and laminators for processing flexible packaging. Rotogravure presses for special materials

C.M.R. Srl

Viale Industria 59-20037, Paderno D,
Milan, Italy

Phone : (2)99045363
Fax : (2)99045355

Products : Rotogravure-flexographic-dry offset or letter press printing machines, dry-wet-solvent based and solvent less coating and laminating machines, mono and bi-shaft slitting rewinding machine, sheeters, die-cutting machines.

Coates of India Limited

10, Transport Depot Road,
Calcutta - 700 088

Phone : 033-4965913
Fax : 033-4795267

Products : Printing inks, coatings, resins & adhesives.

Converting Machinery

233/B, Netaji Subhash Road,
Howrah - 711 101 (West Bengal)

Phone : 68-3530
Fact. : 6671238

Products : Rotogravure printing machine, wet & dry lamination machine, slitting cum rewinding machine.

C.R. Enterprises

E-26, Nehru Ground,
Faridabad - 121 001
(Haryana)

Phone : 8-216275, 2283303, 85-23063

Products : Screen printing machine.

Didde Web Press

1200, Graphic Arts Road,
Emporia, KS 66801

Phone : (316)342-4740
Fax : (316)342-7383

Products : Narrow web offset printing presses and a collator.

Engineers India Research Institute

4449, Nai Sarak, Main Road,
New Delhi - 110 006

Phone : 2918117, 2916431, 2920361
Fax : 91-11-2916431

Products : Industrial Books, Project Reports, Detailed Project Reports & Industrial Directories on Printing, Packaging and Allied Industries.

Expert Converters (P) Ltd.

274-C, Kiadb Industrial Area,
Bommasandra, Anekal Taluk,
Bangalore - 562 158

Phone : 8422690, 8423177
Fax : 8422037

Products : Multicolour rotogravure printing machine, coating & laminating machine, slitting machine, inspection machine, doctoring machine, cylinder proofing machine.

Fair Deal Engineers

89, Ram Sarup Colony,
Mujessar, Near Sector - 24,
Faridabad - 121 005 (Haryana)

Phone : 0129-8 237143, 234314
Fax : 0129-8 213289

Products : Sheet fed offset printing machine.

Flexotecnica Srl

Strada Per Pezzolo 20080
Tavazzano (Lodi)

Phone : 0371-760572, 760573
Fax : 0371-760574

Products : Flexo printing presses both C.I. and STACK version, from a min. print width of 300 to a max. print width of 3200 mm, from 1 to 12 print elements suitable for printing all flexible materials used for packaging.

Graphic (India)

E-43/3, Okhla Indl. Area, Phase - II,
New Delhi - 110 020

Phone : 6841997, 6841865, 6829357
Fax : (011) 6841873, (022) 2625300

Products : Complete plants for the production of flexible packaging material, printing and converting equipment, cylinder making equipment.

HMT Limited

59, Bellary Road,
Bangalore - 560 032

Phone : 91-(0)80333033,3338546
Fax : 91-(0)803337899

Products : Two colour offset printing machine som 225, single colour offset printing machine som 125 G, programmable guilotine FG 92, automatic paper folding machine.

Holostic India Ltd.

50, Apmchini,
Sri Aurobindo Marg,
New Delhi - 110 017

Phone : 665690,669725
Fax : 6868828

Products : Holograms, holographic films.

Indo-Polygraph Machinery Pvt. Ltd.

88, Okhla Industrial Estate,
New Delhi - 110 020

Phone : 6820531,6842865
Fax : 6848763

Products : Sheet fed offset printing machine, paper cutting machine, stitcher & perfect binder.

Intergrafica Print & Pack Gmbh

401, Bhikaji Cama Bhavan,
11, Bhikaji Cama Place, Ring Road,
New Delhi - 110 066

Phone : 6885882,6885304,673143
Fax : 6872731

Products : Web offset machines, stationery manufacturing machines, label printing and punching machines, plate processing machines, laminating machines.

Iron Craft Industries

A-43-A-Anand Parbhat Industrial Area,
NewDelhi - 110005

Phone : 5751367,5745588

Products : Rotogravure printing machine, slitter-reqinder, flexographic printing machine.

J. Mahabeer & Co. Private Ltd.

3620-21, Netaji Subhash Marg, New Delhi - 110 002

Phone : 3266055 Fax : 3273130

Products : Fast-300 WEB offset printing machines (4 hi + folder, 4 colour satellite, y unit, I unit), dominant - 715 A single colour sheet fed offset printing machine, Dominant - 725 P/A two colour sheetfed offset printing machine, Delta-664 four colour offset printing machine, Dominant - 715 A with numbering, perforating & Imprinting attachment.

Kohli Industries

6/4, Sona Udyog Industrial Estate,
Parsi Panchayat Road,
Andheri (E), Mumbai - 400 069

Phone : 91-22-8324267,8329023
Fax : 91-22-8390729

Products : Rotogravure printing machine.

Komori Chambon Sa

6, Rue Auguste-Rooin-BP 6329
45063 Orleans Cedex 2,
France

Phone : (33)38-64-5500
Fax : (33)38-69-3730

Products : Web fed rotogravure, offset & flexo printing presses with in line rotary die cutters.

Manugraph Industries Limited

Sidhwa House, 2nd Floor, N.A. Sawant Marg,
Colaba, Mumbai - 400 005

Phone : 91-22-2874815,2874788
Fax : 91-22-2870702

Products : Sheet fed offset machines (single & multicolour).

Ohio Electronic Engravers Inc.

4105, Executive Drive, Dayton,
Ohio - 45430 USA

Phone : 513-427-1022
Fax : 513-427-1375

Products : M500 Scanner/engraver/composing system, M820 engraver, Large format colour printer, colour prepresss, alliance systems medallion system, flat bed colour & B/W scanner, novajet, cylinder composition system.

Patel Enterprises

B-1, Navratna, Gulmohar Cross Road No. 12,
J.V.P.D. Scheme, Juhu Vile-Parle (W),
Mumbai - 400 049

Phone : 6232587

Products : Small offset printing press models OM-1015 & OM-1520

Popli Graphics (P) Ltd.

B-39, J.F.F. Complex,
Rani Jhansi Road,
New Delhi - 110 055

Phone : 738513,7778523,7537513

Products : Nova offset machines, size : 18"X25", 18"X28", 29"X30". Plate making equipments : paper cutting machines & allied machinery, technova P.S. plates & chemicals, polyster masters nova dom & consumables & press material.

Rotomec S.p.A.

Strada Statale Casale-Asti Km 5,
15020, San Giorgio Monferrato - Italy

Phone : (0142)4071
Fax : (0142)805501

Products : Rotogravure printing presss ROTOPACK 3000-3.

Speed-O-Graphics (India)

167/37/1, IInd Main Road, Indl. Town,
Rajajinagar, Bangalore - 560 044

Phone : 3355752,3351837
Fax : 3355752

Products : Single colour sheetfed offset printing machine 'Printoram 164', CNC programmable paper cutting machine Parks-92, Pawan-Air pressure vacuum pump.

Stovec Industries limited

N.I.D.C., Near Lambha Village,
Post Narol, Ahmedabad - 382 405 (Gujarat)

Phone : 5890460,5980470
Fax : 079-5890352

Products : Presensitized offset plates, chemicals, plate processor, films and blankets.

Sud & Waren Private Limited

Plot No. 72, Sector - 6, Industrial Estate,
Faridabad - 12_ 006 (Haryana)

Phone : 8-242402,242342
Fax : 91-1_-646-8991

Products : Rotary printing machine, slitter rewinder, rewinding/doctoring machine, printing & paper conversion machinery, computer stationery plant, web offset , letter press & gravure printing machines.

The Graphic House

23, Radha Nagar,
Ballabgarh, (Haryana)

Phone : 8-241887,244104

Products : Single colour sheet-fed offset printing machine (Padmini).

The Printers House Limited

10, Scindia House,
New Delhi - 110 001

Phone : 3313071/72/73/75
Fax : 011-3310490

Products : Orient web offset press for printing newspapers, magazines & books, Reel-fed offset machine etc.

V.S. Resources

4, Alankar Society, Above 'NADCO'
S.V. Road, Andheri (W),
Mumbai - 400 058

Phone : 022-6282976,6283877
Fax : 022-6282976

Products : "Gallentic" small offset press.

Vulcan Polyprint

128, New Apollo Estate, Mogra Lane,
Off. New Nagardas Road, Andheri (E),
Mumbai - 400 069

Phone : 8382424
Fax : 8382423

Products : Flexographic, rotogravure printing machines, dry lamination, slitter, reqinders side, bottom sealing machines.

103. ALUM FOR WATER TREATMENT
104. ALUMINIUM PAINT
105. ALUMINIUM HYDROXIDE GEL
106. ALUMINIUM INGOTS FROM BAUXITE
107 AMLA PLANTATION
108. AMPICILLIN TRIHYDRATE IN CAPSULES WITH STRIP PACKING
109. AMMONIUM CHLORIDE TABLETS
110. AMMONIUM DI-CHROMATE
111. AMMONIUM SULPHATE
112. AMMONIA GAS
113. AMMONIA PAPER
114. AMMONIUM NITRATE
115. AMUSEMENT PARK
116. AMMONIUM CHLORIDE BLOCK
117. AMMONIA LIQUOR
118. AMINO ACID FOR POULTRY FEED
119. AMINES & ALLIED PRODUCTS
120. ANODIC ALUMINIUM LABELS
121. ANGORA RABBIT WOOL
122. ANTI CORROSION LUBRICANTS (No Costing)
123. ANTI SCALE COMPOUND for Adding Sugar Juce Boiling
124. ANTHRAQUINONE
125. ANTIMONY TRI-OXIDE
126. ANTI STATIC POLYTHENE BAGS
127. ANHYDROUS CALCIUM CHLORIDE
128. ANTIMONY
129. APPLE JUICE CONCENTRATE & DEHYDRATED FRUITS & VEG. MANUFACTURING
130. APPLE POMACE PECTIN
131. APPLE JUICES
132. AQUA CULTURE SHRIMP FARM (EOU)
133. AQUA CULTURE PRAWN FARMING (100% EOU)
134. ARTIST COLOURS
135. ARTIFICIAL FLOWERS
136. ARTIFICIAL FISH MEAL for PoultryFeed
137. ARMOURED CABLES
138. ASBESTOS CEMENT PIPE & Fitting for Bldg. Sewerage & Drainage
139. ASBESTOS RIDES & ROOFING SHEET
140. ASBESTOS CEMENT PIPES AND FITTING FOR BUILDING SEWIRAGE & DRAINAGE
141. ASPHALTIC ROOFING SHEET
142. ASH TRAYS FOR MARUTI CARS
143. ASBESTOS FIBRE MOULDED PRODUCTS
144. ASBESTOS GASKET SHEET
145. ASPIRIN
146. ASAFOETIDA (HING)
147. ATRAZIN PESTICIDE
148. AUTO CLUTCH PLATE
149. AUTO TUBE (All Type)
150. AUTO BULBS (HEAD & TAIL)
151. AUTO FLAPS
152. AUTO PISTON & PISTON RING (Piston Assembly - Al. Alloy)
153. AUTO SPOKES
154. AUTO TYRE, TUBE & FLAPS
155. ATTA (MINI FLOUR MILL)
156. AUTOMATIC BISCUIT PLANT
157. AUTOMATIC BREAD PLANT
158. AUTOMATIC BREAD & BISCUIT MAKING PLANT
159. AUTO CABLES
160. AUTO PINS
161. AUTO LEAF SPRING
162. AUTO TELEPHONE RECORDING & ANSWERING M/C.
163. AUTO GEARS
164. AUTO PART (Rubber)
165. AUTO FLOUR MILL
166. AUTO INJECTION MOULDED PLASTIC COMPONENTS

Readily available 15000 Detailed Project Reports

167. AUTO WIRES FOR 2/3 WHEELERS CLUTCH WIRES, BRAKE WIRES, SPEEDO METER WIRE & GEAR WIRES
168. AUTO VOLTAGE STABILIZERS
169. AUTOMOBILE FILTER
170. AUTOMOBILE BUSHES
171. AUTOMATIC BRICK PLANT
172. AUROMINE- O
173. AUTOMOBILE PAINTS
174. AUDIO CASSETTES ASSEMBLY & RECORDING
175. AUDIO & VIDEO CASSETTES
176. AUTOMATIC BOOK BINDING
177. AUTOBODY BUILDING
178. AUTOMOBILE REFRIGERATORS
179. AUTOMOBILE RADIATORS
180. AUTOMATIC VOLTAGE STABILIZER
181. AUTOMOBILE BRAKE SHOES
182. AUDIO MAGNETIC TAPES
183. AUTOMOBILE WORKSHOP & SERVICE CENTER
184. AUTOMOBILE PISTON RINGS
185 AUTOMOBILE PISTONS
186. AUTOMOBILE CYLINDERS FOR TWO WHEELERS
187. AUTOMOBILE WIRES FOR TWO/THREE WHEELERS, CLUTCH WIRE, BRAKE WIRE, SPEEDO METERS WIRE & GEAR WIRES
188. AUTOMATIC PLANT FOR TOFFEE/CANDY MANUFACTURE
189. AUTOMATIC CANDLE UNIT
190. AUTOMATIC VENDING MACHINE FOR HOT & COLD BEVERAGES
191. AUTOMOBILE POLISH
192. AUTOMOBILE BLINKERS
193. AUTOMOBILE GASKET
194. AUTOMOBILE PARTS FOR MARUTI VEHICLE
195. AUTOMOBILE GARAGE/ WORKSHOP FOR TRUCKS (12-15 TRUCKS)
196. AUTOMOBILE PARTS
197. AUTOMOBILE RUBBER PARTS
198. AUDIO CASSETTES SCREW
199. AYURVEDIC MEDICINES
200. AYURVEDIC SHARBAT
201. AYURVEDIC PAIN BALM OINTMENT
202. AZO-DYE STUFFS
203. BABY DIAPERS
204. BACTERICIDA FOR CANE JUICE
205. BADMINTON RACKETS
206. BADMINTON SHUTTLE COCKS
207. BAKELITE MOULDED PRODUCTS
208. BAKERS YEAST
209. BAKELITE SHEETS (PHENOLIC SHEETS) ELECTRICAL GRADE
210. BAKELITE ELECTRICAL ACCESSORIES (SWITCH, SOCKET, PLUG)
211. BAKERY UNIT (BUNS, BREAD, PASTRY, CAKES & TOFFEES)
212. BAKING POWDER
213. BALL POINT PEN REFILLS (100% EOU)
214. BALL POINT PEN REFILLS & INKS
215. BALL BEARING
216. BALLOONS (All Type)
217. BAMBOO STICKS FOR AGARBATTIES
218. BANANA & ITS BYE PRODUCTS

Price Rs. 2500/- for each "Detailed Project Report" Payable in advance through Draft/Cash/M.O. in favour of "ENGINEERS INDIA RESEARCH INSTITUTE". Or Ask by V.P.P. PH.: 291 8117, 291 6431, 292 0361 Fax: 91-11-291 6431 (24 Hrs.)

219. BANANA POWDER
220. BANQUET HALL
221. BAND SAW BLADES
222. BANANA PUREE
223. BARBED WIRE
224. BARIUM CARBONATE
225. BARIUM COMPOUND
226. BARIYAN & PAPPAD
227. BASMATI RICE TRADING
228. BATTERY PLATE
229. BATTERY CONTAINER
230. BAYGON SPRAY
231. BESAN PLANT
232. BED SHEET, BED COVERS, FURNISHING, ETC.
233. BEER PLANT
234. BEES WAX REFINING & BLEACHING
235. BEES WAX
236. BENEFICATION OF CHROMITE ORE PROCESSING CHARGE CHROME
237. BENZENE
238. BENZENE HEXA CHLORIDE
239. BENZYL BENZOATE
240. BENZYL PEROXIDE
241. BETA NAPHTHOLS
242. BI-METAL BUSHES
243. BI-CHROMATES OF SODIUM POTASSIUM & AMMONIUM
244. BINDIA & SINDUR
245. BITUMINIZED COMPOUND FOR WATER PROOFING
246. BITUMINOUS ROAD EMULSION
247. BI-CYCLE MANUFACTURE AND ITS PARTS
248. BI CYCLE PARTS
249. BIO COAL FROM AGRO WASTE
250. BITUMEN
251. BLANKETS
252. BLACK & WHITE T.V. PICTURE TUBE
253. BLEACHING DYEING, PRINTING/ FINISHING OF CLOTH
254. BLEACHING POWDER
255. BLEACHING & REFINING OF BEES WAX
256. BLEACHING & MORDANT DYEING OF YARN
257. BLACK/WHITE TV PICTURE TUBE
258. BLACK PEPPER
259. BLISTER FILM PVC
260. BLOCK BOARD
261. BLOCK MAKING
262. BLOOD BAGS
263. BLOW MOULDED PLASTIC CONTAINER
264. BLACK & GALVANIZED STEEL CONDUIT PIPES
265. BLEACHING LIQUOR (CALCIUM HYPO CHLORITE LIQUOR)
266. BLOWING AGENT
267. BLUE DETERGENT POWDER
268. BOILER DE-SCALING COMPOUNDS
269. BOOT/SHOE POLISH
270. BORIC ACID
271. BONE MILL
272. B.O.P.P. FILMS
273. BOPP TAPES
274. BORAX
275. BOARD MILL BASED ON RICE STRAW

276. BONE CRUSHING
277. BOLTS (MILD STEEL)
278. BOTTLING PLANT
279. B.P HARD COKE
280. BRAKE LININGS
281. BRAKE OIL, COOLANT & PACKING OF LUBE OIL & GREASE
282. BRAKE OIL
283. BRASS/COPPER SHEET CIRCLES & UTENSILS
284. BRA & PANTY (HOSIERY)
285. BREAD PLANT
286. BRICK FROM FLY ASH
287. BRASS HOLDERS
288. BRASS & COPPER TUBES
289. BRANDY
290. BRIQUETTED FUEL FROM AGRO WASTE
291. BRASS UTENSILS
292. BRASS SHEET ROLLING
293. BRASS PIPES
294. BRASS WARES
295. BROILER CHICKEN
296. BRASS STAIRCASE & WROUGHT IRON, RODS, RAILING, GATE & GRILL
297. BULK DRUGS
298. BUTTON FROM HOOVES & HORNS
299. BUILDING HARDWARE OF ALUMINIUM
300. BUTT HINGES OF BRASS SHEET
301. BUFFING & POLISHING COMPOUNDS
302. BUS TRANSPORT COMPANY
303. BUBBLE GUM & CHEWING GUM
304. .BUFFALO MEAT PROCESSING
305. BUTTONS (PLASTIC) FROM POLYESTER SHEETS & RODS
306. BUSINESS CENTRE (JOB WORK)
307. BUS AND TRUCK BODY BUILDING
308. CABLE JELLY COMPOUND
309. CASSETTE RECORDER/ PLAYER (STEREO)
310. CAMPHOR
311. CATTLE & POULTRY FEED
312. CARBON DIOXIDE
313. CARBON BRUSHES
314. CARBON ZINC CELL
315. CARBON-ACTIVATED
316. CARBON- ONE TIME
317. CARBON - HIGH FERRO
318. CARBON BLACK
319. CARBON BLACK FROM NATURAL GAS
320. CARBON ELECTRODE
321. CARBON BLACK FROM NATURAL GAS
322. CARBON POTENTIO METERS
323. CARBON MONO-OXIDE FOR WATER GAS
324. CARBON SEAL
325. CARBON POWDER
326. CARBON PAPER
327. CARBON PLATES - GRAPHITE
328. CARBON/METAL FILM RESISTORS
329. CARBON - (CINE-ARC)
330. CARD BOARD SLATE
331. CAPACITORS
332. CALCIUM CARBIDE
333. CALCIUM SILICATE BLOCKS
334. CARBONATED BEVERAGES
335. CAR BURGLAR ALARM
336. CAUSTIC SODA
337. CALCIUM CARBONATES
338. CAR AIR FRESHNER
339. CAR SHAMPOO
340. CASTOR OIL
341. CATTLE FEED
342. CATTLE & POULTRY FEEDS
343. CAST STEEL PANS FOR MELTING FURNACE
344. CAST IRON PIPES & FITTINGS (VERTICAL) FOR DOUBLE FLANGED PIPES
345. CALCINING OF MANGANESE & DEAD BURNT MANGANESE
346. CALCIUM CARBONATE BASED ON STEAM COAL
347 CASING UNIT OF SAUSAGE FOOD (100% EOU)
348. CARPET WOOL YARN SPINNING
349. CANNING OF MANGO PULP & MANGO SLICES
350. CAFFEINE BY TEA WASTE
351. CALCINED PETROLEUM COKE
352. CALCIUM CARBONATE, MAGNESIUM CARBONATE & METAL FROM DOLOMITE
353. CALCIUM CASEINATE & SODIUM CASEINATE

354. CAMERA (35 M.M)
355. CARTONS FOR DISTILLERY
356. CASHEWNUT SHELL LIQUID & KERNELS (CNSL)
357. CARPET WOOLLEN YARN DYEING
358. CASTOR OIL HYDROGENATION
359. CASTOR OIL REFINING
360. CANDLE (Semi Automatic)
361. CAST IRON POWDER
362. CASEIN BASED PIGMENTS USED IN SPORT INDUSTRY
363. CASHEWNUT (Dried & Fried)
364. CARD/GREY BOARD
365. CANDLE (NON DRIP)
366. CATTLE FEED BY TAPIOCA
367. CAUSTIC SODA/CHLORINE PLANT MEMBRANE CELL
368. CARBOXY METHYL CELLULOSE
369. CANNING & PRESERVATION OF FRUIT & VEGETABLE
370. CANNING & PRESERVATION OF FRUITS & VEGETABLE WITH COLD STORAGE & RAISIN (KISMISH MAKING)
371. CASSETTE TAPES (COVER)
372. CANVAS SHOES, JUNGLE BOOT, RUBBER KNEES & BOOT COMBAT
373. CALCIUM SILICATE
374. CALCIUM GLUCONATE
375. CANVAS SHOES
376. CASTOR OIL EMULSIFIER
377. CASEIN FROM MILK
378. CARPET WEAVING
379. CABLES FOR CABLE NETWORK
380. CABLE (FLAT/RIBBEN)
381. CABLES FOR AUTOMOBILE
382. CABLES (PVC WIRE)
383. CABLES-ARMOURED
384. CABLES-TEFLON COATED
385. CABLES-TELEPHONE
386. CABLES- XLPE/PVC
387. CABLES-WELDING
388. CABLES-OPTICAL FIBRE
389. CANNING OF ROSGULLAS IN METAL CANS
390. CALCIUM NITRATE
391. CATIONIC SOFTENER
392. CANNING & BOTTLING OF FRUITS & VEGETABE PRODUCTS
393. CATECHU (KATTHA) - CHEMICAL PROCESS
394. CATTLE BREEDING
395. CARPET DRY CLEANING
396. CAR AIR CONDITIONERS
397. CARBOXY METHYL CELLULOSE (C.M.C.)
398. CARD BOARD MATCH BOXES
399. CARDINAL FROM C.N.S.L.
400. CAPACITOR DISCHARGE IGNITION (CIDI Unit)
401. CASHEWNUT KERNEL EXTRACTION FROM CASHEWNUT FRUIT
402. CARBON ZINC CELL (DRY CELL)
403. CANDY HARD BOILED
404. CASHEW FENI (WINE DISTILLATION FROM FRUITS & CASHEWNUT)
405. CARD BOARD BOXES & CARTONS (SYSTEM PACK)
406. CAR PAINTS
407. CAR POLISHES
408. CASTOR OIL DERIVATIVE OLEORESIN
409. CANNED FRUITS & VEGETABLES
410. CANNED FRUITS & VEGETABLES
411. CANNED FRUITS & VEGETABLES
412. CERAMIC INSULATOR
413. CERAMIC CORES & TUBES
414. CEMENT PLANT
415. CHEESE (Processed)
416. CEMENT ROOFING TILES
417 CERAMIC TILES (GLAZED)

EIRI

Pioneer Yesterday, Leader Today & Supremo Tomorrow

418. CELLULOSE ACETATE
419. CEMENT WATER PROOF COMPOUND
420. CEMENT PAINT
421. CEMENT PLANT (800 TPD)
422. CEMENT COLOUR/LIME COLOUR (SYNTHETIC RED IRON OXIDE) USED FOR FLOORING
423. CEMENT FROM RICE HUSK
424. CEMENT (CLINKER)
425. CEMENT FROM FLY ASH AND LIME
426. CEILING FAN
427. CENTRIFUGAL PUMP
428. CELLULOSE POWDER & MICRO CRYSTALLINE CELLULOSE POWDER
429. CELLULOSE ACETATE MOULDING POWDER
430. CERAMIC NOVELTIES
431. CERAMIC TRANSFERS (FOR PRINTING ON CERAMICS)
432. CERAMIC COATED ALUMINIUM THREAD GUIDE
433. CERAMIC THREAD GUIDE
434. CERAMIC FIRING/ DECORATIVE TILES
435. CEMENT POLE, JALLIE & TILE
436. CHEMICAL LABORATORY
437. CERAMIC CROCKERY WARE (Bone China - Hitkari)
438. CHEMICAL RESISTANT IRON & STEEL
439. CERAMIC GLAZED TILES
440. CEMENT GRINDING
441. CEMENT OXIDE
442. CERAMIC MAGNET
443. CEMENT TILES (LAYING OVER RCC ROOFS)
444. CHINA CLAY
445. CHOKES, TRANSFORMERS & ELIMINATORS
446. CHOLORINATED PARAFFIN WAX
447. CHICKEN/MUTTON (SHEEP MEAT) PROCESSING
448. CHICKEN/MEAT PROCESSING AND PACKAGING
449. CHROME PLATED (C.P.) BATH RCOM FITTINGS
450. CHOKES & PATTIES
451. CHAIN LINK FENCING OUT OF PVC COATED WIRE
452. CHEWING TOBACCO
453. CHROMIC ACID
454. CHINESE SOYA SAUCE
455. CHROMIC ACID
456. CHEWING GUM
457. CHLORAM PHENICOL
458. CHELATED ZINC (Zn-EDTA)
459. CHILLI POWDER
460. CHOCOLATE
461. CHEWING GINGER & AMLOKI
462. CHROME PLATING
463. CHOKE & STARTER
464. CHOKE OF FLUORESCENT TUBES
465. CHEMICAL ETCHING OF STAINLESS STEEL
466. CHEMICAL LAMINATION OF PHOTO
467. CHLORINATED RUBBER BASED PLANT
468. CITRONELLA OIL
469. CINEMA HALL
470. CIGARETTES
471. CIGARETTES- HERBAL
472. CINNAMON BARK OIL
473. CINE-ARC- CARBON
474. C.I. CASTINGS (FOUNDRY) BY INDUCTION FURNACE
475. CITRIC ACID BY MOLASSES
476. CIGARETTE & BIDI
477. CIDER PLANT (APPLE WINE)
478. CITRONELLA OIL
479. C.I. POWDER BY GRINDING PROCESS
480. CLOVE OIL
481. CLOTH (COTTON PROCESSING & FINISHING OF CLOTH)
482. CLUTCH WIRE FROM DRAWN WIRE
483. CLEANING OF COOLING SYSTEM & BOILER

484. CLAY PLATES FOR ELECTRIC HEATERS
485. CLUTCH PLATE FOR 4 WHEELERS
486. CLUTCH PLATE FOR 3 WHEELER
487. CLEANING POWDER (VIM)
488. CLUTCH FACING & BRAKE LINING
489. CLEAR TRANSPARENT LACQUER FOR COATING ON BRASS BANGLES TO MAKE IT WEATHER RESISTANT
490. CLINICAL THERMOMETER
491. C.N.S.L. BASED RESIN IN LIQUID & Powder Form
492. COPPER WIRE DRAWING & ENAMELING
493. CORDLESS PHONE
494. CONCENTRATION OF MANGANESE ORE
495. COPPER & BRASS TUBES
496. CORRUGATED SHEET BOARD & BOXES
497. COPPER BOTTOM STAINLESS STEEL UTENSILS
498. COOLING COILS FOR AIR CONDITIONERS
499. COLOUR LAB (QSS-PHOTO)
500. COMPUTER CONTINUOUS STATIONERY
501. COMPUTER ASSEMBLY
502. COMPUTER MONITOR
503. COMPUTER RIBBON
504. COMPUTER RIBBON REFILLING & REINKING
505. COMPUTER MONITOR TUBE & T.V. PICTURE TUBE (B/W)
506. COMPUTER SOFTWARE (100% EOU)
507. COMPUTER FORMS AND SECURITY PRINTING PRESS
508. COMPUTER FORM (COMPUTER STATIONERY)
509. COMPUTER JOB WORK
510. COMPUTER ATTENDANCE REGISTER
511. COMPUTER PRINTER
512. COMPUTER KEYBOARD
513. COMPUTER EDUCATION INSTITUTE
514. COMPUTER (MINI/ PERSONAL)
515. COMPUTER-LAPTOP
516. COMPUTER PERIPHERALS
517. COMPUTER STATIONERY AND IMPORTED HARDWARE PARTS
518. COOLANT ENGINE
519. COLLEGE
520. COLD DRINKS
521. COLD PROCESSED TYRE RETREADING
522. COLD STORAGE
523. COLD STORAGE & ICE
524. COLD ROLLING MILL
525. COLD PROCESSED TREAD RUBBER
526. COLD CREAMS
527. COLD ROLLING OF STEEL STRIPS
528. COLD ROLLED PRESSED STEEL DOORS, WINDOW FRAMES
529. COTTON ADHESIVE TAPES & PLASTER OF PARIS BANDAGES For Hospital
530. COLOUR & B/W TV
531. COLOUR TELEVISION
532. COSTUME JEWELLERY
533. COTTON SEED OIL
534. COTTON YARN
535. CONDUIT IRON PIPES (C.I.PIPES)
536. CONDENSED MILK SWEETENED
537. COIR FOAM (RUBBERIZED COIR) CUSHION & MAT ETC.
538. CONCRETE HOLLOW BRICK/ BLOCKS
539. CONDENSED MILK
540. COCONUT OIL
541. COFFEE PLANTATION
542. COBALT OCTOATE
543. COIR PITH
544. COPPER NITRATE
545. CONCENTRATE OF TOMATO (TOMATO PASTE)

546. CONFERENCE BAG, FOLDERS ETC. (PLASTIC)
547. CORN FLAKES
548. COATING ON PLASTICS
549. COPPER OXY-CHLORIDES
550. COPPER PHTHALOCYNINE BLUE & GREEN
551. COATED PAPER & BOARD
552. CONVERTER
553. COPPER CLAD LAMINATES FOR PCB'S (PAPER & FABRIC BASED)
554. COPPER RODS FROM SCRAPS
555. COLLECTION OF MILK & PACKAGING IN POLYTHENE POUCHES (MILK CHILLING)
556. COURIER SERVICES
557. CONFECTIONERY
558. CONFECTIONERY INDUSTRY-SEMI AUTOMATIC PLANT (TOFFEE & CANDY MANUFACTURING)
559. COAL BRIQUETTING FROM COAL
560. COAL BRIQUETTES FROM AGRO WASTE
561. COUNTRY LIQUOR
562. COPPER STRIPS COILS
563. CONCAST STEEL BAR
564. COATING & PRINTING OF LAMINATED PAPER POUCH
565. COATING & LAMINATION ON PAPER (HOT MELT FILM LAMINATION METHOD)
566. COUNTRY LIQUOR FROM MOLASSES
567. COSMETIC UNIT
568. COMPOSITE CONTAINER
569. COPPER BERYLLIUM ALLOY SPRINGS
570. COLOUR MASTER BATCH FOR VARIOUS PLASTICS
571. COMPACT DISC PLAYER
572. COMPACT DISC (CD)
573. COTTON FINISHING
574. CONSTANT VOLTAGE TRANSFORMER (C.V.T.)
575. CORROSION CONTROLLING CHEMICAL (PIPE LINE)
576. COPPER FOIL
577. COPPER & BRASS INGOTS
578. COMPRESSOR (HERMETIC) FOR AIR CONDITIONER
579. COATING ON PLASTICS & GLASS
580. COATING OF CLEAR TRANSPARENT LACQUER ON BRASS BANGLES TO MAKE IT WEATHER RESISTANT
581. COCONUT PLANTATION
582. COCONUT PRODUCTS & BYE PRODUCTS PROCESSING COMPLEX (WET FRESH) 100% EOU
583. CONVEYER BELTS
584. COPPER SULPHATE
585. COIR INDUSTRY
586. COSMETIC (HERBAL & SYNTHETIC)
587. COTTON & ACRYLIC YARN SPINDLES
588. CO-EXTRUSION MULTI-LAYER FILM
589. COLOURED FLAME CANDLE
590. COMMUTATOR FOR ELECTRIC MOTOR
591. COTTON BUDS/SWABS
592. COATING ON METALLIZED POLYE-STER FILM/ METALLIZED PAPER/ ALUMINIUM FOILS
593. COOLER BODY & TRUNK (FABRICATION UNIT)
594. COSMETIC, DETERGENT POWDER & PERFUMERY COMPOUND
595. COLOUR MASTER BATCHES FOR VARIOUS PLASTICS
596. COUNTRY LIQUOR
597. COBALT OCTOATE

598. CONDENSER FOR MOTOR
599. COAL GRINDING
600. COCOA POWDER
601. COTTON ROLLS
602. COSTUME/IMITATION/ ARTIFICIAL JEWELLERY (CHAINS & BANGLES)
603. CONCENTRATE OF ROSE, JASMINE & LILLY EXTRACT
604. COPPER WINDING FOR SUBMERSIBLE PUMP & MOTOR
605. COMPACT FLUORESCENT TUBES
606. CONE FOR SOFTY ICE CREAM
607. CORRUGATION OF PLAIN GALVANIZED SHEET
608. CORN FLAKES
609. COTTON GINNING & PRESSING
610 COMPUTER PERIPHERALS
611. COMPUTER HARDWARE
612. COMPACT DISC PLAYER (AUDIO/VIDEO)
613. CO_2 WELDING WIRE
614. COPPER POWDER
615. COPPER EXTRACTION FROM PCB WASTES
616. CRYSTAL TABLEWARE
617. CRUCIBLE BY FIRE CLAY
618. CRACKING OF KERNELS (DESHELLING/DECORTICATING)
619. CRICKET BAT/BALL
620. CROCKERY WARES
621. CRAYON WAX
622. CRITICAL AUTO BODY SHEET METAL PARTS
623. CREPE BANDAGES
624. CUBICAL ELECTRICAL PANEL BOARD (SWITCH BOARD)
625. CUSHION COMPOUND, THREAD & VULCANIZING SOLUTION, FORMULATION AND MANUFACTURE
626. CUTLERY & SILVER JEWELLERY (GOLD PLATED)
627. CUTLERY (STAINLESS STEEL)
628. CURRY POWDER
629. CUTTING OIL
630. CYCLE & RIKSHAW FRAMES
631. CYANIDE ZINC BRIGHTENER
632. CYCLE TYRE & TUBES
633. CYLINDER LINERS FOR AUTOMOBILES
634. CYCLE HANDLE BAR GRIPS
635. CYCLE SPOKES
636. DAIRY FARM & PRODUCTS
637. DAIRY FARM AND DAIRY (MILK) PRODUCTS (PASTEURISED MILK, BUTTER, CAKE & PANEER)
638. DAIRY PRODUCTS
639. DAIRY PRODUCTS & MILK PACKAGING IN POUCHES
640. DALL/PULSE MILL
641. DAIRY FARM & MILK PDTS.
642. DAIRY PLANT
643. DETERGENT POWDER
644. DETERGENT CAKE & POWDER
648. DECORATIVE LAMINATED SHEET (SUNMICA)
649. DESK TOP PUBLISHING(DTP)
650. DEHYDRATED ONIONS & ONION POWDER
651. DEHYDRATION OF FRUITS & VEGETABLES
652. DEXTROSE SALINE
653. DEXTROSE FROM POTATO
654. DEHYDRATED GARLIC FLAKES
655. DEXTRIN & STARCH BASED ADHESIVE
656. DEXTRIN
657. DEXTROSE 5%
658. DEXTROSE (ANHYDROUS) FROM STARCH
659. DESICCATED COCONUT POWDER

660. DEXTROSE POWDER FROM STARCH
661. DEAD BURNT DOLOMITE
662. DETERGENT CAKE
663. DEXTROSE SALINE (I.V. FLUID) IN PLASTIC BOTTLES
664. DETERGENT WASHING POWDER (ARIEL TYPE)
665. DEHYDRATED CASTOR OIL
666. DENIM JEANS & JACKETS
667. DENIM CLOTH (INTEGRATED UNIT WITH BLEACHING, DYEING & PRINTING)
668. DETTOL TYPE ANTISEPTIC LOTION
669. DEPARTMENTAL STORE
670. DEHYDRATION OF VEGETABLES
671. DENIM CLOTH
672. DEHYDRATION AND CANNING OF FRUITS & VEGETABLES
673. DEHYDRATION OF FRUITS, VEGETABLES & NON-VEGETABLE PRODUCTS
674. DE-HULLING OF JAUN FOR BEER INDUSTRY
675. D.G. SET
676. DHOOP BATTI STICK
677. DISPOSABLE PLASTIC SYRINGES (STERILIZED)
678. DISPOSABLE PLASTIC CUPS, GLASSES, ETC.
679. DISTILLED WATER AMPOULES
680. DI-OCTYL PHTHALATE(DOP)
681. DISTRIBUTION TRANSFORMER
682. DIRECT COTTON DYE (NO COST ESTIMATION)
683. DIARY EQUIPMENT
684. DIAZO COATING LUMINESCENT PIGMENT
685. DISTILLED WATER
686. DISPOSABLE CIGARETTE GAS LIGHTER
687. DISPOSABLE NEEDLES
688. DIE MAKING FOR SHEET METAL WORKING
689. DIAMOND TOOLS FOR CUTTING / DRILLING & POLISHING
690. DIRECT BLACK DYE
691. DISH ANTENNA
692. DI-CALCIUM PHOSPHATE FROM ANIMAL BONES
693. DI-CALCIUM PHOSPHATE FROM ROCK PHOSPHATE
694. DIGITAL ELECTRONIC WATCHES
695. DISTILLATION OF ROSIN AND TURPENTINE
696. DIAMOND IMPREGNATED SEGMENTS (METAL BONDED) FOR MARBLE SAWING
697. DI-NITRO CHLORO BENZENE (D.N.C.B.)
698. DI-ETHYL PHTHALATE (DEP)
699. DISH ANTENNA & SATELLITE EQUIPMENTS.
700. DIAMOND CUTTING & EXPORT
701. DI-ETHYL OXALATE
702. DISPOSABLE BABY DIAPER
703 DIAGANOSTIC CENTRE
704. DIESEL GENERATOR SETS
705. 4,4-DIAMINO STILBENE 2,2 - DISULPHONIC ACID
706. DOOR BELL
707. DOOR LOCKS/PAD LOCKS
708. DODECYCLE BENZENE SULPHONATE
709. DOUGH MOULDING COMPOUND
710. DRY ICE
711. DRY DISTEMPER & LIME COLOURS
712 DRY GINGER
713. DRY CELL
714. DRYING OF RED CHILLIES, HALDI, DHANIA, PEAS, AND GREEN PEAS
715. DROSS LEAD SCRAP, LEAD POWDER
716. DRY CELLS & STORAGE BATTERIES

717. DRUM CLOSURES
718. DRIP IRRIGATION
719. DRY FRUIT ROASTING & PACKING
720. D.T.P. & OFFSET PRESS
721. D.T.P. CUM TABLE OFFSET
722. DUPLICATING INK
723. DUPLICATING INK (BLACK) FOR GESTENER DUPLICATOR
724. DUPLICATING STENCIL PAPER
725. DUPLEX/FILE BOARD
726. DYE STUFFS
727. DYE INTERMEDIATE
728. DYE FIXING AGENTS
729. DYEING OF HANK YARN FOR POWER LOOM
730. EAF BASED STEEL
731. EARTH LEAKAGE CIRCUIT BREAKERS (ELCB)
732. EASTER GUM (NCCOSTING)
733. E.C.G/E.E.G. PAPER
734. EDIBLE & NON EDIBLE OIL
735. EDTA AND ITS SALT
736. EDIBLE OIL (MUSTARD OIL)
737. EGG POWDER
738. EGG POWDER (100% EOU - AUTOMATIC IMPORTED PLANT)
739. EGG TRAY
740. EHT TRANSFORMER
741. ELECTRICAL GLS LAMP
742. ELECTRIC FANS
743. ELECTRONIC SERVICE CENTRE
744. ELECTRONICCHOKE
745. ELECTRICAL APPLIANCES
746. ELECTRONIC FLASHER FOR AUTOMOBILES
747. ELECTRONIC TOYS
748. ELECTRONIC GAS LIGHTER (MULTI SPARK)
749. ELECTRONIC TIMER
750. ELECTRONIC ENERGY METER
751. ELECTRIC IRON
752. ELECTRICAL INSULATION TAPES (USING BOPP FILM)
753. ELECTRONIC BALLAST (CHOKE)
754. ELECTRICAL LAMP (GLS)
755. ELECTRONIC QUARTZ CLOCK/WALL CLOCK
756. ELECTRICAL STAMPING
757. ELECTRONIC INDICATOR
758. ELECTRONIC TELEPHONES
759. ELECTRO MAGNETICRELAY
760. ELECTROPLATING ON GOLD AND THEIR CHEMICAL TREATMENT IN GOLDEN COLOUR & SILVER THREAD
761. ELECTROPLATING SCHEME PLANT
762. ELECTROPLATING OF SILVER & SILVER
763. ELECTRICAL INSULATION TAPE (USING BOPP FILM)
764. ELECTRICAL LAMP (INCANDESCENT LAMP)
765. ELECTRICAL REPAIR
766. ELECTRICAL HORN FOR AUTOMOBILE
767. ELECTROPLATING BRIGHTNER
768. ELECTROLYTIC CAPACITOR (MOTOR START)
769. ELECTRIC HEATER CLAY PLATES
770. ELECTRIC LAMP ADHESIVE POWDER
771. ELECTRONIC FAN REGULATOR
772. ELECTRICAL ACCESSORIES (SWITCH, SOCKET, PLUG,)
773. ELECTRO CARDIOGRAM MACHINE (ECG MACHINE)
774. ELECTRIC PORTABLE TOOL
775. ELECTRO POLISHING OF STEEL
776. ELECTROPLATING CHEMICALS
777. ELECTRIC MIXER
778. ELECTRIC CABLES (POWER AND CONTROL CABLES, MINING CABLES, FRLS CABLES, INSTRUMENTATION CABLES, SCREENED CABLES, SUBMERSIBLE PUMP CABLE ETC.)

779. ELECTRONIC SECURITY SYSTEMS
780. ELECTRONIC T.V. TUNER
781. ELECTRONIC TEST & MEASURING INSTRUMENT
782. ELECTRONIC TELEPHONES
783. ELECTRONIC TIMER (PROCESSED CONTROL)
784. ELECTRO REFINING OF ZINC
785. ELECTRONIC FLASH GUN
786. ELECTRONIC MAIL (E-MAIL)
787. ELECTRICAL AND ELECTRONIC PANEL METER (ANALOGUE, DIGITAL, VOLTMETER ETC.)
788. ELECTRICAL MOTOR STARTER
789. ELECTRONIC FIRE ALARM
790. ELECTRIC SWITCHES, PLUGS, SOCKETS & OTHER ACCESSORIES
791. ELECTRIC WATER HEATER
792. ELECTRIC MOTOR WINDING (FOR FAN, MIXIES ETC.)
793. ELASTIC & RIGID TAPES
794. ELECTROPLATING BRIGHTNER FOR NICKEL
795. ELECTRICAL FIXTURES (CHOKES & STARTER, PATTIES LIGHTENING FIXTURES ETC.)
796. ELECTROPLATING UNIT
797. ELASTIC THREADS & TWINE
798. ELECTRIC GENERATORS
799. ELECTRIC MOTOR
800. EMERGENCY LIGHT
801. EMBOSSING POWDER OR RESIN COMPOUND
802. EMERY POWDER
803. EMPTY AMPOULES
804. EMULSIFIER FOR PESTICIDE
805. EMPTY GELATIN CAPSULES
806. EMERY PAPER CLOTH
807. EMULSIFIER FOR CUTTING OIL
808. EMULSION PAINTS
809. EMPIRE SLEEVINGS
810. ENAMELING OF COPPER WIRE
811. ENGINEERING WORK SHOP
812. ENAMEL WARE
813. ENDOSULFAN
814. ENGINE VALVE
815. EPABX/EPAX SYSTEM
816. EPOXY RESINS & METAL FILLING COMPOUND
817. EPOXY RESIN BASED PRIMER (PUTTY)
818. EPOXY TRANSFORMER (CURRENT & POTENTIAL)
819. EPOXY RESIN
820. ERW STEEL CONDUIT PIPE
821. E.R.W. PIPES
822. ERW TUBES
823. ESSENTIAL OILS
824. ESSENCE & SOFT DRINK CONCENTRATE
825. ETHYL ALCOHOL FROM MOLASSES
826. ETHYL ACETO ACETATE FROM ALCOHOL
827. ETHYL HEXANOL FROM ETHYL ALCOHOL
828. ETHYLENE GLYCOL MONO STEARATE ETHYLENE GLYCOL DI-STEARATE
829. ETHYL ACETATE
830. ETHYL ACETATE
831. ETCHING OF BRASS
832. ETCHING PROCESS
833. EUCALYPTUS OIL
834. EUCALYPTUS TREE PLANTATION
835. EXERCISE NOTE BOOK & REGISTER
836. EXPANDED POLYSTYRENE MOULDING
837. EXTRACTION OF OIL (CARDAMOM, JEERA ETC.)
838. EXTRACTION OF GLUE POWDER
839. EXPANDED POLYSTYRENE EXTRUSION PROFILE USED FOR MATCH BOX MAKING

840. EXTRACTION OF ALKALOID FROM SOLANIUM KHASIANUM
841. EXTRACTION OF GOLD, SILVER & COPPER
842. EXTRACTION OF ESSENTIAL OIL AND PACKING OF GROUND SPICES (100% EOU)
843. EXTRACTION OF EDIBLE OIL FROM OIL SEEDS (EXPANDER - EXTRUSION COOKING PROCESS)
844. EXTRACTION OF ACID OIL FROM SOAP STOCK
845. EXHAUST FAN
846. EXTRACTION OF OIL FROM WAX, GENERATED AS A BYE PRODUCT FOR PETRO CHEMICALS
847. EXTRACTION OF JASMINE ESSENCE
848. EXTRACTION OF ALKALOIDS FROM VINCA ROSEA
849. EXTRACTION OF CHEMICAL FROM D.M.O
862. FAST COLOUR
863. FATTY ACID FROM WASTE VEGETABLE
864. FASTENERS (NUTS, BOLT, RIVET & WASHER)
865. FERRO ALLOYS
866. FERRIC ALUM
867. FERRO CEMENT
868. FERROUS SILICATE
869. FERRO MANGANESE ON ALUMINA THERMIC PROCESS
870. FERRO SILICON
871. FERRITE COURSE
872. FERRIC CHLORIDE
873. FEED MILLS (CATTLE & POULTRY FEED)
874. FERRO ALLOYS (OF NIOBIUM, MOLYBDENUM, TITANIUM, TUNGSTEN & VANADIUM)
875. FIBRE BASED BITUMINOUS WATER PROOF FELT
876. FROZEN FOODS, FRUIT & VEGETABLE PROCESSING WITH BACKWARD LINKAGES (100% EOU)
901. FLEXO GRAPHIC & ROTO GRAVURE PRINTING INK
902. FLOURSPER BRIQUETTES
903. FLUSHING CISTERN
904. FLOPPY DISKETTES
905. FLORICULTURE (CUT FLOWER) - 100% EOU
906. FLORICULTURE (CUT FLOWER) WITH GREEN HOUSE TECHNOLOGY
907. FLUORESCENT TUBE
908. FLY ASH BRICKS
909. FLOOR POLISH
910. FLUORESCENT TUBES & GLS LAMPS
911. FLUSH DOOR, CHIP BOARDS, INSULATING BOARDS & HARD BOARD
912. FLOAT GLASS
913. FLOOR COVERING SHEET
914. FLOUR MILL (ROLLER)
915. FLOUR MILL (GRINDER/ PULVIRIZED)
916. FLUORESCENT TUBE & CHOKE
917. FLUORESCENT POWDER FOR FLURESCENT TUBES

850. EXTRACTION OF SOYBEAN OIL FROM SOYBEAN (EXPANDER EXTRUSION - COOKING PROCESS) WITH SOYA GRITS
851. EXTRACTION AND FILTRATION OF EDIBLE OIL
852. EXTRACTION & FILTRATION UNIT FOR EDIBLE OIL
853. EXTRUDED ALUMINIUM SECTION
854. EXTRACTION & REFINING OF VEGETABLE OIL
855. FABRICATION WORKSHOP TO MANUFACTURE TRUSSES & TANKS (PRESSURE VESSELS)
856. FABRICATION OF STORAGE TANKS AND M. S. DRUMS
857. FAT LIQUOR
858. FAST FOOD PARLOR
859. FACSIMILE/FAX MACHINE
860. FABRICATION INDUSTRIES (WORKS) FOR S.S & M.S VESSELS WITH ELECTRO-PLATING UNIT (TOOLROOM)
861. FATTY ACID
877. FERRITE MAGNETS
878. FERROUS SULPHATE
879. FERRITE CORE TRANS-FORMERS
880. FERRO SILICON
881. F.H.P. MOTOR
882. FILE /DUPLEX BOARD
883. FILTERS FOR ALL VEHICLES
884. FIBRE REINFORCED PLASTIC
885. FISH FARMING
886. FISH CANNING & POUCHING
887. FISH OILS
888. FIRE BRICKS
889. FIBRE GLASS
890. FIRE WORKS & PYRO TECHNIQUE
891. FILM STUDIO (VIDEO)
892. FISH (PRAWN & OTHERS) & MARINE PRODUCTS
893. FISH MEAL
894. FISH NET
895. FIRE EXTINGUISHER
896. FLAT/RIBBON CABLES
897. FLUSH DOORS
898. FLOCK PRINTING
899. FLAVOURED MILK
900. FLIP TOP CANS
918. FLEXOGRAPHIC & ROTOGRAVURE PRINTING
919. FLEXOGRAPHIC PRINTING INKS
920. FOAM AND ITS PROD-UCTS AS MATTRESSES (CUSHION, PILLOWSHEET)
921. FORMALDEHYDE
922. FOOD COLOUR
923. FORGING (NON FERROUS)
924 FORGING PLANT (FOR MANUCATURING OIL/GAS PIPE FITTINGS
925. FOUNDRY & MACHINING JOB WORK UNIT
926. FORMIC ACID
927. FOOD GRADE CALCIUM CHLORIDE
928. FOODDEHYDRATION
929. FORMAL DEHYDE RESIN
930. FORMULATION FOR DDT, BHC, MELETHION
931. FORGING PLANT (FOR MANUFACTURING OIL/GAS PIPE FITTINGS)
932. FOUNDRY/C.I. CASTINGS
933. FOAM BOOSTERS

Price Rs. 2500/- for each "Detailed Project Report" Payable in advance through Draft/Cash/M.O. in favour of "ENGINEERS INDIA RESEARCH INSTITUTE". Or Ask by V.P.P. PH.: 291 8117, 291 6431, 292 0361 Fax: 91-11-291 6431 (24 Hrs.)

934. FRACTIONAL DISTILLATION OF D.M.O
935. FRACTIONAL DISTILLATION OF ESSENTIAL OIL & MEDICINAL PLANT EXTRACTS
936. FRUIT JUICES, SQUASHES, KETCHUP ETC.
937. FRUIT JUICE MAKING AND PACKING IN PLASTIC CONTAINERS (POUCHES)
938. FROZEN FRUITS & VEGETABLES
939. FRUIT DRINKS IN TETRA PACKS (FROOTI TYPE)
940. FRUIT JUICE MAKING & PACKING
941. FRP PRODUCTS
942. FRICTION DUST (LIQUID & POWDER) FROM CNSL
943. FRIED & ROASTED GROUNDNU, GRAM, PEA, ETC. IN POUCHES
944. FRUIT PULP & JUICE CONCENTRATE (i.e. MANGO AND PINEAPPLE PULP & CONCENTRATE)
945. FRENCH POLISH
946. FRUIT JUICES BOTTLING
947. FRUITS & VEGETABLE DRYING BY FREEZE DRYING METHOD
948. FRUIT JUICES, PICKLE PROCESSING & CANNING
949. FRUIT FLAVOURS (WHISKEY, VODKA, GRAPE, BUTTER SCOTCH & RUM)
950. FROZEN FINGER CHIP
951. FURNISHING FABRICS ON POWER LOOM
952. FURFURAL FROM RICE HUL
953. FUEL OIL
954. FUEL BRIQUETTES FROM AGRO WASTE
955. FUEL BRIQUETTES FROM JUTE CADDIES (BIO COAL FROM AGRO WASTE)
956. FURNACE OIL
957. GARLIC FLAKES
958. GAS PIPE (LPG)
959. GARLIC POWDER
960. GALVANIZED ERW PIPES
961. GAS LIGHTER
962. GALION THREAD
963. GAS FILLING OF LPG CYLINDER (LPG GAS BOTTLING PLANT)
964. GALVANIZING PLANT
965. GARLIC OIL & POWDER
966. GAS MANTLES
967. GAS DETECTOR FOR L.P.G.
968. GATE, GRILL, WROUGHT IRON & BRASS STAIRCASE, RODS & RAILING
969. GASKET SHEET
970. GENERATOR SET (PORTABLE)
971. GEMS & JEWELRY
972. GEMS MANUFACTURE
973. GEM CLIPS, PAPER PINS & STAPLE
974. GELATIN & OSSEIN FROM BONE
975. GEOMETRY BOX (MATHEMATICAL INSTRUMENTS)
976. GELATIN
977. GENERATOR (MUSICAL SOUND)
978. GENERATOR (D.G. SET)
979. GELATIN CAPSULES (HARD)
980. GRINDING UNIT (CEMENT)
981. G.I. WIRES
982. GINGER POWDER
983. GINGER OIL, SANDAL WOOD OIL, NAGARMUTHA OIL
984. G.I. PIPES
985. G.I. PIPE FITTINGS
986. GLAZED CERAMIC TILES
987. GLASS BOTTLE BY SCRAPS
988. GLS LAMPS & FLUORESCENT TUBE
989. GLASS SILVERING (MIROR)

990. GLACIAL ACETIC ACID
991. GLASS SHEET (AUTOMATIC PLANT)
992. GLASS WARE
993. GLASS TUBES- Report - Rs.2500/-
994. GLOW SIGNS
995. GLASS BOTTLES
996. GLS LAMPS/BULBS
997. GLASS WOOL
998. GLUE FROM LEATHER WASTE
999. GLASS SHEET FOR WINDOW PANES
1000. GLUE EXTRACTION & GLUE WHITE POWDER
1001. GLUCOSE & GLUCOSE SALINE
1002. GLASS MARBLES
1003. GLUE & GELATIN
1004. GLYCERIN PURIFICATION
1005. GLYCERIN EXTRACTION PLANT FROM COCONUT OIL
1006. GLASS FLOORING TILES
1007. GLASS SYRINGES
1008. GLUE POWDER FOR TECHNICAL GLUE FLAKES
1009. GOSSY POL (POLY PHENOL) FROM COTTON SEED OIL- COST Rs.2500/-
1010. GOAT FARMING
1011. GOAT SLAUGHTERING & BREEDING FARM
1012. GOLD EXTRACTION USING CYANIDE SOLUTION & ACID
1013. GOBAR GAS (BIO GAS)
1014. GOLDEN COLOUR SHADE
1015. GOLD ELECTROPLATING
1016. GOLD PLATING ON GLASS
1017. GOAT & SHEEP FARMING
1018. GOLF COURSE
1019. GOLD, ROLLED GOLD & SILVER PLATING
1020. GOLD JEWELLERY
1021. GOLD ELECTROPLATING OR METALLIC JEWELLERY ARTICLE INCLUDING METALLIC WATCH STRAPS
1022. GOLD & SILVER PLATING ON PVC & NYLON
1023. GOLD SALT
1024. GOLD PLATED SILVER JEWELLERY
1025. GOLD PLATED SILVER JEWELLERY AND CUTLERY
1026. GOLD COLOUR (POWER) FOR MORE BRIGHTNESS PROCESS AND FORMULATION FOR OBTAINING MORE BRIGHTNESS AND YELLOW COLOUR FOR PRECIPITATED GOLD POWDER
1027. GOLD COLOUR ELECTROPLATING ON CHEAPER ORNAMENTS WITHOUT USING GOLD
1028. GOLD CYANIDE POWDER
1029. GRAPE DEHYDRATION
1030. GRAPE WINE
1031. GRINDING OF SPICES (TURMERIC, RED CHILLIES, MASALA)
1032. GRANITE SLAB / TILE
1033. GRAPHITE POWDER FROM GRAPHITE ORE
1034. GRANITE MONUMENT
1035. GRANITE CUTTING & POLISHING UNIT
1036. GREEN HOUSE, PLANT MICRO PROPAGATION
1037. GRANULES (PLASTIC) FROM WASTE
1038. GRANULES (PLASTIC) FROM RESIN
1039. GROUND NUT OIL MILL
1040. GROUND NUT OIL REFINING
1041. GREASES MANUFACTURE
1042. GRANITE & MARBLE TILES
1043. GREETING CARD BY OFFSET PRINTING PRESS
1044. GRAPHITE CARBON PLATES

Price Rs. 2500/- for each "Detailed Project Report" Payable in advance through Draft/Cash/M.O. in favour of "ENGINEERS INDIA RESEARCH INSTITUTE". Or Ask by V.P.P. PH.: 291 8117, 291 6431, 292 0361 Fax: 91-11-291 6431 (24 Hrs.)

1045. GRAPHIC DEVELOPER FOR GRAPHIC ART FILM AND GUM SOLUTION FOR PRINTING
1046. GHEE, BUTTER & PANEER
1047. GREASES FROM CASTOR OIL
1048. GRINDING WHEELS
1049. GRINDING MEDIA BALLS
1050. GRANITE CRUSHING
1051. GRAM DALS & FLOUR MILLS
1052. GRAM DALL/PULSE MILL
1053. GREENPEAS PROCESSING & CANNING
1054. GRAPHITE ORE BENIFICATION UNIT
1055. GRADED & M.I. CASTING
1056. GRADES OF GUAR GUM
1057. GRIPE WATER
1058. GRANULATED MIXED FERTILIZER
1059. GRAVURE PRINTING CYLINDER
1060. GUM FROM TAMARIND SEED POWDER
1061. GUAR GUM
1062. GUAR GUM POWDER
1063. GUNNY BAGS
1064. GUM FOR PASTING LABELS/OFFICE PASTE (GUM)
1065. GUAR GUM POWDER (FOOD GRADE)
1066. HAZMOLA TYPE AYURVEDIC TABLET
1067. HAWAI CHAPPAL (RUBBER)
1068. HARD RUBBER BATTERY CONTAINER
1069. HATCHERY FARMING (BROILER)
1070. HAND BLOCK PRINTING
1071. HAND TOOLS
1072. HAIR SHAMPOOS
1073. HAIR DYE IN CREAM FORM
1074. HAMMERS
1075. HAIR FIXER
1076. HALOGEN LAMPS
1077. HAIR DYE POWDER
1078. HARD CHROMIUM & NICKEL CHROMIUM PLATING
1079. HANDKERCHIEF
1080. HANDICRAFTS
1081. HARD GREASE
1082. HAIR DYE IN HAIR OIL FORM
1083. HARD & SOFT FERRITES
1084. HARD GELATIN CAPSULES (EMPTY)
1085. HANK YARN DYEING FOR POWER LOOM
1086. HAMMER TONE PAINTS
1087. HARD COKE
1088. HARD CHROMIUM PLATING
1089. HAND MADE PAPER
1090. HAND LOOM PRODUCTS-KHES, BEDSHEET, BED COVERS, FURNISHING
1091. HARD BOARD FROM RICE HUSK
1092. HARD BAORD FROM BAGASSE
1093. HAWAN SAMAGRI
1094. HACK SAW BLADE
1095. HYDRATED LIME
1096. HDPE/LDPE MANUFACTURING FROM ETHYL ALCOHOL
1097. HOLIDAY RESORTS
1098. HOSPITALS
1099. HOSPITAL (Rs. 100 Cr. PROJECT)
1100. HOSPITAL/NURSING HOME
1101. HOLLOW CONCRETE BLOCK/ Brick
1102. HDPE FILM / SHEET
1103. HOTEL (3 STAR)
1104. HOTEL (5 STAR)
1105. HOTEL (NO STAR)
1106. HOT ROLLING MILL

1107. HOSE PIPE (RUBBER)
1108. HING (ASAFOETIDA)
1109. HOT DIP GALVANIZING
1110. HYDROGEN PEROXIDE
1111. HDPE/LDPE PIPES
1112. HIGH VOLTAGE WIRE
1113. HOSIERY INDUSTRY (FOR MEN)
1114. HOSIERY INDUSTRY (for WOMEN -BRA & PANTY)
1115. HOSPITAL RUBBER GOODS & SHEETS
1116. HDPE/PP WOVEN SACKS (BAGS)
1117. HDPE PIPE & FITTING
1118. HDPE & LDPE PIPE FITTING
1119. HDPE TARPAULINS
1120. HDPE BOX STRAPPINGS
1121. HDPE/LDPE PIPES & FITTINGS
1122. HDPE PIPE
1123. HERBAL KUM -KUM ROLI
1124. HEAT TRANSFER LABEL FOR RUBBER
1125. HEXAMINE FROM FORMALDEHYDE
1126. HEAT TRANSFER LABEL by SCREEN PROCESS
1127. HEAT TREATMENT OF LEAF SPRING
1128. HELICAL SPRING (COIL SPRINGS)
1129. HELMET
1130. HEALTH CENTRE
1131. HERBAL MEDICATED CIGARETTES
1132. HERBAL COSMETIC
1133. HERBAL TOOTH PASTE & TOOTH POWDER
1134. HESSIAN BAGS (LAMINATED) WITH PRINTING
1135. HESSIAN CLOTH
1136. HEPTAL DEHYDE
1137. HERBAL SHAMPOO/CREAM
1138. HEALTH CLUB CUM BEAUTY PARLOUR WITH HAIR SALOON & SONA BATH
1139. HELMET FOR COAL MINES
1140. HEAT CHAMBER PAINTING
1141. HINGES (PianoType)
1142. HINGES (M.S.)
1143. HIGH ALUMINA CERAMICS
1144. HIGH RUPTURING CAPACITY (HRC) FUSES
1145. HIGH TENSILE FASTENERS
1146. H.M BAGS
1147. HOMOEOPATHIC MEDICINES
1148. HOSIERY & TAILORS LABELS
1149. HOT DIP GALVAINZING
1150. HOSIERY PRODUCTS LIKE CHILDREN KNITWEAR, T-SHIRTS & ACRYLIC FIBRE
1151. HOMOEO & BIO MEDICINES WITH MOTHER TINCTURE
1152. HOT ROLLED (HR) COILS
1153. HOSIERY MERCERIZING
1154. HOSIERY CLOTH (COTTON) PROCESSING-BLEACHING, DYEING & FINISHING OF CLOTH
1155. HOIST & CRANES (MATERIAL HANDLING EQUIPMENTS)
1156. HOOKS & CLIPS (METAL)
1157. HOT MIX PLANT
1158. H - ACID
1159. H.T. & M.V. INDUSTRIAL CUBICAL SWITCH BOARDS
1160. HUME PIPES
1161. HURRICANE LANTERN/ STOVE
1162. HYDROGENATION OF CASTOR OILS

1163. HYDROCHLORIC ACID (HCL)
1164. HYDROGEN PEROXIDE BY AUTO OXIDATION PROCESS
1165. HYDRAULIC BRAKE CYLINDER
1166. HYDROFLUORIC ACID
1167. HYDRAULIC DOOR CLOSER
1168. HYBRID SEED
1169. HYDRATED CALCIUM SILICATE BRICKS
1170. HYPODERMIC NEEDLES FOR DISPOSABLE SYRINGE
1171. HYDRAULIC LIFTING DEVICES (FOR AUTOMO-BILE SERVICING & REPAIR)
1172. HYDROGENATED CASTOR OIL
1173. HYDROGEN GAS PLANT (HYDROGEN & OXYGEN)
1174. IBUPROFEN
1175. ICE MAKING PLANT
1176. ICE CUBE PLANT
1177. ICE CREAM OF DIFFERENT FLAVOURS
1178. ICE CREAM STABILIZERS
1179. ICE CREAM & ICE CANDY
1180. ICE CREAM
1181. ICE CREAM CUPS OF PLASTIC
1182. ICE & COLD STORAGE
1183. IDLER ROLLERS FOR CONVEYERS (PLAIN & RUBBER COVERED)
1184. IF/RF COILS
1185. IGNITION CONDENSERS
1186. IGNITION CONDENSER
1187. IMMERSION HEATER
1188. IMITATION JEWELLERY
1189. INDUCTION FURNACE (M.S.
1190. STAINLESS STEEL PATTA
1191. INJECTION WATER & SALINE
1192. INSULATING VARNISH
1193. INJECTION MOULDED PLASTIC ARTICLES
1194. INDUSTRIAL REFRIGERA-TION
1195. INJECTION & BLOW MOULDED PLASTIC Products
1196. INJECTION MOULDED HOUSE HOLD ITEMS
1197. INSECTICIDES FROM NEEM OIL, LEAVES & NEEM SEEDS
1198. INJECTION MOULDED PLAS-TIC COMPONENTS
1199. INSTANT FOODS (IDLI MIX, SAMBAR MIX, VADA MIX, GULAB JAMUN, TOMATO SOUP MIX ETC.)
1200. INDUCTION FURNACE BASED C.I. CASTING
1201. INDUCTION HARDENING OF MACHINE COMPOUNDS
1202. INFORMATION MOVING DISPLAY
1203. INJECTION MOULDED PLASTIC COMPONENTS FOR ELECTRICAL/ ELECTRONICS INDL.
1204. INSULATING VARNISH (POLY VINYL BUTYRAL BASED FFC GRADE)
1205. INDUSTRIAL OXYGEN GAS
1206. INTRAVENOUS (I.V.) SET
1207. INDIAN PICKLE
1208. INDIAN MADE FOREIGN LIQUOR (IMFL)
1209. INDUCTION FURNACE

1210. INSULATING VARNISH(DryType)
1211. INTERNAL COMBUSTION ENGINE (for Agricu-ltural Equipments)
1212. INTEGRATED COMPLEX OF EASTERS & ALLIED PRODUCTS (DOP, DBP, ETHYL ACET-ATE, BUTYL ACET-ATE, WIRE ENAM-EL, JELLY CABLE COM-POUNDS)
1213. INSULATING VARNISH & WIRE ENAMEL
1214. INDUSTRIAL KNIFE
1215. INDIGO BLUE
1216. INVESTMENT CASTINGS
1217. INVESTMENT CAS-TINGS OF BRASS
1218. INVERTER
1219. INDUSTRIAL HARD OIL USED IN SOAP MAKING
1220. INDUSTRIAL GLOVES
1221. INVERTER & CONVERTER
1222. INSTANT ICE CREAM MIX
1223. INTEGRATED CIRCUITS
1224. INDUSTRIAL ALCOHOL FROM MOLASSES
1225. INVESTMENT CASTINGS FOR SS & HIGHER ALLOYS
1226. INDUSTRIAL ALCOHOL FROM ETHYLENE
1227. INSTANT TEA & COFFEE
1228. INJECTABLE FOR PHARMACEUTICALS
1229. INSTANT SOUP
1230. INSTANT NOODLES
1231. INSULATING LAGGING OF BOILERS & STEAM TUBES
1232. INTIMATE SCENT, CHEMICALS ETC. FROM ALL TYPES OF FLOWERS
1233. IONES FROM LEMON GRASS OIL
1234. IODIZED SALT
1235. IODIZED SALT (MOISTURELESS-FREE FLOWING)
1236. IRON POWDER FROM MILL SCALE SCRAP ARISING from Iron & Steel Rerolling Mill
1237. IRON TAWA
1238. IRON & STEEL WIRE & NETTING
1239. IRON OXIDE PIGMENT
1240. IRON (WROUGHT) & BRASS STAIRCASE, RODS, RAILING, GATE & GRILL
1241. ISO PROPANOL (ISO PROPYL ALCOHOL)
1242. ISOPRENE & NEOPRENE BASED RUBBER ADHESIVE
1243. I.V. CANNULA
1244. I.V. FLUID
1245. I.V. SET
1246. I.V. PLASTIC BOTTLES
1247. JAM & JELLY
1248. JAM, CHUTNEY, PICKLE & SQUASHES

1249. J-ACID
1250. JASMINE & LILY FLOWER OIL
1251. JACQUARD FABRICS
1252. JAUN DEHULLING FOR BEER INDUSTRY
1253. JEANS & JACKETS (DENIM)
1254. JEAN DYEING & FIXING BY INDIGO BLUE (JIGGER DYE & DIP DYE)
1256. JELLY FILLED CABLES
1257. JELLY & JAM
1258. JEWELLERY (Gold)
1259. JOB WORK UNIT (FOUNDRY & MACHINING)
1260. JUTE TAR FELT
1261. JUTE BAGS
1262. JUTE BATCHING OIL
1263. JUTE WASTE PRODUCTS
1264. JUTE PROCESSING TWIN & GUNNY BAGS
1265. JUTE TWIN INCLUDING COTTON & COIR
1266. JUTE BAGS FROM RAW JUTE
1267. JUTE, COIR, GRASS, ROPE SUTLI MAKING
1268. JUICES (Fruit)
1269. KATECHU (Kattha)
1270. KALI MEHNDI (HAIR DYE)
1271. KATTHA & CUTCH
1272. KATTHA
1273. KANTHAL/NICHRO-ME FURNACE HEATING WIRE
1274. KERNAL (CASHEW NUT KERNAL EXTRACT)
1275. KHANDSARI SUGAR
1276. KIMAM MANUFACTURE
1277. KITCHEN SINK (S.S)
1278. KNITTING FABRICS
1179. KNITTED CLOTH
1280. KRAFT PAPER (FROM WASTE PAPER)
1281. KRAFT PAPER & MILL BOARD
1282. KRAFT PAPER FROM WASTE CARTON BOXES
1283. KRAFT PAPER & SPECIAL PAPER
1284. LAMINATED OF PAPER WARE (CARDS) WITH GLOSSY PP (POLYESTER FILM)
1285. LAUNDRY & DRY CLEANER
1286. LACTIC ACID
1287. LACTIC ACID FROM WHITE SUGAR (BY FERMENTATION PROCESS)
1288. LATEX RUBBER THREAD
1289. LAMINATED SAFETY GLASS
1290. LAMINATED SAFETY & TOUGHENED GLASS-
1291. LAMINATED PARTICLE BOARD & HARD BOARD
1292. LATEX RUBBER ADHESIVE
1293. LAUNDRY & WASHING SOAP
1294. LAUNDRY SOAP
1295. LAMINATED HESSIAN BAG
1296. LAMINATED SPRAY BRASS ARTICLES/BADGES
1297. LAMP CAPS
1298. LAMINATED JUTE BAGS
1299. LABORATORY CHEMICAL UNIT
1300. LATEX RUBBER CONDOM
1301. LATHER SHAVING CREAM
1302. LAPTOP COMPUTERS
1303. LAMP FILAMENT
1304. LATEX FOAM PRODUCTS
1305. LADDU
1306. LACTOSE & BYE PRODUCT PROCESSING FROM MILK
1307. LAMINATION OF CO-EXTRUSION, THREE LAYERS-FILM WITH LAMINATION & PRINTING
1308. LAMINATION OF CO-EXTRUSION MULTI LAYER FILM IN ROLL FORM
1309. LAUNDRY FOR '5' STAR HOTEL
1310. LDPE/HDPE FROM ETHYL ALCOHOL
1311. LDPE/HDPE PLANT
1312. LDPE/HDPE PIPES
1313. LEATHER GARMENTS
1314. LEMON GRASS OIL BASED IONES

1315. LEAD CRYSTAL
1316. LEATHER GOODS
1317. LEATHER TANNING & COLOURING
1318. LEATHER SHOE & CHAPPAL
1319. LEATHER BINDER (RESIN BASED)
1320. LEVELING & DISPERSING AGENT
1321. LEATHER STRAPS FOR WRIST WATCHES
1322. LEATHER SHOES
1323. LEATHER BOARD
1324. LECITHIN (SOYA BASED)
1325. LEATHER TANNING
1326. LEATHER GOODS
1327. LETTER PRESS PRINTING
1328. LEATHER AUXILIARIES & CHEMICAL
1329. LEATHER TANNING & LEATHER GARMENTS
1330. LEATHER DYES
1331. LEASING BUSINESS
1332. LEASING & HIRE PURCHASE
1333. LEAD STEARATE
1334. LEMON GRASS OIL
1335. LEAD REFINING USING LEAD DROSS, LEAD SCRAP, LEAD POWDER
1336. LEAD NITRATE
1337. LEATHER GARMENTS, SHOES & CHAPPALS
1338. LEATHER WASHERS
1339. LEAD MONOXIDE
1340. LEATHER SUIT-CASES, BRIEF CASES & TRAVELING BAGS
1341. LEAD EXTRACTION FROM SCRAP BATTRIES
1342. LEAD BATTERY PLATES & BATTERY ASSEMBLY
1343. LEAD PENCILS
1344. LEAD SMELTING
1345. LEAD OXIDE (A) LEAD MONOXIDE (B) REA LEAD (LEAD TETROXIDE) (C) GREY LEAD OXIDE
1346. LEAD EXTRACTION (SECONDARY) FROM SCRAPS (A) BATTERY PLATE (B) PIPES (C) SHEET
1347. LIQUID BINDI & SINDUR
1348. LIQUID GLUCOSE & ITS BYE PRODUCTS FROM MAIZE
1349. LIQUID SOAP
1350. LIQUID DETERGENTS
1351. LIQUID SHOE POLISH PUFF
1352. LITHOPONE
1353. LIQUID GLUCOSE FROM POTATOES
1354. LIQUID OXYGEN BOTTLING
1355 LIGHTNING ARRESTER AND ISOLATOR
1356. LIGHT LIQUID PARAFFIN
1357. LILLY FLOWER & JASMINE
1358. LIQUID SOAP BY PINE OIL
1359. LINK CHAIN
1360. LITMUS PAPER
1361. LIGHT EMITING DIODE (LED)
1362. LIME STONE, DOLOMITE CHIPS & POWDER
1363. LIME STONE CRUSHING, GRINDING AND PULVERISING (FOR MFG. CHIPS & POWDER)
1364. LIQUID DETERGENTS (NON IONIC)
1365. LIME COLOUR/CEMENT COLOUR/SYNTHETIC RED IRON OXIDE USED FOR FLOORING
1366. LIMIT SWITCHES & METAL PLUG SOCKETS
1367. LIQUID DETERGENT
1368. LIPSTICKS
1369. LINSEED OIL
1370. LICHEN (JHYAU) (CHARILA)
1371. LIQUID GLUCOSE
1372. LIST OF 100% EOU/EOU UNIT
1373. LINING MATERIAL FOR FLUID FLOWING PIPE (LIQUID PETROLEUM)
1374. LOW PRESSURE CELLULOSE LIQUID
1375. LOUDSPEAKER
1376. LOOM OIL
1377. LOW TENSILE TRANSFORMERS (L.T) upto 400 KVA

1378. LPG STOVE
1379. LPG CYLINDER TESTING CENTER
1380. LPG CYLINDER
1381. LPG GAS REGULATOR
1382. LPG GAS BOTTLING PLANT
1383. LPG GAS STOVE
1384. LPG GAS PIPE
1385. LPG GAS DETECTOR
1386. L.T TRANSFORMER REPAIRING (400 KVA)
1387. LUBE OIL FROM CNSL TO REDUCE FRICTION
1388. LUBE OIL & GREASES
1389. LUBE OIL RECLAMATION
1390. LUBE OIL BLENDING
1391. LUBRICATING OIL & GREASES (BLENDING OF LUBRICATING OILS) & MANUFACTURE OF GREASE
1392. LUBRICANT VISCOSITY INDEX IMPROVERS
1393. LUBRICANT (WIRE DRAWING)
1394. MACARONI & VERMICELLI
1395. MANUFACTURE OF T-SHIRTS WITH KNITTING FABRICS
1396. MANGO PEEL BASED PECTIN
1397. MASALA/SPICES
1398. MATCH BOX MAKING UNIT
1399. MARBLE & GRANITE TILES
1400. MANGANESE ORE CONCENTRATION
1401. MAGNESIUM CARBONATE, MAGNESIUM METAL, CALCIUM CARBONATE FROM DOLOMITE
1402. MAGNESIUM SILICATE (TALC)
1403. MAIZE/CORN STARCH
1404. MALTED MILK FOOD
1405. MARINE CONTAINERS
1406. MANILA ROPES
1407. MALACHITE GREEN
1408. MANGO PULP & MANGO SLICES CANNING
1409. MAIZE STARCH
1410. MAGNESIUM HYDROXIDE POWDER
1411. MAGNESIUM SULPHATE
1412. MAGNESIUM TRI-SILICATE
1413. MAIZE/CORN OIL
1414. MALEIC ANHYDRIDE
1415. MALTING PLANT
1416. MARKING INK FOR FIBER TIP PENS
1417. MACARONI
1418. MANGALORE TILES & BRICKS
1419. MAN POWER EXPORT
1420. MACHINE SCREWS & SELF TAPPING SCREWS
1421. MANGO POWDER
1422. MANGO JUICE
1423. MANGO KERNEL POWDER
1424. MAGNET
1425. MAGNESIUM CARBONATE & BI-CARBONATE
1426. MAGAZINE
1427. MATCH SPLINTERS & INNER BOX MAKING PLANT FROM POPLAR WOOD
1428. MATERIAL HANDLING EQUIPMENTS (HOISTS & CRANES)
1429. MANUFACTURING OF PHARMACEUTICALS-TABLETS, CAPSULES ETC.
1430. MANGO PROCESSING & CANNING (MANGO PULP)

1431. MANGO PRODUCTS, MANGO JUICE, PICKLES, CHUTNEY ETC.
1432. METAL CUTTING DIE DESIGN
1433. MEASURING TAPES (STEEL, METALLIC & PLASTIC)
1434. MENTHOL CRYSTAL & OTHER CHEMICALS
1435. METHANE GAS
1436. METAL SPECTACLE FRAME
1437. MELAMINE CRYSTALS
1438. METTOL FROM HYDRO QUINENE & METHYL AMINE
1439. MEDICAL X-RAY FILM, SLITTING & REPACKING
1440. MEDICAL PLANT EXTRACT
1441. METAL FINISHING
1442. MENTHOL & D.M.O.
1443. MELAMINE CROCKERY
1444. METHYL METHA CRYLATE
1445. MELAMINE FORMALDEHYDE POWDER
1446. METAL HARDENING
1447. METAL FITTINGS FOR LEATHER GOODS & GARMENTS
1448. METAL CONTAINER
1449. MECHANICAL TOY
1450. MENTHOL CRYSTAL
1451. METAL BONDED DIAMOND IMPREGNATED SEGMENT FOR MARBLE SAWING
1452. METHYLATED SURGICAL SPIRIT
1453. METALLIZED POLYPROPYLENE FILM
1454. METAL NAPHTHANATE
1455. METALLIC GASKET (SPIRAL WOUND)
1456. METAL PRE TREATMENT CHEMICALS
1457. MENTHA OIL
1458. METALLIC ACID
1459. MERCURIC OXIDE
1460. METHYL METHACRYLATE MONOMER & VARIOUS CHEMICAL ADDITIVES FOR PLASTIC BANGLES
1461. METAL POLISH SOAP
1462. METAL HOOKS & CLIP
1463. METALLIC STEARATES
1464. METHYLINE GLUE
1465. METHYL SALICYLATE
1466. MEAT PROCESSING (BUFFALO)
1467. METAL POLISHING BAR
1468. METHYL ETHYL KETONE
1469. M.G. KRAFT PAPER FROM WASTE PAPER
1470. MICRO SCALE STEEL PLANT
1471. MICROWAVE OVEN
1472. MINI CEMENT PLANT (BY ROTARY KILN PROCESS-800 TPD)
1473. MILK PRESERVATION & MARKETING TO WHOLESALERS (IN POUCH)
1474. MILK/DAIRY PRODUCTS
1475. MINI RE-ROLLING MILL
1476. MINI PAPER PLANT FORM JUTE STICK & WHEAT HUSK/ RICE HUSK
1477. MILK/DAIRY PRODUCTS
1478. MILK CHOCOLATE
1479. MINI STEEL PLANT BY INDUCTION FURNACE
1480. MINI CEMENT PLANT
1481. MICA PAPER FOR ELECTRICAL INSULATION
1482. MINI SUGAR PLANT
1483. MICRO CRYSTALLINE WAX
1484. MINIATURE CIRCUIT BREAKER (MCB)
1485. MINI FLOUR MILL (ROLLER)
1486. MINI FLOUR MILL (PULVERISED)
1487. MINI PAPER PLANT (KRAFT PAPER)
1488. MINI PAPER PLANT FROM SISAL WOOD

Price Rs. 2500/- for each "Detailed Project Report" Payable in advance through Draft/Cash/M.O. in favour of "ENGINEERS INDIA RESEARCH INSTITUTE". Or Ask by V.P.P. PH.: 291 8117, 291 6431, 292 0361 Fax: 91-11-291 6431 (24 Hrs.)

1489. MITHAI/NAMKEEN
1490. MICRO CRYSTALLINE WAX FROM SLUDGE OF PETRO CHEMICAL REFFINERY
1491. MINIATURE WATCH BATTERY
1492. MICRO NUTRIENT MIXTURE (SOLID)
1493. MISHRI PEARL SUGAR CANDY
1494. MINI PAPER PLANT FROM EUCALYPTUS WOOD
1495. MILL & KRAFT PAPER FROM WASTE CARTON BOXES
1496. MINI PAPER PLANT (WHITE WRITING & PRINTING)
1497. MINERAL WATER IN POUCHES
1498. MINERAL WATER IN POUCHES & PLASTIC BOTTLES
1499. MIRIT SANJEEVNI SURA
1500. MINI STEEL PLANT
1501. MILK PRESERVATION & MARKETING (MILK CHILLING PLANT)
1502. MICRO NUTRIENTS MIXTURES
1503. MICRO WAVE TUBES USED IN MICRO WAVE OVEN
1504. MILK POWDER
1505. MILD STEEL BOLT
1506. MILD STEEL NUTS
1507. MINI (PERSONAL) COMPUTER
1508. MINIATURE TRANSFORMER
1509. MINI PAPER PLANT USING BAGASSE
1510. MILK POWDER, GHEE & SPICES
1511. MICRO PAPER
1512. MIRROR (GOLDEN, SILVER AND PINK)
1513. MICROVEE & ABSOLUTE FILTER
1514. MICRO MOTORS
1515. MIXERS/GRINDERS (MIXIE)
1516. MILK POWDER & GHEE
1517. MICRO CELLULAR SHEET FOR SHOE SOLE
1518. MILK TOFFEE
1519. MILK CHILLING PLANT & PACKING IN POUCHES
1520. MODERN COSMETIC INDUSTRY
1521. MOSQUITO COILS & MATS
1522. MOULDED CASE CIRCUIT BREAKER (MCCB)
1523. MOTHER BOARD
1524. MONOCHROME MONITOR FOR COMPUTER
1525. MOULDED LUGGAGE
1526. MOULDED LUGGAGE (V.I.P. TYPE)
1527. MOULDED LUGGAGE (CHEAP QUALITY)
1528. MOSQUITO REPELLENT MAT
1529. MOTHER TINCTURE & BIO-CHEMIC MEDICINES
1530. MOTEL/SMALL HOTEL
1531. MOSQUITO COILS
1532. MODERN RICE MILL
1533. MOSAIC TILES
1534. MOTOR START ELECTROLYTIC CAPACITORS
1535. MOSQUITO MAT RECHARGER

1536. MONO CHLORO ACETIC ACID
1537. MOBILE CATERING VAN
1538. MODERN VEHICLE WORKSHOP
1539. MODERN BREAD AND BAKERY UNIT
1540. MONOCHROTOPHOS (TECHNICAL)
1541. MOSQUITO REPELLENT OIL
1542. MOTEL/SMALL HOTEL, BANQUET HALL WITH RESTAURANT
1543. MOSQUITO COILS USING EUCALYPTUS LEAVES
1544. MODERN ADVERTISING AGENCY WITH DTP & FILM STUDIO
1545. M.S. INGOTS (INDUCTION FURNACE)
1546. M.S. WIRE DRAWING PLANT & ANNEALING
1547. M.S. HINGES
1548. M.S. INGOTS & H.R. STEEL STRUCTURES
1549. M.S. WELDING ELECTRODES
1550. M.S. DRUM & FABRICATION OF STORAGE TANK
1551. MUSTARD OIL (EDIBLE OIL)
1552. MULTI PURPOSE SPRAY DRIER
1553. MUSICAL DOOR BELL
1554. MUSHROOM CULTIVATION
1555. MUSHROOM CULTIVATION & PROCESSING WITH CANNING
1556. MULTI LAYER PRINTED CIRCUIT BOARD (PCB)
1557. MULTI PURPOSE COLD STORAGE FOR MEDICINES, FRUITS & VEGETABLES
1558. MULTIPLE RELAY FOR LOW VOLTAGE APPLICATION
1559. MUSHROOM(EOU) CULTIVATION & PROCESSING UNIT (DEHYDRATION & PICKLING OF OYSTER & PADDY STRAW MUSHROOM)
1560. MUTTON TALLOW FOR INDUSTRIAL USE
1561. MUFFLERS & SILENCERS FOR TWO WHEELERS
1562. MUFFLER & SILENCER PIPES FOR FOUR WHEELER
1563. MUSHROOM & PROCESSED FOOD
1564. MUSICAL SOUND GENERATOR
1565. MULTI LAYER FILM
1566. MULTI STOREY COMMERCIAL COMPLEX ALONGWITH RESIDENTIAL & DELUXE FLATS FOR FOREIGN TOURISTS & REVOLVING RESTAURANT
1567. MUSTARD OIL EXTRACTION & REFINING
1568. MURABBA
1569. MULTI LAYER CO-EXTRUSION, THREE LAYERS-FILM WITH LAMINATION PRINTING
1570. NAPHTHALENE BALLS
1571. NAMKEEN & SWEETS
1572. NAIL ENAMEL (NAIL POLISH)
1573. NAMKEEN INDUSTRY
1574. NAPHTHALENE BALLS
1575. NAPHTHA BASED THINNER
1576. NAIL CUTTER WITH FILER & MANICURE
1577. N-ACETYL, L-TYROSINE
1578. N.C. PUTTY
1579. N.C. THINNER USED IN AUTO PARTS
1580. N.C. SENDING SEALERS
1581. NEWS PRINT PAPER FROM RICE STRAW/BAGASSE
1582. NEWS PAPER
1583. NEOPRENE BASED ADHESIVES
1584. NEON SIGN
1585. NEON BULB
1586. NEEM OIL FROM SEEDS
1587. NEON LAMP INDICATORS
1588. NEON INDICATOR
1589. NEEM SEEDS INSECTICIDES
1590. NEEDLE ROLLERS FOR BEARING
1591. NEROL LAUNDRY SOAP
1592. NEWS PAPER FOR CHILDREN (DAILY)-EVENING NEWS PAPER

1593. NITRO CELLULOSE (LACQUER)
1594. NICHROME WIRE
1595. NICHROME/KANTHAL FURNACE HEATING WIRE
1596. NICKEL PLATING BRIGHTNER (PRIMARY OR CARRIER BRIGHTNER AND SECONDARY)
1597. NICKEL SALT
1598. NICKEL/CADMIUM BATTERY
1599. NICKEL PLATING
1600. NICKEL PLATING BRIGHTNER
1601. NICKEL LINED SCREENS
1602. NICKEL SULPHATE
1603. NICKEL CATALYST
1604. NICKEL CATALYST FOR HYDROGENETION OF VEGETABLE OIL
1605. NICKEL ELECTROPLATING SALTS (ONLY MARKET SURVEY)
1606. NICKEL CHROMIUM PLATING & HARD CHROMIUM
1607. NICKEL RECLAMATION FROM SPENT CATALYST OF VANASPATI INDUSTRY
1608. NITROGEN & OXYGEN UNIT
1609. NILGIRI OIL
1610. NICOTINIC ACID
1611. NIRMA TYPE DETERGENT POWDER
1612. NITROCELLULOSE
1613. NITRO MUSK
1614. NICOTINE SULPHATE FROM TOBACCO WASTE
1615. NON-STICK KITCHEN WARES (TEFLON COATED UTENSILS)
1616. NON-FERROUS SCRAP MELTING ROD CASTING & WIRE DRAWING
1617. NON-IONIC SURFACTANTS WETTING AGENTS
1618. NOODLES
1619. NON-BASMATI RICE FROM PADDY
1620. NON-IONIC LIQUID DETERGENT
1621. NON-ALCOHOLIC FLAVOUR
1622. NON-CARBONATED SOFT DRINK
1623. NON-FERROUS METAL ALLOY
1624. NON-FERROUS FORGING
1625. NON-EDIBLE & EDIBLE OIL MILL
1626. NOTE BOOK, REGISTER & FILES
1627. NON-WOVEN CARPETS (WADDED WITH POLYESTER FIBER)
1628. NUMBER COMBINATION AUTO LOCKS FOR LUGGAGES
1629. NUT, BOLTS, RIVETS/ WASHER
1630. NURSING HOME
1631. NURSERY SCHO-OL (PRE-NURSERY & NURSERY)
1632. NYLON YARN CRIMPING DOUBL-ING, BLEACHING, DYEING ETC.
1633. NYLON POLYESTER & P.P. ROPE MAKING
1634. NYLON ZIP FASTENERS
1635. NYLON SOCKS
1636. OCTYL ALCOHOL
1637. OFFSET PRINTING PRESS
1638. OFFSET SECURITY PRINTING PRESS
1639. OFFSET COLOUR & TREADLE TYPE PRINTING PRESS
1640. OFFSET PRINTING INK
1641. OIL (COTTON SEED)
1642. OIL (MUSTARD)
1643. OIL (GROUND NUT)
1644. OIL MILL
1645. OIL SEALS
1646. OIL (CASTOR)

1647. OIL (RICE BRAN)
1648. OIL (ESSENTIAL)
1649. OIL BOND DISTEMPER PAINT
1650. OLEORESIN OF SPICES
1651. OLEORESIN FROM CHILLY
1652. ONE TIME CARBON PAPER
1653. ONION POWDER
1654. ONION & POTATO POWDER
1655. OPTICAL GLASS GRINDING
1656. OPTICAL FIBER CABLE
1657. OPTICAL WHITENER
1658. OPEN END SPINNING PLANT
1659. OPTICAL WHITENER
1660. ORTHO BORIC ACID
1661. ORGANIC SOLVENT PURIFICATION PLANT
1662. ORTHO TOLUENE SOLVENT
1663. ORGANIC MANURE
1664. OSSEIN & GELATIN
1665. OSSEIN FROM ANIMAL BONES
1666. OXYGEN GAS
1667. OXALIC ACID
1668. OXALIC ACID FROM WASTE VEGETABLES
1669. OXYGEN & NITROGEN PLANT
1670. OXALIC ACID FROM SAW DUST
1671. OXIDISED WAX
1672. OYSTER MUSHROOMS (CULTIVATION & PROCESSING UNIT)
1673. PAINT INDUSTRY
1674. PACKAGING OF NAMKEEN, BHUJIA, DALMOTH ETC. IN FLEXIBLE POUCHES
1675. PARAFFIN WAX FROM SLACK WAX
1676. PAINT BRUSHES
1677. PAPER BAGS
1678. PALM OIL
1679. PARACETAMOL
1680. PAPPAD PLANT
1681. PAN MASALA IN POUCHES & TIN PACKS
1682. PAPER FROM BAMBOO
1683. PAPER FROM WASTE PAPER (KRAFT PAPER)
1684. PAPER FROM WASTE PAPER (WRITING & PRINTING PAPER)
1685. PAPER FROM BAGASSE
1686. PAPER FROM RICE STRAW
1687. PAPER CONES & TUBES
1688. PAPER & PULP
1689. PAPER FROM EUCALYPTUS
1690. PAPER ENVELOPS
1691. PAPER FROM RICE HUSK & WHEAT HUSK
1692. PAPER FROM PAPYRUS GRASS
1693. PAPER (HAND MADE PAPER)
1694. PAPER CUPS
1695. PAPER PLANT FROM TREE BARK & EUCALYPTUS WOOD
1696. PAPER BASED PHENOLIC SHEET (FOR ELECTRICAL APPLIANCES)
1697. PAPER WASTE RECYCLING
1698. PAPER & PAPER BOARD
1699. PAPER PRODUCTS
1700. PAPAIN
1701. PAPAIN FROM PAPAYA
1702. PAPAYA CULTIVATION
1703. PAPAYA & TOMATO CULTIVATION
1704. PAPAYA CULTIVATION & PAPAIN MANUFACTURE
1705. PARTICLE BOARD
1706. PAPER COATED ALUMINIUM & COPPER WIRES
1707. PANEL, FLUSH DOOR, WINDOWS, OFFICE FURNITURE & HOUSE HOLD FURNITURE
1708. PANEER
1709. PAPER PLATES
1710. PAINT & VARNISH
1711. PARACETAMOL BY PNCB
1712. PARAAMINO BENZOIC ACID

1713. PAINT INDUSTRY (LIME COLOUR, DRY DISTEMPER, OIL BOUND DISTEMPER, ENAMEL PAINT, RED OXIDE PRIMER/RESIN, MICA BASED PAINT)
1714. PAN MASALA & POUCH MAKING PLANT
1715. PARA CHLORO NITRO BENZENE
1716. PASTEURIZATION OF MILK (FLAVOURED MILK)
1717. PARTICLE BOARD FROM RICE HUSK
1718. PAN MASALA, TOBACCO, ZARDA & KIMAM
1719. PAINT-BITUMINOUS BASED CORROSION RESISTANT
1720. PAINT REMOVERS
1721. PALM OIL CRUSHING UNIT
1722. PAPER VARNISH
1723. PAPER FROM AKRA
1724. PARTICLE BOARD WOOD CHIPS
1725. PARTICLE BOARD & BLOCK BOARD WITH SENDING & LAMINATION OF PARTICLE BOARD
1726. PAPER CONES FOR LOUDSPEAKER
1727. PATCHES (TUBE REPAIR MATERIAL)
1728. PAINT INDUSTRY (PRIMER)
1729. PAPER PLANT (KRAFT & WHITE WRITING & PRINTING PAPER)
1730. PAPAIN FROM PAPAYA (PAPAYA LATEX)
1731. PCB SHEETS
1732. PCC ELECTRIC POLES
1733. PCC/RCC PIPES
1734. PEPSI COLA IN POLY TUBES
1735. PETROMAX CONTAINER
1736. PERFUMERY COMPOUND
1737. PERFUMERY COMPOUND, COSMETICS ETC.
1738. PERFUMED PHENYL (PINE OIL DISINFECTANT)
1739. PERFUMERY COMPOUNDS (AROMATIC)
1740. PERFUME (SPRAY)
1741. PERFUMERY COMPOUND (SYNTHETIC AGARBATTI)
1742. PERFUMES (SCENT) FROM LEMON GRASS OIL AND JASMINE OIL
1743. PET BOTTLE/CONTAINERS
1744. PERSONAL COMPUTER
1745. PECTIN BY RAW PAPAYA
1746. PECTIN FROM APPLE POMACE
1747. PECTIN FROM CITRUS, LEMON & ORANGES
1748. PECTIN BY MANGO PEELS
1749. PECTIN FROM ORANGE/ LIME PEELS
1750. PERFUME FOR SOAP, DETERGENT & AGARBATTI (YARA YARA)
1751. PERFUME & SCENTS
1752. PERFUMED PHENYL (THICK)
1753. PETROLEUM COKE
1754. PESTICIDE FORMULATIONS
1755. PETROLEUM JELLY
1756. PESTICIDES (MELATHION, MANCOZEV, COPPER OXY-CHLORIDE, WATTABLE SULPHUR, ZINC PHOSPHIDE)

1757. PEANUT COATING (SPICES, HONEY, CHEESE, CHOCOLATE, SALT)
1758. PENCIL (LEAD)
1759. PELLETIZER PLANT (FOR CATTLE FEED, POULTRY FEED, SHEEP FEED, PIG & OTHER FEED)
1760. PETHA PACKAGING
1761. PEPPERMINT OIL
1762. PHARMACEUTICAL
1763. ALCOHOL FROM NON-MOLASSES BASED
1764. POWER LOOM
1765. POWDER COATING (CHAMBER TYPE)
1766. POUCH FILLING for SAUNF, SUPARI & ELAICHI ETC.
1767. PUBLISHING & PRINTING UNIT
1768. POTATO STARCH
1769. POLYTHENE BAGS & AUTOMATIC PRINTING
1770. PVC FABRIC YARN ON POWER LOOM (TERRYCOT)
1771. PVC CONDUIT PIPE
1772. PVC PIPE & FITTINGS
1773. PHARMACEUTICAL UNITS (TABLETS, CAPSULES, SYRUPS, LOTION, OINTMENT, POWDER INJECTABLE, EYE DROPS & EYE OINTMENT ETC.)
1774. PHENACETIN
1775. PHTHALOCYNINE BLUE & GREEN
1776. PHOTO POLYMER COATING FOR PLATE & BLOCK MAKING
1777. PHOTO GRAVURE & FLEXO GRAPHIC PRINTING INK FOR PLASTIC FILM PRINTING
1778. PHOSPHORIC ACID FOR POLLUTION CONTROL
1779. PHOTO ALBUM ADHESIVES
1780. PHENOLIC RESIN
1781. PHENOLIC FORMALDEHYDE RESIN (PF RESIN)
1782. PHOTOGRAPHIC DEVELOPERS & FIXERS
1783. PHENYL ACETIC ACID
1784. PHOTO DEVELOPER & FIXER
1785. PHENOL
1786 PHOTO ETCHING OF STAINLESS STEEL PLATES
1787. PHOTO TYPE SETTING
1788. PHENYL (BROWN & WHITE)
1789. PHENYL (BLACK) IN LIQUID FORM
1790. PHOSPHORIC ACID FROM ROCK PHOSPHATE
1791. PHOTO COLOUR LAB (QSS)
1792. PHOTO EMULSION FOR ROTARY SCREEN PRINTING
1793. PHOSPHORIC ACID (Purification) FROM CRUDE
1794. PILFER PROOF CAPS & CROWN CAPS
1795. PILFER PROOF CAPS (P.P. CAPS)
1796. PIG IRON
1797. PICKLES, MURABBAS, SAUCES ETC. (VEGETARIAN & NONVEG. PICKLES)
1798. P.I.D. CONTROLLER
1799. PIGMENTS (DYE PIGMENTS)
1800. PISTON ASSEMBLY (ALUMINIUM ALLOY)

1801. PISTON ASSEMBLY (ALUMINIUM ALLOY)
1802. PIGGERY/MEAT/CHICKEN PROCESSING
1803. PINEAPPLE JUICE & CANING
1804. PINE APPLE SLICE CANNING
1805. PIGMENT DYE & DYE INTERMEDIATES
1806. PICKLE & SAUCES
1807. PIGMENT BINDER FOR TEXTILE PRINTING
1808. PIGGERY FARM
1809. PICKLES
1810. PICTURE VARNISH
1811. PLASTIC MOULDED T.V CABINETS
1812 PLASTIC INJECTION MOULDED AUTO COMPONENTS
1813. PLASTIC PRODUCT-AUDIO, VIDEO CASSETTE SHELL)
1814. PLASTIC BUCKETS & DOLI
1815. PLASTIC DRINKING STRAW
1816. PLASTIC FILM CAPACITOR
1817. PLAIN PAPER COPIER
1818. PLASTIC GRANULES (HDPE, LDPE, PP) FROM PLASTIC SCRAPS/WASTE
1819. PLATINUM LABORATORY APPARATUS
1820. PLASTIC SPRAY LAMINATED BRASS ARTICLES/BADGES
1821. PLASTIC TOOTH PICK
1822. PLASTIC I.V. BOTTLES
1823. PLASTIC FILM & SHEETS WITH PRINTING (FLEXO & ROTO) LDPE/HDPE/PP/HM/PVC
1824. PLASTIC CORRUGATED SHEET & BOXES
1825. PLASTIC BUTTONS FROM POLYESTER SHEET & RODS
1826. PLASTIC ADVERTISEMENT BALLOONS
1827. PLASTIC CONTAINER (BLOW MOULDED)
1828. PLASTIC INJECTION MOULDING PROJECTS
1829. PLASTIC SHEET FROM PLASTIC SCRAPS
1830. PLASTIC CANES
1831. PLASTIC SYRINGE (DISPOSABLE)
1832. PLASTER OF PARIS BANDAGES
1833. PLASTER OF PARIS
1834. PLASTER OF PARIS BANDAGES & COTTON ADHESIVE TAPE
1835. PLASTIC BUTTONS
1836. PLASTIC CONFERENCE BAGS, FOLDERS ETC.
1837. PLASTIC MOULDED FURNITURE
1838. PLASTIC WASTE REPROCESSING
1839. PLASTIC SUTLI
1840. PLANT PROTECTION EQUIPMENTS

EiRi

Areas of Expertise

IDENTIFICATION OR PRODUCT

CONDUCTING MARKET SURVEY

PREPARATION OF PROJECT PROFILES & FEASIBILITY STUDIES

PREPARATION OF TECHNOECONOMIC FEASIBILITY STUDIES

PREPARATION OF FINANCING SCHEME & LOAN APPLICATION

GUIDANCE OF PROCEDURES FOR GOVERNMENT CLEARANCE

TURNKEY SERVICES

TECHNOLOGY TRANSFER

1841. PLASTIC COLLAPSIBLE TUBES
1842. PLASTIC TANKS (WATER STORAGE SINTEX TYPE TANKS)
1843. PLASTIC MOULDED TOYS
1844. PLASTIC WARES
1845. PLASTIC SPRAY LAMINATED ARTICLES
1846. PLASTIC MOULDED ARTICLES
1847. PLY WOOD & PLY BOARD
1848. PLY WOOD
1849. PLY WOOD BOARD
1850. PLY WOOD & PLY BOARD (PHENOL BONDED, BOILING WATER PROOF, TERMITE, RESISTANCE, LAMINATED & COMMERCIAL PLY WOOD & PLY BOARD)
1851. PLASTIC STRIPPABLE COATING MATERIAL
1852. PLASTER OF PARIS (CALCIUM SULPHATE)
1853. POLYSTYRENE MOULDING (EXPANDED)
1854. POTATO POWDER
1855. POLYESTER RESIN
1856. POULTRY & CATTLE FEED
1857. POULTRY FEED
1858. POLYESTER YARN
1859. POUCH PACKING FOR MILK
1860. POWER PLANT
1861. PORK PROCESSING & FARMING
1862. POUCHES FOR OIL & GHEE PACKING
1863. POLYPROPYLENE BOX STRAPPING
1864. POWER SUPPLY (LINER&SWITCHMODE)
1865. POWER TRANSFORMER
1866. POLYURETHANE FOAM FLEXIBLE & RIGID
1867. POTATO CHIPS/WAFERS
1868. POWER SUPPLY (SWITCH MODE)
1869. POTATO GRANULE
1870. PROCESSED FRUITS
1871. POLYPROPYLENE/HDPE BOX STRAPPING
1872. POULTRY & BROILER FARMING
1873. POULTRY & HATCHERY FARMING
1874. POULTRY FARM
1875. POTABLE ALCOHOL FROM GRAINS & ROTTEN FRUITS
1876. POTASSIUM SILICATE
1877. POLY VINYL ALCOHOL
1878. POLY BUTENS FROM CAREFFINATES
1879. POLYESTER HOSIERY LABELS & PATCHES
1880. POLYURETHANE FOAM (P.U. FOAM)
1881. POLYPROPYLENE SPINNING FILAMENT YARN

Price Rs. 2500/- for each ``Detailed 'Project Report'' Payable in advance through Draft/Cash/M.O. in favour of ``ENGINEERS INDIA RESEARCH INSTITUTE''. Or Ask by V.P.P. PH.: 291 8117, 291 6431, 292 0361 Fax: 91-11-291 6431 (24 Hrs.)

1882. PORTABLE TELEVISION
1883. POLYSTER YARN FROM WASTE
1884. POLYSTER BEADING
1885. POUCH MAKING & GRAVURE PRINTING
1886. POWDER COATING
1887. POLY VINYL ACETATE
1888. POLYTHENE PRINTING BAG (P.P & H.M. FLEXIBLE FOUR COLOURS ROTO GRAVURE PRINT)
1889. POWER TRANSFORMERS UPTO 600 KVA
1890. POLYTHENE BAGS & TUBES
1891. POLYESTER RESIN FOR WIRE ENAMEL
1892. PORTABLE GENERATOR SET
1893. POTASSIUM NITRATE
1894. POTASSIUM PERMANGANATE (IN SOLUTION FORM)
1895. POWER COATING PAINT (EPOXY, ACRYLIC & POLYESTER BASIS)
1896. POTATO & ONION POWDER
1897. POTATO CHIPS WITH IMPORTED MACHINERY
1898. POLYURETHANE RIGID FROM MOULDING
1899. POLYURETHANE SOLE
1900. POLYURETHANE FOAM & ITS PRODUCTS
1901. POUCH PACKING FOR MILK
1902. POWER PLANT
1903. PORKPROCESSING & FARMING
1904. POTASSIUM IODIDE
1905. POTATO POWDER AUTOMATIC IMPORTED PLANT
1906. POTABLE LIQUOR
1907. POLYESTER YARN
1908. POLISH (WAX)
1909. POLISH (CAR)
1910. POTASSIUM DI-CHROMATE/BI-CHROMATE
1911. POWER INVERTER
1912 POLYPROPYLENE & MULTIFILAMENT SPINNING YARN
1913. POLYESTER MICRO FIBER
1914. POWER PLANT (HYDRO BASED)
1915. POLYETHENE POUCHES FOR GHEE, BUTTER, OIL, MILK ETC.
1916. POLYTHENE BOTTLES FOR MINERAL WATER, I.V. FLUIDS ETC.
1917. POPLAR PLANTATION
1918. PRINTED TIN CONTAINERS
1919. PRINTING INKS
1920. PRINTING INKS (FLEXO GRAPHIC)
1921. PRINTED CIRCUIT BOARD (PCB)
1922. PROCESSING OF FRUIT & VEGETABLE
1923. PRUSSIAN BLUE
1924. PRINTING PLATE FOR OFFSET PRINTING MACHINE
1925. PROCESSED FOOD (READYMADE)
1926 PRECIPITATED CALCIUM CARBONATE
1927. PROCESSED CHEESE
1928. PRE STRESSED CONCRETE RAILWAY SLEEPER

1929. PRINTING PRESS (LETTER PRESS)
1930. PRINTING PRESS (OFFSET)
1931. PRESSURE DIE CASTING ALUMINIUM
1932. PROTEIN & PROTEIN BASED PRODUCTS
1933. PRECIOUS METAL PLATING & MANUFACTURE OF THEIR SALTS
1934. PRESSURE COOK-ER & ALUMINIUM UTENSILS
1935. PRESSURE COOKER (ALUMINIUM/STAINLESS STEEL) & WATER FILTER
1936. PRESSURE SENSITIVE ADHESIVE TAPES
1937. PRESSURE SENSITIVE ADHESIVE FOR BOPP TAPES (ACRYLIC BASED)
1938. PRECIPITATED CALCIUM CARBONATE FROM BYE-PRODUCTS LIME SLURRY & CARBON DIOXIDE
1939. PRINTING INK (ROTO GRAVURE & FLEXO GRAPHIC)
1940. PRINTING INK (OFFSET)
1941. PROCESSED FOOD & MARINE PRODUCTS
1942. PRINTING INDUSTRY (DTP & OFFSET)
1943. PRESSURE COOKER
1944. PRESSURE COOKER (ALUMINIUM & STAINLESS STEEL)
1945. PRECIPITATED SILICA
1946. PRODUCTS BASED ON INDUSTRIAL WASTE (COVERING TEN PROJECT PROFILES)
1947. PROCESSED FOOD & SPICES
1948. PROCESSED CONTROL TIMER (Electronic Timer)
1949. PRAWN FISH FARMING
1950. P.U. (POLYURETHANE) RIGID FOAM
1951. PUMIC WHITE ABRASIVE CAKE/STICK
1952. PULVERIZED FLOUR MILL
1953. PULSE MILL (DAL MILL)
1954. PULP FROM WOOD, BAMBOO OR GRASS
1955. PULP FROM BAMBOO & WOOD
1956. PUTTY (METAL CASEMENT PUTTY)-ASIAN PAINT TYPE
1957. PUTTY & WATER PROOFING PLANT
1958. PURIFICATION OF CASEIN
1959. PVC INSULATION TAPES
1960. PVC WIRES & CABLES
1961. PVC WIRES/TWIN FLAT CABLE
1962. PVC PIPES & FITTINGS
1963. PVC GRANULES/ COMPOUNDS BY CHEMICAL PROCESS
1964. PVC GRANULES FROM PVC SCRAPS (POLLUTION CONTROL)
1965. PVC GRANULES/ COMPOUNDS BY PLASTIC WASTE
1966. PVC RIGID PIPE
1967. PVC INSULATED CABLES
1968. PVC PROFILES (DOOR & WINDOW)
1969. PVC FOOTWEAR

Price Rs. 2500/- for each "Detailed Project Report" Payable in advance through Draft/Cash/M.O. in favour of "ENGINEERS INDIA RESEARCH INSTITUTE". Or Ask by V.P.P. PH.: 291 8117, 291 6431, 292 0361 Fax: 91-11-291 6431 (24 Hrs.)

1970. PVC SOLES FOR LEATHER SHOE UPPERS
1971. PVC STABILIZERS
1972. PVC/XLPE (ARMOURED) CABLES
1973. PVC WIRE & CABLES/PIPES & FITTINGS
1974. PVC CASING CAPING MATERIAL FOR ELECTRICAL FITTING
1975. PVC/PLASTIC/SOFT/RIGID/ FILM SHEETS
1976. PVC LEATHER CLOTH
1977. PVC CABLES
1978. PVC FLOOR TILES
1979. PVC ELECTRICAL INSULATION TAPE WITH PRINTING (STEEL GRIP TYPE)
1980. PVC COATING ON LEATHER SHEETS
1981. PVC BATTERY SEPARATOR
1982. PVC PIPES & FITTINGS (RIGID PIPE, FLEXIBLE PIPE, CONDUIT PIPE, ELBOW FITTING, T-JOINTS ETC.)
1983. PVC RULLER
1984. PVC SOLVENT CEMENT
1985. PVC SUCTION HOSES
1986. PVC FLEXIBLE PIPES
1987. PVA BASED ADHESIVES
1988. PVC ON G.I. WIRE
1989. PVC ROOFING SHEET
1990. PVC FILM
1991. QSS COLOUR PHOTO LAB
1992. QUICK LIME
1993. RAILWAY SLEEPERS (PRE STRESSED CONCRETE)
1994. RAISING COMPOUNDS OR EMBOSSING POWDER
1995. RABBIT FARMING
1996. RAINBOW COLOUR ON PVC FILM & SHEET
1997. RAINBOW COLOUR ON METALS
1998. RAZOR BLADE
1999. RCC SPUN PIPES
2000. REACTIVE DYES
2001. READY MADE PROCESSED FOOD
2002. RECTIFIED SPIRIT FROM MOLASSES & MAHUA FLOWER
2003. REROLLING OF SARIYA (TOR)
2004. RESTAURANT
2005. REFINED OILS (COTTON SEEDS, GROUNDNUT, SUNFLOWER ETC.)
2006. RESIN BASED LEATHER BINDER
2007. REROLLING OF STEEL
2008. RECOVERY OF LEAD FROM DISPOSED LEAD ACID BATTERY
2009. REFRIGERATOR & MINI REFRIGERATOR
2010. RESIN CORED SOFT SOLDERING WIRE
2011. RECLAMATION OF TRANSFORMER OIL
2012. RED IRON OXIDE
2013. RE-ROLLING MILL (ALUMINIUM) & UTENSILS
2014. REFINED SUNFLOWER SEED OIL
2015. RESIDENTIAL APARTMENT
2016. RESIDENTIAL & DELUXE FLATS
2017. RECLAMATION OF USED ENGINE OIL
2018. RECLAMATION OF WAX SLUDGES FOR MANUFACTURING OF MICROCRYSTALINE WAX
2019. READY MADE GARMENTS

2020. READY MADE GARMENTS AND HOSIERY
2021. REFINING OF GROUNDNUT OIL
2022. RECONDITIONING OF EMPTY CEMENT JUTE BAG
2023. RED OXIDE PRIMER
2024. REFINING OF CASTOR OIL
2025. RECHARGEABLE TORCHES
2026. READY MADE GARMENTS MERCHANDISE PLANT
2027. RECOVERY OF SILVER NITRATE FROM PHOTO GRAPHIC WASTE FIXERS
2028. REMOTE CONTROL SYSTEMS (FOR STARTING DOOR, OPEN & CLOSE HEADLIGHT ON & OFF FOR CAR)
2029. RECOVERY OF SILVER FROM WASTE FIXTURE BLEACH OBTAINED FROM PHOTO COLOUR LAB BY SULPHIDE PROCESS
2030. RECYCLING OF WASTE CELLULOSE ACETATE INTO CELLULOSE ACETATE SHEETS
2031. RED OXIDE PIGMENTS FROM IRON PICKLING PLANT WASTE
2032. REFRACTORIES
2033. REFINED OIL & GROUNDNUT OIL
2034. REROLLING OF STEEL CUTTING
2035. RED MUD PVC PIPES & FITTINGS
2036. REXINE CLOTH & ALIKE PRODUCTS
2037. RECONDITIONING OF T.V PICTURE TUBE
2038. RECONDITIONING OF FLUORESCENT TUBE
2039. RECTIFIED SPIRIT FOR POTABLE ALCOHOL, INDUSTRIAL ALCOHOL & MEDICAL ALCOHOL
2040. RE-REFINING OF USED LUBRICANT
2041. RECTIFIED SPIRIT FROM RICEPADDY STRAW
2042. RED OXIDE PRIMER (ANTI CORROSIVE)
2043. READY MADE GARMENTS (100% EOU)-STITCHING, WASHING, DYEING, PRINTING & FINISHING ETC.)
2044. REFINED VEGETABLE OILS
2045. REROLLING OF STEEL SECTIONS
2046. REFINING OF MUSTARD OILS
2047. REPACKING OF MEDICINES
2048. READY MADE SALWAR SUITS
2049. RED OXIDE PIGMENTS
2050. RECLAMATION OF HYDRAULIC OIL
2051. RED MIRROR BY ELECTROLESS DIPPING METHOD
2052. REACTIVE DYE M5B DYE
2053. RIGID PVC PIPES & FITTINGS (RIGID PIPES, PIPE FITTINGS LIKE ELBOW FITTINGS, T-JOINTS ETC.)
2054. RE-WINDING OF BURNT ELECTRIC MOTOR
2055. RECLAMATION OF NICKEL FROM SPENT CATALYST OF VANASPATI INDUSTRY
2056. RECLAMATION OF SPENT BLEACHING EARTH
2057. REFRIGERANT ALFA-R134
2058. RESISTORS (WIRE WOUND)
2059. RESIN CORED SOFT SOLDERING WIRE
2060. RESIN COATED SAND (SHELL MOULDING SAND)
2061. RED PHOSPHORUS
2062. RICE HUSK BASED CEMENT
2063. RICE&CORNFLAKE
2064. RICE MILL
2065. RICE FLAKES (CHUDA)
2066. RICE POLISHING AND PACKAGING IN POUCHES
2067. RIGID PVC PIPES
2068. RIGID PVC PIPES & FITTINGS
2069. RICE BRAN OIL
2070. RICE TRADING (BASMATI)
2071. RICE POLISHERS
2072. RIVETS
2073. ROLLING BEARING FORGING OF OUTER/INNER RINGS
2074. ROLLER FLOUR MILL

2075. ROLLING MILL
2076. ROLLING OF STAINLESS STEEL SHEET (PATTA)
2077. ROTARY PRINTING & DYEING ON COTTON/ SYNTHETIC TEXTILE
2078. ROOFING TILES (CEMENT)
2079. ROSIN & TERPENTINE DISTILLATION
2080. ROSE CRYSTALS
2081. ROSE PLANTATION & ROSE OIL EXTRACTION
2082. ROLLER FLOUR MILL & MUSTARD OIL MILL
2083. ROTO GRAVURE PRINTING
2084. ROASTED & FRIED DRY FRUITS, GROUNDNUTS/ PEANUTS WITH PACKAGING
2085. ROUND GLASS MARBLES
2086. ROASTED/SALTED/COATED CASHEWNUT, PEANUT, ALMOND (IMPORTEDAUTOMATIC)
2086A.RIGID & ELASTIC TAPES
2087. RUBBER BALLOONS (DECORATIVE, TOYS & INDUSTRIAL BALOONS)
2088. RUBBER HAWAI CHAPPALS
2089. RUBBER ADHESIVES
2090. RUBBER CHAPPALS & GENTS LEATHER SHOES
2091. RUBBERISED CORK SHEETS
2092. RUBBER SHEET & ALLIED HOSPITAL GOODS
2093. RUBBERIZED COIR FOAM
2094. RUBBER FOAM MATTRESS
2095. RUBBER SHEET FROM USED TYRE
2096. RUBBER SHEET FOR SHOE SOLE
2097. RUBBER LATEX FOAM PRODUCT
2098. RUBBER CONDOM
2099. RUBBER SOLUTION
2100. RUBBER AUTO PARTS
2101. RUBBER LINING
2102. RUBBER GOODS FROM WASTE RUBBER
2103. RUBBING COMPOUND FOR AUTOMOBILE
2104. RUBBER BANDS
2105. RUM FLAVOUR
2106. RUBBER TOYS
2107. RUBBER PLASTIC STAMP & PAD (AUTOMATIC)
2108. RUBBER HOT WATER BOTTLES
2109. RUBBER COTS & APRONS
2110. RUBBERIZED CLOTH
2111. RUST PREVENTIVE (PETROLEUM)
2112. RUBBER COMPOUND TOYS (USING PLASTER OF PARIS)
2113. RUBBER BUSHING
2114. RUBBER HOSE PIPES & RUBBER GLAZING
2115. RUBBER PLANTATION
2116. RUBBER MOULDING & LINING OF RUBBER SHEETING

2117. RUBBER ADHESIVE (All PURPOSE)-NEOPRENE & ISOPRENE BASED
2118. RUBBER ADHESIVE
2119. RUBBER ROLLERS
2120. RUBBER ROLLER FOR PRINTING MACHINE
2121. RUBBER ROLLER FOR RICE MILL
2122. RUBBER CONVEYOR BELT
2123. RUBBER HOSE PIPE
2124. RUBBER RECLAMING
2125. RUBBER CAPS FOR PHARMACEUTICAL USE
2126. RUBBER ROLLERS FOR TEXTILE MILLS & PAPER INDUSTRIES
2127. RUBBER ROLLER& EBONITE ROLLER
2128. RUBBER (LATEX) LINED JUTE MATS
2129. RUBBER PROCESS OIL
2130. RUBBER BELTING (FAN/V BELT)
2131. RUBBER (FIELD) CONVERTED TO THE 60% LATEX RUBBER
2132. RUBBER ERASERS (SCHOOL RUBBER)
2133. RUBBER AUTO GASKET
2134. RUBBERISED CANVAS SHOES
2135. RUBBER (SYNTHETIC)
2136. RUBBER HOSES FOR AUTOMOBILE
2137. SAFETY GLASS
2138. SANITARY WARE & WALL TILE/FLOOR TILE
2139. SALINE & INJECTION WATER
2140. SANITARY NAPKIN
2141. SANITARY NAPKIN & DISPOSABLE BABY DIAPERS
2142. SAW MILLS
2143. SAFETY MATCHES (MATCH BOX)
2144. SAND PAPER (ABRASIVE PAPER)
2145. SALT GLAZED STONE WARE PIPES & FITTINGS
2146. SAND LIME BRICKS
2147. SAGOL
2148. SAUSAGED FOOD CASING (100%EOU)
2150. SAFETY PINS
2151. SALINE & INJECTION WATER
2152. SALTED GROUNDNUT
2153. SAGO SEED FROM POTATO & SWEET POTATO (SABOO DANA)
2154. SAFETY MATCH & FIREBOX
2155. SALT LICKS FOR CATTLES
2156. SANITARY NAPKINS (TAB ENDED-TUBE FILLED)
2157. SAFETY BELT
2158. SABOO DANA
2159. SCOOTER TYRE & TUBE
2160. SCREEN PRINTING INKS
2161. SCREEN PRINTING ON PAPER/CARDS
2162. SCREEN PRINTING
2163. SCREEN EMULSION
2164. SCREWS FOR AUDIO CASSETTE
2165. SCENT & PERFUME FOR AGARBATTI
2166. SCENTS/PERFUME
2267. SCENT BY LEMON GRASS OIL & JASMINE OIL
2168. SCENTED SUPARI
2169. SCENT (INTIMATED SCENT, CHEMICALS ETC.)

2170. SCREEN PRINTING ON TEXTILES
2171. SCHOOL
2172. SCOOTER RIMS
2173. SECURITY SYSTEM
2174. SECONDARY LEAD EXTRACTION FROM SCRAPS (A) BATTERY PLATE (B) PIPES (C) SHEETS
2175. SNACK FOOD (CRAX TYPE-ROLL & BALL TYPE)
2176. SNUFF FACTORY
2177. SELF TAPPING STEEL SCREWS
2178. SEWING NEEDLES (FOR USED WITH DOMESTIC/ INDUSTRIAL SEWING MACHINE)
2179. SECURITY OFFSET PRINTING PRESS
2180. SEWING THREADS, REELS & BALLS
2181. SEMI CONDUCTORS FOR TRANSISTORS & DIODE
2182. SEMI CONDUCTOR DEVICES
2183. SESAME OIL FROM SESAME SEEDS
2184. SERVO CONTROLLED STABILIZERS (1-100 KVA)
2185. SEWING MACHINE (PARTS MACHINING & ASSEMBLY)
2186. SEMI AUTOMATIC BRICKS PLANT
2187. SEMI AUTOMATIC CONFECTIONERY PLANT
2188. SEAMLESS M.S. TUBES
2189. SEALING MATERIAL COMPATIBLE TO CERAMIC & NICHROME WIRE
2190. S.G. IRON & MALLEABLE IRON CASTING
2191. S.G. IRON & ALLOY STEEL CASTINGS
2192. SHEET GLASS
2193. SHAMPOOS
2194. SHOE POLISH PUFF
2195. SHOVELS
2196. SHOCK ABSORBERS
2197. SHAMPOOS FOR DOGS
2198. SHAMPOO & CREAM (COLD CREAM, ALL PURPOSE & VARNISHING CREAM)
2199. SHUTTLELESS LOOM
2200. SHAVING CREAM & SHAVING SOAP
2201. SHAWLS (POWER LOOM)
2202. SHOE UPPER
2203. SHOE POLISH (BOOT POLISH)
2204. SHEET METAL PRODUCTS (FERROUS/NON-FERROUS)
2205. SHIP CONTAINERS
2206. SHEEP & GOAT FARMING
2207. SHOE LACES
2208. SHOES, CANVAS AS WELL AS BOOT, RUBBER KNEES, JUNGLE BOOT COMBAT, RUBBER LINED
2209. SHAVING CREAM (LATHER)
2210. SHERBAT
2211. SHOTS & GRITS OF HIGH CARBON STEELS
2212. SHUTTLE COCKS FOR BADMINTON
2213. SHOE TACKS
2214. SHEHNAZ HUSSAIN'S INSTITUTE FOR SKIN, HEALTH & HAIR CARE (HEALTH CLUB CUM BEAUTY PARLOUR TRAINING INSTITUTE)
2215. SILK COCOON CULTIVATION (GROWING OF SILK COCOON FROM SILK WORM)
2216. SILICA GEL
2217. SINGLE SUPER PHOSPHATE (S.S.P)
2218. SILICON COMPOUND
2219. SILICON EMULSION (MOULD RELEASING AGENTS)
2220. SILK SCREEN PRINTING ON SAREES (BLOCK & SCREEN PROCESS)

2221. SILK WASTE PROCESSING & SPINNING
2222. SILK REELING UNIT
2223. SILICA SAND
2224 SILICON RELEASE PAPER
2225. SILVER NITRATE
2226. SILVER DIP (CLEANING SOLUTION)
2227. SIZING OF YARN
2228. SINTERED BUSHES
2229. SINTERED BUSHES (SELF LUBRICATED)
2230. SINTERED METAL PRODUCTS
2231. SHISHAM PLANTATION
2232. SILICON RUBBER NIPPLE/ TEAT
2233. SILENCERS FOR TWO/ THREE WHEELERS
2234. SINGLE CORE TWIN FLAT CABLE
2235. SILICON EMULSION
2236. SILVER EXTRACTION FROM WASTE HYPO SOLUTION BY CHEMICAL PROCESS
2237. SILVER EXTRACTION BY WASTE HYPO SOLUTION, X-RAY FILM
2238. SILVER JEWELLERY & CUTLERY (GOLD PLATED)
2239. SILVER & GOLD JEWELLERY
2240. SINGLE SUPER PHOSPHATE (S.S.P) & SULPHURIC ACID
2241. SILVER & GOLD PLATING ON PVC & NYLON
2242. SILICON
2243. SINDHUR
2244. SILVER DIP (CLEANING SOLUTION)
2245. SILVER PLATED UTENSILS
2246. SINTERED BEARINGS
2247. SILVER JEWELLERY
2248. SILVER BRAZING FOIL
2249. SILK FABRICS (POWER LOOM)
2250. SILICON FROM RICE HUSK
2251. SKIMMED MILK (LIQUID)
2252. SKIMMED MILK POWDER
2253. SKYLATED PHENOL
2254. SKY BAGS
2255. SKIMMED MILK POWDER & GHEE
2256. SMOKE LESS COAL
2257. SOFT DRINKS (NON CARBONATED)
2258. SODIUM DICHROMATE & SODIUM SULPHATE
2259. SOLVENT EXTRACTION & REFINING OF SOYA BEAN
2260. SORBITOL
2261. SODIUM TRI-POLY PHOSPHATE
2262. SODIUM THIO-SULPHATE FROM SODIUM SULPHATE
2263. SODIUM SULPHATE
2264. SOLID FUEL CAKE
2265. SODIUM HEXA META PHOSPHATE
2266. SODIUM SULPHIDE FROM AMMONIUM SULPHITE & SODIUM CHLORIDE
2267. SOFT DRINK CONCENTRAT (SACCHARINE BASED)
2268. SOAP COATED PAPER
2269. SODIUM BENZOATE
2270. SOLVENT EXTRACTION PLANT
2271. SOCKS KNITTING
2272. SODA ASH
2273. SODA LIME
2274. SOLAR CELL
2275. SOLAR COOKER
2276. SOLAR PHOTO VOLTAGE MODULES (SOLAR ELECTRICAL CELLS & PANEL)
2277. SOLAR PHOTO VOLTAIC SYSTEM
2278. SOLAR PUMP
2279. SOLAR ELECTRICAL CELLS & PANELS
2280. SOLAR PUMP
2281. SOLAR ENERGY WATER HEATER (GEYSER)
2282. SOLAR POWER EQUIPMENTS

2283. SOLAR MODULES
2284. SOYABEAN PRODUCTS
2285. SOYABEAN BARIYAN
2286. SOFT DRINKS CONCENTRATES & ESSENCES (ORANGE, COLA, LIME, PINE APPLE) FLAVOURS FOR BAKER & SODA WATER
2287. SOLVENT EXTRACTION PLANT FROM COCONUT CAKE
2288. SODIUM BICARBONATES
2290. SOLDERING PASTE
2291. SOYA MILK FROM SOYABEAN
2292. SOYA SAUCE (CHINESE)
2293. SOLDER WIRE (SOFT RESIN CORED)
2294. SOAP RIVETS (HOLLOW TYPE)
2295. SOYABEAN BARIYAN
2296. SOAP FROM SOAP STOCK (SOAP INDUSTRY)
2297. SOFTWARE (COMPUTER)
2298. SOYABEAN OIL
2299. SOLVENT & THINNERS
2300. SOFT DRINK (COLD DRINKS)
2301. SODIUM META SILICATE
2302. SODIUM ACETATE
2303. SODIUM SULPHITE FROM SODIUM DIOXIDE
2304. SODIUM THIO-SULPHATE BY SODIUM SULPHATE
2305. SODIUM SILICATE FROM SILICA SAND
2306. SODIUM SULPHATE (ANHYDROUS)
2307. SODIUM SILICATE FROM RICE HUSK/PADDY HUSK
2308. SODIUM DICHROMATE (BICHROMATE)
2310. SODIUM SULPHIDE
2311. SODIUM SULPHIDE BY BARIUM SULPHATE PROCESS
2312. SODIUM CAFFINATES & CALCIUM CAFFINATES
2313. SODIUM SULPHITE
2314. SODIUM NITRATE
2315. SODIUM NITRITE
2316. SODIUM LAURYL SULPHATE
2317. SODIUM ALUMINATE
2318. SODIUM HYDRO SULPHITE (ZINC REDUCTION PROCESS)
2319. SODIUM HYDRO CHLORITE (BLEACH LIQUOR)
2320. SODIUM NAPHTHOANATE
2321. SODIUM BI-SULPHITE
2322. SODIUM SULPHIDE FROM SALT CAKE
2323. SODIUM PETROLEUM SULPHONATE
2324. SODIUM PERBORATE (TETRA HYDRATE)
2325. SODIUM CYCLAMATE
2326. SODIUM ALGINATE
2327. SODIUM META SILICATE
2328. SODIUM CHROMATE
2329. SODIUM TRI-POLY PHOSPHATE
2330. SODIUM ALUMINIUM SULPHATE
2331. SODIUM FLUORIDE
2332. SODIUM HYPO-CHLORITE (BLEACH LIQUOR)
2333. SODIUM BENZOATE
2334. SODIUM PERBORATE (TETRAHYDRATE)
2335. SODIUM SALT (2,4-D)
2336. S.W.PIPES
2337. SOLVENT EXTRACTION & REFINING PLANT (COTTON SEED OIL
2338. SOFT DRINK ESSENCES
2339. SOFT & HARD FERRITES
2340. SOAP SHOP
2341. SOYA MILK & PANEER
2342. SPONGE RUBBER (LATEX FOAM RUBBER)
2343. SPECIAL STEEL (HIGH ALLOY)
2344. SPRAY DRIED DETERGENT POWDER
2345. SPRAY LAMINATED BRASS ARTICLES/BADGES (PLASTIC)
2346. SPARK PLUGS
2347. SPORT SHOES

Cost
Rs. 2500/-
for each
Detailed
Project Report

2348. SPORT SHOES (IMPORTED) AUTOMATIC PLANT-ACTION, LIBERTY TYPE
2349. SPONGE IRON
2350. SPECTACLE FRAMES (PLASTIC)
2351. SPIRAL WOUND METALLIC GASKET
2352. SPECTACLE FRAMES (METAL)
2353. SPICES (MASALA)
2354. SPRAY DRIER
2355. SPEAKER PARRY RING (FORMULAE)
2356. SPINNING OF VISCOSE STAPLE FIBER INTO YARN
2357. S.S. HINGES
2358. STEP DOWN TRANSFORMER
2359. STEEL DRUM & BARRELS
2360. STENCIL COATING SOLUTION
2361. STARCH & DEXTRIN BASED ADHESIVES
2362. STENCIL PAPER (DUPLICATING)
2363. SOAP JELLY
2364. SPIKENARD (JATAMANSI)
2365. SPRAY PERFUME
2366. SPINDLE OIL
2367. SPICE OILS OR OLEORESINS (EXTRACTION OF ESSENTIAL OILS- CARDAMOM, JEERA, AJWAIN, GINGER OIL & OTHER SPICES)
2368. STARCH (MAIZE/CORN)
2369. STAINLESS STEEL CASTINGS BY INDUCTION FURNACE
2370. STAINLESS STEEL SHEET ROLLING & MANUFACTURE OF STAINLESS STEEL UTENSILS
2371. STAINLESS STEEL PATTA
2372. STAMP PADS & PAD INKS
2373. STAPLES, GEM CLIPS & PAPER PINS
2374. STRAW BOARD & MILL BOARD
2375. STEEL PLANT (EAF-BASED)
2376. STANNOUS CHLORIDE
2377. STEEL ROLLING MILL
2378. STEEL/ALUMINIUM COAST FOR WINDING OF TEXTILE YARNS
2379. STITCHING WIRE
2380. STEEL WOOL
2381. STUFFING JOINT BOX OF PLASTIC
2382. STARCH & ALLIED PRODUCT FROM MAIZE
2383. STEAM IRON (LIGHT WEIGHTED)
2384. STEARIC ACID
2385. STRAW BOARD
2386. STEEL WIRE ROPES
2387. STEEL TUBE/ PIPE
2388. STEEL FOUNDRY
2389. STARCH, DEXTROSE, SORBITOL, VITAMIN - C, ETC. FROM MAIZE
2390. STEARATES MANUFACTURE
2391. STRIPPERS FOR ROTAORY PRINTING EMULTION
2392. STAINLESS STEEL UTENSILS (COPPER BOTTOM)
2393. STEEL BALL BEARINGS
2394. STEEL FURNITURE
2395. STEREO CASSETTE RECORDERS/PLAYERS
2396. STABLE BLEACHING POWDER
2397. STRAW BOARD & GREY BOARD
2398. STEEL CASTING FOR RAILWAYS
2399. STONE CRUSHER
2400. STAINLESS STEEL UTENSILS (COPPER ELECTROPLATED)

Price Rs. 2500/- for each "Detailed Project Report" Payable in advance through Draft/Cash/M.O. in favour of "ENGINEERS INDIA RESEARCH INSTITUTE". Or Ask by V.P.P. PH.: 291 8117, 291 6431, 292 0361 Fax: 91-11-291 6431 (24 Hrs.)

2401. STEEL FORGING (AUTOMOBILE PARTS)
2402. STEEL WIRE HEALDS
2403. STARCH FROM TAPIOCA
3323. STREET LIGHT FITTING
2404. STAMPING HOT FOILS
2405. STEEL REROLLING MILL (STEEL RODS & COILS FROM SCRAPS)
2406. STAINLESS STEEL TIFFIN BOX (LUNCH BOX)
2407. STEEL TAPES FOR CABLE ARMOURING
2408. STICKER MAKING-AUTOMATIC PLANT
2409. STEEL BALLS
2410. STEEL BALLS FOR BALL POINT PENS
2411. STICKER & LABELING PLANT
2412. STAIN REMOVERS
2413. SURAT JARI
2414. STARCH BOOK BINDING CLOTH
2415. STEEL STRIPS (COLD ROLLED)-ELECTRICAL SILICON WITH ORIENTED GRAINS FOR ELECTRICAL MACHINES & TRANSFORMERS
2416. STARCH BOOK BINDING CLOTH
2417. STEEL TANKS FOR DRINKING WATER (WATER STORAGE TANKS OF M.S)
2418. STEEL PLANT (25-T UHF ELECTRIC ARC FURNACE & HOT ROLLING)
2419. STEEL STRIPS (COLD ROLLED)-ELECTRICAL SILICON WITH ORIENTED GRAINS FOR ELECTRICAL MACHINES & TRANSFORMERS
2420. STEEL WIRE DRAWING & GALVANIZING
2421. STORAGE BATTERY
2422. STUFF TOYS
2423. STAINLESS STEEL VACUUM FLASK (UN-BREAKABLE)
2424. STARCH FROM WHEAT FLOUR
2425. STAINLESS STEEL KNIFE
2426. STEEL PIPES
2427. STAINLESS STEEL CUTLERY
2428. STEEL INGOTS (GAS FIRE FURNACE)
2429. STARCH & ALLIED PRODUCTS FROM BROKEN RICE, LIQUID GLUCOSE, DEXTROSE ANHYDROUS
2430. STEEL WIRE/ROD
2431. SUNFLOWER PLANTATION
2432. SUBMERGED ARC WELDED PIPES (SAW PIPE)
2433. SUNFLOWER OIL
2434. SUBMERSIBLE PUMP
2435. SULPHUR POWDER FROM SULPHUR CRYSTALS/LUMP
2436. SUGAR CANE WAX FROM PRESS MUD
2437. SURGICAL/ABSORBENT COTTON
2438. SURFACE FLOOR & CAR POLISHES
2439. SUPER ENAMELED COPPER WIRE (COPPER SCRAPS)
2440. SUGAR MANUFACTURING PLANT BY CARBONATION PROCESS
2441. SURGICAL EXAMINATION GLOVES (DISPOSABLE)
2442. SULPHUR CRYSTAL
2443. SUGAR CANE JUICE PRESERVATION
2444. SUNMICA
2445. SURAT ZARI (ZARI MANUFACTURE FOR SAREE)
2446. SURGICAL COTTON & BANDAGES
2447. SURGICAL COTTON AND SURGICAL ADHESIVE TAPES
2448. SULPHUR BLACK DYES

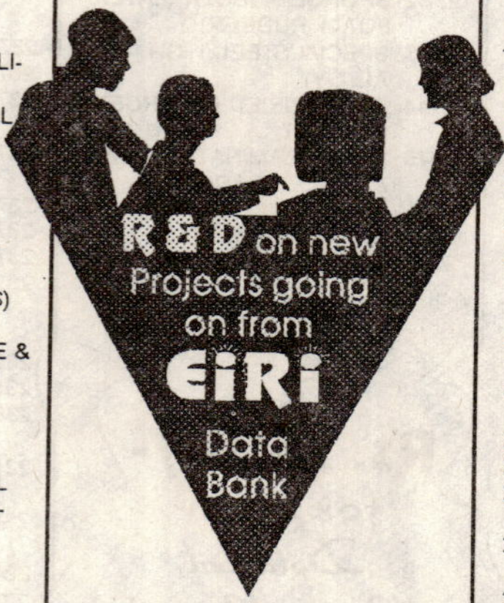

2449. SURGICAL GLOVES FROM LATEX
2450. SURGICAL BANDAGE, SANITARY NAPKINS & ALLIED PRODUCTS
2451. SURGICAL ADHESIVE TAPE ON CLOTH SURFACE
2452. SURGE SUPPRESSER
2453. SULPHUR RECOVERY FROM SLUDGE
2454. SUNFLOWER SEED OIL EXTRACTION
2455. SURGICAL BANDAGES
2456. SUPER ENAMELED COPPER WIRE
2457. SUGAR PLANT
2458. SULPHURIC ACID (H_2SO_4)
2459. SURA
2460. SUGAR CUBES
2461. SUPER ENAMELING FOR WINDING
2462. SURGICAL METHYLATED SPIRIT
2463. SUGAR COATED CASHEWNUT, ALMONDS.
2464. SWITCH MODE POWER SUPPLY (SMPS)
2465. SWEATER, MUFF-LER & KNITTING INDUSTRY
2466. SWITCH BOARD
2467. SWEET AROMA OF BETAL NUT
2468 SYNTHETIC IRON OXIDE (YELLOW)
2469 SYNTHETIC IRON OXIDE (RED)
2470. SYNTHETIC RED & YELLOW IRON OXIDE
2471. SYNTHETIC ASAFOETIDA(HING)
2472. 2-4-D SODIUM SALT
2474. SYNTHETIC ALMOND OIL
2475. SYNTHETIC TALLOW
2476. SYNTHETIC DETERGENT (BLUE POWDER)
2477. SYNTHETIC ADHE-SIVE FOR DECORATIVE LAMINATE BONDING
.2478. SYNTHETIC PEARL COATING ON POLYSTYRENE BEADS
2479. TARTARIC ACID
2480. TAPE DECK MECHANISM
2481. TAB ENDED PULP FILLED NAPKINS (Sanitary Napkin)
2482. TABLET & CAPSULE
2483. TABLET, CAPSULE, SYRUPS, LOTION & OINTMENT
2484. TAMARIND JUICE CONCENTRATE
2485. TARTARIC ACID FROM MALEIC-ANHYDRIDE
2486. TAR FROM PINE WOOD
2487. TABLE FAN
2488. TABLE WARE & CERAMIC TILES
2489. TALCUM POWDER (FACE & TOILET)
2490. TALC (MAGNESIUM SILICATE)
2491. TAPER ROLLER BEARINGS
2492. TAILORS CHOKES
2493. TANTALUM CAPACITOR
2494. TABLE OFFSET & D.T.P
2495. TANNIC ACID
2496. TABLE TENNIS BALL
2497. TALLOW PROCESSING FOR SOAP MANUFACTURING
2498. TABLET, CAPSULE, SYRUP & LOTION
2499. TEA PACKAGING & DISTRIBUTION JOB WORK
2500. TETRA PACK FOR MILK PACKAGING & OTHER LIQUIDS
2501. TENNIS BALL & CRICKET BALL
2502. TEA PLANTATION
2503. TEA INDUSTRY
2504. TEA & COFFEE PROCESSING AND PACKAGING
2505. TEAK & MUSHROOM PLANTATION

Price Rs. 2500/- For each "Detailed Project Report" Payable in advance through Draft/Cash/M.O. in favour of "ENGINEERS INDIA RESEARCH INSTITUTE". Or Ask by V.P.P. PH.: 291 8117, 291 6431, 292 0361 Fax: 91-11-291 6431 (24 Hrs.)

2506. TEAK PLANTATION
2507. TEFLON MANUFACTURING
2508. TEFLON COATED ELECTRIC CABLES
2509. TELEPHONE CABLES/CORD
2510. TERELENE PRODUCTS
2511. TENT & TARPAULINE
2512. TEFLON TAPES
2513. TEA PACKAGING
2514. TELEPHONE AMPLIFIER
2515. TEXTURISED POLYESTER YARN
2516. TENNIS BALL
2517. TEFLON COATED UTENSILS (NON-STICKS)
2518. TEXTILE GOLD STAMPING PASTE
2519. TEXTILE PRINTING PIGMENT BINDERS
2520. TELEVISION ANTENNA
2521. TELEVISION (COLOUR AND BLACK & WHITE)
2522. TELEVISION (PORTABLE)
2523. TEXTILE DYEING BLEACHING FINISHING & PRINTING
2524. TERRY TOWEL
2525. TEXTILE AUXILLIARIES & CHEMICALS
2526. TEFLON TAPES & CABLE
2527. TEFLON COATED UTENSILS (NON-STICK)
2528. TEXTILE PRINTING PASTE (GUM)
2529. TELEVISION
2530. TEA PACKAGING & DISTRIBUTION
2531. TERRY TOWELS/TERRY FABRICS WEAVING UNIT
2532. TELEVISION (B/W)
2533. TELEPHONE CABLE (JELLY FILLED)
2534. TEA BAGS
2535. TEA (INSTANT)
2536. THREE STAR HOTEL
2537. THERMOMETER (CLINICAL)
2538. THINNERS
2539. THERMOCOLE MOULDING
2540. THREAD, CUSHION COMPOUND AND VOLCANIZING SOLUTION FORMULATION & MANUFACTURE
2541. THERMO PLASTIC ELECTRICAL SWITCHES & FITTINGS
2542. THERMOCOLE PACKAGING
2543. THERMO COUPLE TIPS
2544. THERMOCOUPLES
2545. THERMOCOLE SHEET & MOULDED PRODUCTS
2546. THERMO PLASTIC POLYURETHANE
2547. THERMOCOLE
2548. THERMOFORMED PACKAGING (BLISTER & POUCH PACKING)
2549. THREE WHEELER ASSEMBLY
2550. THINNER/SOLVENTS & ITS ALLIED PRODUCT
2551. THERMOSTATE FOR REFRIGERATOR
2552. TIN PRINTING & ANODIZING ON ALUMINIUM
2553. TIN CONTAINER
2554. TILES (MOSAIC)
2555. TILES (GLAZED CERAMIC)
2556. TIE ROD ENDS
2557. TITANIUM OXIDE
2558. TITANIUM NITRIDING
2559. TISSUE CULTURE (100% EOU)
2560. TITANIUM DIOXIDE BY CHLORINE
2561. TISSUE & AIR MAIL PAPER
2562. TISSUE & TOILET PAPER ROLL & AIR MAIL PAPER
2563. TISSUE PAPER ESPECIALLY FACIAL PAPER, MOIST TOILETTERIES, CLEANSING TISSUE & RELATED PRODUCTS
2564. TIN PRINTING
2565. TIMBER/WOOD SEASONING
2566. TOMATO POWDER
2567. TOMATO CONCENTRATE
2568. TOYS (PLASTIC)
2569. TOYS (ELECTRONICS)
2570. TOMATO PULP
2571. TOMATO WAFFERS
2572. TOBACCO & ITS PRODUCTS
2573. TOILET PAPER
2574. TOXIC COMPOUNDS EFFECTS ON HUMAN BODY
2575. TOYS (STUFF)
2576. TOILET SOAPS
2577. TOOTH BRUSH
2578. TOOTH PASTE (GEL-COLGATE, CLOSE-UP TYPE)
2579. TOOTH PASTE & POWDER
2580. TOOTH PASTE
2581. TOOTH BRUSH, TOOTH PASTE & POWDER
2582. TOMATO PRODUCT IN POUCHES
2583. TOUGHNED GLASS FOR WRIST WATCH
2584. TORCH & TRI LIGHT UNITS INTEGRATED PLANT INCLUDING MINIATURE BULB & TUBES, ENGINEERING PLASTIC MOULD/DIES MANUFACTURE
2585. TOILET & HERBAL SOAP
2586. TOMATO & PAPAYA CULTIVATION
2587. TOILET PAPER & NAPKIN
2588. TOY BALLOONS, DECORATIVE BALLOONS
2589. TOFFEE (MILK)
2590. TOWEL, SOCKS & HOSIERY
2591. TOMATO PASTE
2592. TOMATO KETCHUP, JAMS, JELLY ETC.
2593. TOGGLE SWITCHES
2594. TONER INK
2595. TOILET SEATS & COVERS
2596. TOUGHENED GLASS & SILVER MIRROR GLASS
2597. TOBACCO TOOTH PASTE FROM TOBACCO DUST
2598. TOBACCO TOOTH PASTE FROM TOBACCO
2599. TRANSPARENT LACQUER (CLEAR) FOR COATING ON BRASS BANGLES TO MAKE IT WEATHER RESISTANT
2600. TREAD RUBBER (CAMEL BLACK)
2601. TRI-PHENYL PHOSPHITE
2602. TRI SODIUM PHOSPHATE
2603. TRICYCLE RIKS-HAW ASSEMBLY
2604. TRI-METHOPRIME
2605. TRI BASIC LEAD SULPHATE
2606. TRANSFORMER OIL RECLAMATION
2607. TRANSFORMER
2608. TRANSFORMER (DISTRIBUTION)
2609. TRANSFORMER OIL
2610. TRAVELLING AGENCY
2611. TRACING PAPER
2612. T-SHIRT & KNITTING FABRIC
2613 T.V. & AUDIO CABINETS & THEIR ASSEMBLING UNIT
2614. TURKEY RED OIL
2615. TUBULAR POLES, TRANSMISSION LINE, HARDWARE & MAIN SWITCH FOR ELECTRICAL TRANSMISSION
2616. TURPENTINE OIL
2617. TURPENTINE OIL FROM EXTRACTIONS OF DIPETROCORPUS TREE
2618. TUTI FRUITY FROM PAPAYA FRUITY
2619. TURMERIC POWDER (EDIBLE GRADE)
2620. TURMERIC OIL OLEORESIN FROM RAW TURMERIC
2621. TUBE VALVES
2622. TUBULAR POLES FOR ELECTRICAL TRANSMISSION
2623. TUNGSTEN FILAMENT
2624. TURPENTINE & ROSIN DISTILLATION
2625. T.V. PICTURE TUBE (B/W) & COMPUTER MONITOR TUBE
2626. T.V CUM VIDEO GAMES
2627. T.V. SIGNAL BOOSTERS
2628. TWISTED YARN (NYLON)
2629. TWO-T 2-STROKE OIL
2630. TWO WHEELERS REPAIR & SERVICE WORKSHOP
2631. TYRE RETREADING
2632. TYRE RETREADING BY COLD PROCESS
2633. TYRE RETREADING (HOT PROCESS)
2634. TYRE & TUBES FOR SCOOTER, MOTOR CYCLE, RIKSHAW, 2/3 WHEELERS
2635. TYRES, TUBES AND FLAP (MOPED TO TRUCK)
2636. 2-4-D SODIUM SALT
2637. U-CLAMPS, U-BOLTS & NUTS
2638. U.J. CROSS & KING PIN
2638. ULTRAMARINE BLUE
2639. UMBRELLA

2640. UNDECYLENIL ACID
2641. UNSATURATED POLYSTER RESINS
2642. UNINTERRUPTED POWER SUPPLY (UPS)
2643. UN ARMOURED, PVC. INSULATED CABLES
2644. UTENSILS (SILVER PLATED)
2645. UTENSILS (ALUMINIUM)
2646. UTENSILS (BRASS)
2647. UREA FORMALDEHYDE POWDER
2648. UREA FORMALDEHYDE RESIN
2649. UREA
2650. UREA FERTILIZER PLANT
2651. UREA FORMALDEHYDE & MELAMINE FORMAL-DEHYDE MOULDING POWDER
2652. UTENSILS (STAINLESS STEEL)
2653. UTENSILS (TEFLON COATED)
2654. U.V. PAINT
2655. VACUUM METALIZING
2656. VANASPATI GHEE
2657. VALVE GUIDES
2658. VARNISH & PAINT UNIT
2659. VASELINE
2660. VARNISH THINNER (SOLVENT)
2661. VACUUM-METALLISING LACQUER
2662. VAT DYES
2663. VACUUM CLEANER
2664. V-BELTS
2665. VCP & VCR
2666. VENETIAN BLIND
2667. VELVET CLOTH BY FLOCKING PROCESS
2668. VEGETABLE OIL REFINING (BY PHYSICAL PROCESS)
2669. VEGETABLE OIL (EXTRACTION & REFINNING)
2670. VELCROW FASTENING TAPE (FASTNER HOOP LOOP TAPE & SYNTHETIC)
2671. VETENERY MEDICINES
2672. VERMICELLI
2673. VERMICELLI & MACARONI
2674. VIDEO & T.V. GAMES
2675. VIDEO & AUDIO CASSETES
2676. VIDEO CASSETES
2677. VIDEO STUDIO
2678. VIDEO & AUDIO MAGNETIC TAPES
2679. VINEGAR & MALT VINEGAR FOR INDUSTRIAL & DOMESTIC USE
2680. VIDEO CASSETE ASSEMBLING & RECORDING
2681. VITAMIN-C FROM POTATO EXTRACT
2682. VISCOSE RAYON YARN FROM COTTON LINIERS
2683. VIDEO CAMERA
2684. VIDEO FILM STUDIO
2685. VIDEO CASSETTES (COMPLETE MANUFACTURING & ASSEMBLING UNIT)
2686. VIDEO TAPE
2687. VIDEO FILM STUDIO TO MAKE FILMS ETC. IN VIDEO CASSETTES & FILM ROLLS
2688. VIDEO CASSETTES LIBRARY
2689. VISCOSE STAPLE FIBRE (RAYON STAPLE FIBER)
2690. VOLTAGE REGULATOR (FOR AUTOMOBILES)
2691. VOLTAGE STABILIZER
2692. VOLTAGE STABLIZER
2693. VODKA FROM WASTE GRAIN
2694. WAX CRAYON
2695. WAX FLOOR POLISH
2696. WASHING & LAUNDRY SOAP
2697. WALL TILES/FLOOR TILES/ SANITARY TILES
2698. WASHING MACHINE (AUTOMATIC ELECTRO COMPUTERISED)
2699. WAX (PARAFFIN)
2700. WAX (MICRO CRYSTALLINE)
2701. WATCH LEATHER STRAP
2702. WALL PAPER PRINTING
2703. WAX EMULSION
2704. WAX FOR PAPER
2705. WATER PROOF CEMENT COMPOUND
2706. WAX EMULSION
2707. WATER FILTER CANDLES
2708. WATER FILTER & PRESSURE COOKER
2709. WASHING MACHINE & GEYSER
2710. WATER PROOFING BITUMINISED COMPOUND
2711. WAX FOR PAPER INDUSTRY
2712. WATCH CASE BUFFING
2713. WATER FOR INJECTION AMPOULES PLANT
2714. WATER PROOF MARKING INK
2715. WATTLE EXTRACT (TANNIN POWDER)
2716. WAX PAPERED MATHC STICK
2717. WATCH GLASS
2718. WAX & CHEMICAL COATED BRAIDED TINSEL WIRE
2719. WALL PAPER
2720. WASHING CAKE, DETERGENT CAKE & POWDER
2721. WATER PROOFING FORMULATIONS FOR PAPER CONES USED FOR SPEAKERS
2722. WATER PROOFING FOR COTTON CLOTH
2723. WATER METER
2724. WATER STORAGE TANK
2725. WATER PROOFING PAINT
2726. WATER (MINERAL)
2727. WATER METER
2728. WATER STORAGE TANK
2729. WATER PROOFING PAINT
2730. WATER (MINERAL)
2731. WASHING POWDER & WASHING SOAP
2732. WELDING FLUXES
2733. WELDING RODS (SPECIAL) & M.S. WELDING ELECTRODES
2734. WELDING BRASS ROD
2735. WETTING OIL
2736. WELDED WIRE MESH
2737. WEET AROMA OF BETAL NUT
2738. WELDING CABLE
2739. WEET AROMA OF BETAL NUT
2740. WELDING CABLE

2741. WELDING ELECTRODES
2742. WELDING WIRE ELECTRODES (CO2)
2743. WHITE CEMENT
2744. WHTIE OIL FROM KEROSENE OIL
2745. WHEAT PUFF
2746. WHEAT PORRIDGE (DALIA)

2747. WHEAT FLOUR MILL
2748. WHEEL RIMS
2749. WHITE PHENYL
2750. WHITE OIL
2751. WHISKY FROM COMMERCIAL ALCOHOL
2752. WIRE (MILD STEEL)
2753. WIRE & CABLE (PVC)
2754. WIRE (COPPER)
2755. WRITING & PRINTING PAPER
2756. WIRE DRAWING & ENAMEL
2757. WIRE MESH
2758. WIRE RODS (ALUMINIUM)
2759. WINE & BEER
2760. WINE
2761. WIRE DRAWING (ALUMINIUM)
2762. WIRE DRAWING (COPPER)
2763. WIRE DRAWING (MILD STEEL)
2764. WIRE WOUND RESISTORS
2765. WIRE DRAWING & ANNEALING
2766. WIRE DRAWING LUBRICANT
2767. WIRE NAIL
2768. WINDING WIRES, PVC INSULATED SUBMERSIBLE MOTOR
2769. WICK STOVE
2770. WIRE ROPE (STEEL)
2771. WIRE PRODUCTS
2772. WIRE ROPE SLING
2773. WIRE ROPE (STEEL)
2774. WIRE PRODUCTS
2775. WIRE ROPE SLING
2776. WIRE MESH & GAUGE
2777. WIND MILL
2778. WINE, BRANDY, WHISKY & CHAMPAGNE
2779. WINE (I.M.F.L)
2780. WIRE NAILS & WIRE DRAWING
2781. WIND ENERGY POWER
2782. WOOD CHARCOAL & BYE PRODUCTS
2783. WOODEN BOXES
2784. WOOLLEN KNITWEAR
2785. WORSTED WOOLLEN YARN
2786. WOODEN ACCESSORIES FOR SEWING MACHINE
2787. WOOLLEN YARN
2788. WOOLLEN YARN SPINNING
2789. WOOLLEN YARN CARPET DYEING
2790. WOODEN DOOR & WINDOW
2791. WOOD WOOL INDUSTRY
2792. WOOD POLISH
2793. WOODEN DRUM FOR AA/ ACSR CONDUCTOR STORAGE
2794. WOOL BATCHING OIL
2795. WOOLLEN FELT
2796. WOOD SEASONING
2797. WOODEN FURNITURE
2798. WOOLLEN YARN SPINNING PLANT
2799. WOOLLEN SWEATERS
2800. WOVEN HOSIERY LABELS
2801. WOOLLEN CARPETS
2802. WOODEN CANE FURNITURE
2803. WOOD GASIFIER
2804. WRIST WATCH DIAL
2805. WRIST WATCHES
2806. WROUGHT IRON & BRASS STAIRCASE RODS
2807. XANTHATES
2808. XEROX PAPER
2809. XLPE CABLES
2810. X-RAY MACHINE
2811. X-RAY DEVELOPERS
2812. X-RAY FILM SLITTING & REPACKING (MEDICAL)
2813. X-RAY TUBES
2814. X-RAY FILMS
2815. YARN INDUSTRY
2816. YARN - COTTON
2817. YARN - WOOLLEN
2818. YARN DYEING (COTTON)
2819. YARA YARA
2820. YARN DYEING & TEXTURISING
2821. YARN DYEING (COTTON)
2822. YARN (PVC FABRIC)
2823. YARN (VISCOSE RAYON)
2824. YARN (POLYESTER YARN FROM WASTE)
2825. YARN DYEING (CARPET WOOLLEN)
2826. YARN (NYLON)
2827. YARN (TWISTED)
2828. YARN SPINDLES
2829. YARN - SIZING
2830. YARN - HANK
2831. YEAST INDUSTRY
2832. ZARDA & KIMAM
2833. ZARDA-BABA CHHAP
2834. ZARDA & PAN MASALA
2835. ZINC OXIDE
2836. ZINC SULPHATE
2837. ZINC CHLORIDE
2838. ZINC METAL
2839. ZINC BRIGHTNER
2840. ZINC COATING ON WIRE
2841. ZINC STEARATE

NEWLY
PREPARED
DETAILED PROJECT REPORTS

during publishing of this chemical book

(from Sl. No. 2842-2919)

2842. AUTOMOBILE WORKSHOP/ GARAGE & SERVICE CENTRE FOR TRUCK
2843. COTTON CLOTH
2844. PACKAGING FOR NAMKEENS, BHUJIA, DAL MOTH ETC. IN FLEXIBLE POUCHES
2845. ROTO GRAVURE PRINTING & POUCH MAKING
2846. P.V.C. COMPOUNDS (ELECTRICAL GRADE)
2847. STEEL WIRE/ROD (CONTINUOUSLY CAST)-5 M.M. DIAMETER
2848. SYNTHETIC ADHESIVE FOR DECORATIVE LAMINATES BONDING
2849. LPG VALVES & REGULATOR
2850. HERBAL HAIR OIL (AYURVEDIC) LIKE BANPHOOL OIL
2851. TELEPHONE (PUSH BUTTON & CORDLESS)
2852. PHOTO POLYMER COATING FOR PLATE BLOCK MAKING
2853. STOVING PAINT
2854. CLUTCH PLATES FOR 4 WHEELERS
2855. PRINTING FLEXO & PHOTO/ LDPE/HDPE/PP/HM/PVC (FLEXO GRAPHIC & ROTO GRAVURE PRINTING
2856. BALL POINT TIPS (NOZZLES)
2857. ACRYLIC CO-POLYMER EMULSION
2858. STEEL TRANSMISSION LINE TOWER & HOT ROLLING MILL TO PRODUCE STEEL SECTIONS
2859. ACETYLENE & OXYGEN GAS (INTEGRATED UNIT)
2860. ANTISEPTIC CREAM (BORO PLUS BRAND TYPE)
2861. PLASTIC INJECTION MOULDED T.V. CABINETS
2862. GATE GRILL & WINDOW FRAME
2863. FABRICATION OF HEAT EXCHANGER
2864. CARAMEL COLOUR (FOOD COLOUR)
2865. SANITARY NAPKINS (TAB ENDED-PULP FILED) AUTO MATIC IMPORTED PLANT
2866. PLASTIC BOTTLES & CAPS
2867. LAMINATED HDPE WOVEN SACKS
2868. MINERAL WATER (Rs.3 CRORE PROJECT)
2869. HAND MADE PAPER FROM WASTE PAPER
2870. CERAMIC COATED STEEL PIPE
2871. BLOW MOULDED PLASTIC CONTAINER (POLYETHYLENE BOTTLES FOR MINERAL WATER, I.V. FLUIDS ETC.
2872. ESTER GUMS (NO COST ESTIMATION PART
2873. TERPINEOL FROM TURPENTINE
2874. FIBRE CORRUGATED SHEET (FRP, AUTO SCOOTER ROOF/ CEILING)